THE CAUGHT IMAGE

FIGURATIVE LANGUAGE
IN THE FICTION
OF HENRY JAMES

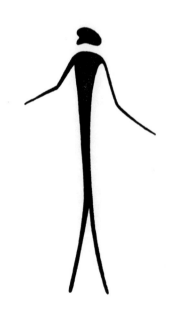

THE CAUGHT IMAGE

FIGURATIVE LANGUAGE

IN THE FICTION

OF HENRY JAMES

BY ROBERT L. GALE

THE UNIVERSITY OF NORTH CAROLINA PRESS   •   CHAPEL HILL

PRINTED BY THE SEEMAN PRINTERY, DURHAM, N. C.

Manufactured in the United States of America

He flashed his faculty of playing with the caught image and liberating the wistful idea over the whole scheme of manners or conception of intercourse of his compatriots, among whom there were evidently not a few types for which he had little love (XVI "AofB" 28).

FOREWORD

The first extensive study of imagery was a book by Henry Willis Wells, called *Poetic Imagery: Illustrated from Elizabethan Literature,* which appeared in 1924 and which in my opinion has rarely been properly praised for its fine insights. Eleven years later, in 1935, Caroline F. E. Spurgeon published *Shakespeare's Imagery and What It Tells Us.* Miss Spurgeon's approach, to be sure, was ridiculed in several reviews, and the apparent limitations of her method have rendered it somewhat out of fashion of late. Furthermore, it may be true that *Shakespeares Bilder* by Wolfgang Clemen, which appeared only a year after Miss Spurgeon's work (but was not translated into English until 1951), is a better book, concerned as it is with the dramatic development and functions of Shakespeare's images and not—as Miss Spurgeon's was—with Shakespeare's personality and with rigid categories into which the figures were forced to fall. Nonetheless, much subtle and important Shakespeare criticism of our time owes a great debt to Miss Spurgeon; and so do many studies of imagery in the works of poets other than Shakespeare. For examples, one might cite the work of Milton Rugoff on Donne's imagery, that of C. Willard Smith on Browning's "star imagery," Richard Harter Fogle on the imagery of Shelley and Keats, and Theodore Banks on Milton's imagery. On the other hand, Miss Rosemund Tuve, following the lead provided by Mrs. Lillian Herlands Hornstein in her "Analysis of Imagery: A Critique of Literary Method," *PMLA*, LVII (September, 1942), 638-53, fiercely rejected Miss Spurgeon's method and produced a significant but difficult work in *Elizabethan and Metaphysical Imagery: Renaissance Poetic and Twentieth-Century Critics* (1947), which defines images in terms of all physical sensations (not rhetorically, after Miss Spurgeon) and seeks the source of metaphysical imagery in the logic of Petrus Remus.

Anyone wanting to review the history of imagistic study in the twentieth century should consult the first half of Chapter XV—entitled "Image, Metaphor, Symbol, Myth"—and its notes in the indispensable *Theory of Literature* by René Wellek and Austin Warren. Further, Stanley Edgar Hyman, in his chapter called "Caroline Spurgeon and Scholarship in Criticism" in *The Armed Vision: A Study in the Methods of Modern Literary Criticism* (1948), has much excellent if bellicose commentary on the whole subject. Finally, a splendid academic review of the critical theory concerning imagery is contained in the first chapter of *Wordsworth's Imagery* (1952), by Florence Marsh.

What I have said thus far has concerned imagery in poetry. Critical writing on imagery in prose had not been extensive.

Miss Spurgeon analyzed Bacon's prose only long enough to hammer home the worn point that Bacon could not have written the plays of Shakespeare. There have been incomplete studies of imagistic language in the works of certain novelists —or treatments of that subject in longer works devoted to larger purposes. Briefly taken up, for example, has been some of the fiction of authors both English and American: Jane Austen, George Eliot, the Brontës, George Meredith, Thomas Hardy, and Graham Greene; also Nathaniel Hawthorne, Herman Melville, Stephen Crane, F. Scott Fitzgerald, William Faulkner, and—of course—Henry James.

Several critics have briefly analyzed imagery in certain segments of the fiction of James. Any list of these critics would include Stephen Spender, A. J. A. Waldock, Austin Warren, F. O. Matthiessen, William M. Gibson, Miriam Allott, R. W. Short, Priscilla Gibson, and Alexander Holder-Barell. But, although the titles of the pertinent essays of some of these persons might lead one to suppose otherwise, no one has considered imagery in all of the 135 novels and short stories of James. In fact, I believe that my present study is the first book-length consideration of imagery in the complete works of any novelist.

It has been a long time in the making. Back in the early 1940's, Philip Wheelwright and John Finch made suggestions for it to me at Dartmouth College. After the war, Vernon Loggins of Columbia University supervised my master's essay on imagery in the three great novels of James's major phase. Still later, under Lionel Trilling, and F. W. Dupee and Lewis Leary as well, I wrote my dissertation at Columbia on imagery in all of James's fiction, completing this work in 1952. To all of these men I should like here to express my gratitude. Since that time, many circumstances caused delays in reworking my material, and publications by other Jamesians on the subject of James's figurative language have sprung up all about me. Many of the countless insights in those works are reflected in my study, which I hope is therefore the better for my delay.

Parts of some of the chapters which follow were first published, usually in rather different form, in *The American Imago, American Literature, Modern Fiction Studies, The Arizona Quarterly, Chess Life,* and *The Optometric Weekly,* and are reprinted by kind permission of the editors of those periodicals.

A key to all abbreviations used in citing James's fiction will be found in Table I, p. 250.

This prefatory note will not be too long if I end it now by dedicating my work on James to ten Gales from various points of the compass:

MG, MG, MG, JG, JG, CG, EG, EG, RG, and KG.

Robert L. Gale
University of Pittsburgh, 1964

TABLE OF CONTENTS

THE CAUGHT IMAGE

FIGURATIVE LANGUAGE
IN THE FICTION
OF HENRY JAMES

We work in the dark—we do what we can—we give what we have . . . (XVI "MY" 105).

I · TOO MANY FIGURES

"I don't think I know what you mean," she said;
"you use too many figures of speech; I could
never understand allegories" (III *PofL* I 395).

Since about 1920—indeed, one might say since Henry James's Prefaces—literary critics have been taking the novel ever more seriously. So it is not surprising to look back over recent decades and note that analytical powers comparable to those earlier devoted to a study of poetry and drama have been turned more and more illuminatingly upon this later literary form. A good novel is now seen to express its author's background, nature, and view reliably, to mirror its times revealingly, to persuade its readers maturely, and withal—containing as it does "the precious life-blood of a master spirit" —to have "a life beyond life."

A study of the figurative language of any master novelist ought to reveal a good deal concerning his nature and that of his age, ought also to tell much concerning his message, and should, in addition, elucidate the organic nature of his works one by one and *in toto*.

My study of imagery in the fiction of Henry James, I hope, will throw varied lights upon his personality and on the modes of his thought; say much about what in reality especially engaged his attention; and finally, help explicate his texts by showing that his imagery habitually paints setting, characterizes, foreshadows, implements plot, and reinforces theme.

And now for a definition and some examples. By "image" I mean simile or metaphor, in the broadest sense, and not a complex of words evoking a mental picture or a sensory impression. I regard imaginative analogy as a type of simile, and extended personification as a type of metaphor; hence both are subsumed under "image." By "imagery" I mean a mass of images. The following examples drawn from James's fiction illustrate his use of (1) simile, (2) metaphor, (3) imaginative analogy, and (4) extended personification:

(1) . . . the sounding torrent gushed beneath us, flashing in the light of the few stars which sparkled in our narrow strip of sky, like diamonds tacked upon a band of velvet ("AtI" 252).

(2) It was but half-hospitality to let her remain outside; to punish him for which Isabel administered innumerable taps with the ferule of her straight young wit (III *PofL* 82-83).

(3) He saw the face of Aurora Coyne whenever he winced with one of those livelier throbs of the sense of "Europe" which had begun to consume him even before his ship sighted land. He had sniffed the elder world from afar very much as Columbus had caught on *his* immortal approach the spices of the Western Isles. His consciousness was deep and confused, but "Europe" was for the time and for convenience the sign

easiest to know it by. It hovered before him, this sign, in places as to which signs were mainly of another sort . . . (XXVI *SeofP* 59).

(4) It [May Bartram's grave] met him in mildness—not, as before, in mockery; it wore for him the air of conscious greeting that we find, after absence, in things that have closely belonged to us and which seem to confess of themselves to the connexion (XVII "BinJ" 120).[1]

Frequently, James creates an image by the choice of a single figuratively used word in preference to one used literally. In the original edition of *The Ambassadors,* for example, James describes Strether questioning himself in the following literal language: "Hadn't he done well enough, for that matter, in being just so dazzled? and in not having too, as he almost believed, wholly hidden from his host [Gloriani] that he knew of the latter's inquiry?"[2] This passage was slightly revised in 1909 for the New York Edition, and the result was a new if unelaborated metaphor where before the words had been only literal: "Hadn't he done well enough, so far as that went, in being exactly so dazzled? and in not having too, as he almost believed, wholly hidden from his host that he felt the latter's plummet?" (XXI *Amb* I 198).

At the other extreme, a single imagistic unit may run to

1. My four examples happen to illustrate the four basic types of figurative comparisons distinguished by Quintilian: "Metaphors fall into four classes. In the first we substitute one living thing for another. . . . Secondly, inanimate things may be substituted for inanimate . . . or [3] inanimate may be substituted for animate . . . or [4] animate for inanimate . . ."; *The Institutio Oratoria of Quintilian,* trans. H. E. Butler, 4 vols., in The Loeb Classical Library (London: William Heinemann, 1922), III, 305, 307 (or Bk. VIII, ch. vi, ll. 8-10). Thus my first example illustrates Quintilian's second class; my second, his third; my third, his first; and my fourth, his fourth. Quintilian just earlier writes that "On the whole *metaphor* is a shorter form of *simile* . . ." (III, 305). I should say that most of James's *tropi* would fall into Quintilian's first and third categories.

2. Henry James, *The Ambassadors: A Novel* (New York: Harper & Brothers Publishers, 1903), pp. 136-37.

five hundred or more words, a proliferation most often encountered in the works written between 1902 and 1909. For example, James suggests the huge problem confronting Maggie Verver's tortured mind in a bizarre figure sprawling across three pages of *The Golden Bowl*:

This situation had been occupying . . . the very centre of the garden of her life, but it had reared itself there like some strange tall tower of ivory, or perhaps rather some wonderful . . . pagoda, a structure plated with . . . porcelain . . . and adorned . . . with silver bells. . . . She had walked around and round it . . . looking up all the while at the fair structure that spread itself so amply. . . . The thing might have been . . . a Mahometan mosque, with which no base heretic could take a liberty . . . it was nevertheless quite as if she had sounded with a tap or two one of the rare porcelain plates. . . . The pagoda in her blooming garden figured the arrangement—how otherwise was it to be named?—by which, so strikingly, she had been able to marry without breaking, as she liked to put it, with her past (XXIV *GB* II 3-5).

We would all agree that the above passage is figurative; however, some might consider that it had four or five images in it, others fewer, still others but one. Since uniformity here is unlikely among image-counters, consistency is essential if counts by any one reader are to be meaningful. It may be helpful—if prosaic—to compare at this point a rhetorical figure to a mathematical statement: $A = $ or $\sim B$, in which A represents the tenor (or literal aspect of the comparison) and B the vehicle (or figurative aspect). Sometimes the precise nature of the tenor is only implied and must therefore be furnished by the reader. In the metaphor from *The Ambassadors* above, Gloriani's inquiring nature (A) equals a plummet (B); in the fantastic simile from *The Golden Bowl* Maggie's problem (A) is similar to a pagoda (B). In my counting, I have considered as a single figure any comparison in which neither the tenor (A) nor the vehicle (B) of the equation changes its identity appreciably. Hence, I consider the whole passage containing the pagoda to have but one image.

It is important next to explain what I do not consider to be figures. Dead metaphors, established in the language as idiomatic expressions or turns of speech or clichés, clutter James's fiction. I do not examine in this study his repetition of mere lifeless tropes. For example, I regard the following passages as non-figurative: "Benyon . . . struck a note more serious than any that had hitherto sounded between them" (xxv "GeR" 313); " 'I think she's an actress, but she believes in her part while she's playing it' " (I *RH* 196); and "I besieged his office, I waylaid his myrmidons, I haunted his path, I poisoned, I tried to flatter myself, his life . . ." (xxvii "JD" 400). Also, I ignore every instance in which James uses a word deriving from a proper noun if it has taken on a special meaning because of a memorable characteristic of the original, since the special meaning is no longer figurative. In the following examples we again have only dead metaphors: "[that] was what, for a Parthian shot, Jane's husband would have liked to leave with her" (xxviii "MM" 277); "Her judgements, as you probably know, are Rhadamanthine' " (VII *TM* I 60); and "she believed herself born, I think, to be the lawful Egeria of a cabinet minister" ("SofB" 764). In addition, James often tediously uses hackneyed idioms, which are no longer figurative. Thus, "Her friend hung fire but a moment" (XVI "BW" 146), and " 'My dear fellow, at night all cats are grey!' " (II *Ame* 338). Unless James adds something to rejuvenate such clichés—and he often does so—I do not call them images. And finally, (1) hyperbole, (2) literal similarity, (3) mere imaginativeness, (4) foreign idioms, and (5) unelaborated translations of foreign phrases into English I also uniformly reject, on the grounds that they do not present figurative comparisons. The following passages, and all others of which they are examples of James's not-quite-imagistic phrasing, therefore play no part in this study:

(1) Schinkel . . . [was] putting away his pipe in a receptacle almost as large as a fiddle-case (V *PC* I 361).

(2) Agreeably to this fact, his most frequent feeling when he was with her was a consciousness of the liberty to be still—a sensation not unlike that which in the early afternoon, as he lounged in his orchard with a pipe, he derived from the sight of the hot, vaporous hills (xxv "PR" 458).

(3) . . . the descent of Mary Antrim opened his spirit with a great compunctious throb for the descent of Acton Hague. It was as if Stransom had read what her eyes said to him (XVII "AofD" 56).

(4) "Parents in society? D'ou tombez-vous? . . ." (XVIII "Pan" 141).

(5) "Petherton will tell you—I wonder he hasn't told you before—why Mrs. Grendon, though not perhaps herself quite the rose, is decidedly in these days too near it" (IX *AA* 101-2).[3]

Even after we coldly reject much, what remains for treatment is considerable. Appearing in the 135 fictional pieces of James are 16,902 figures of speech.[4] Now, if you will permit another total, I should like to add that James's fiction comes to 4,189,800 words. Hence, his imagistic density is four images per one thousand words. Throughout his career of half a century he varied remarkably little from this average; his fiction before 1900, especially that of the 1880's, is slightly below it, while his fiction after 1900, especially that of the first decade of the new century, is noticeably above. Further, James used

3. The original is "Je ne suis pas la rose, mais j'ai vécu avec elle." If James figuratively elaborates the idiom, as he does in the following passage, it turns imagistic: "He had become, in the brief space of a moment, the man she once had loved; but if he was no longer the rose, he stood too near it to be wantonly bruised" (xxiv *WandW* 191).

4. Or perhaps I should say there were at one moment of time, since anyone's standards shift somewhat!

a slightly higher density of imagery in short stories and in long novels than in long short stories and nouvelles.[5] Also, James was inspired to create slightly more images in stories and novels set principally or entirely in England and in France than those set in America, Italy, Germany, Switzerland, or elsewhere. Finally, his unrevised pieces have relatively fewer images than his revised ones.

Counts, wordage, and imagistic densities mean little until explained and also compared with those of other novelists. But when we consider that James often embroidered a single image until it dominated an entire long paragraph, and then that four images per one thousand words can be translated to mean roughly an image per page in the New York Edition, we have more meaningful facts. Further, as every reader senses, both the density and the proliferation of James's images exceed those in the works of almost every other important American fiction writer. Cooper uses almost no tropes. Hawthorne and Melville compare well with James. For example, *The Scarlet Letter* contains slightly more figures of speech per one thousand words than James averages, partly because Hawthorne very rarely elaborates a simile or metaphor; most of his short fiction, however—even "The Gentle Boy" and "Young Goodman Brown," but not "Ethan Brand" and "Rappaccini's Daughter"—is relatively barren of images. *Moby Dick* is rich in suggested and developed tropes, averaging roughly what James's entire fiction does, as do several of Melville's shorter pieces, such as "Bartleby" and "Benito Cereno." Howells and Twain, for different reasons, almost never indulge in figurative language: *Huckleberry Finn,* for example, has an image for

5. I define a short story as under 25,000 words; a long short story, 25,000 to 50,000 words; a short novel, 50,000 to 75,000 words; and a novel, over 75,000 words. According to these standards, James wrote a hundred and one short stories, twelve long short stories, eleven short novels, and eleven novels.

only every five or so pages, and *The Rise of Silas Lapham* even fewer. Stephen Crane's fiction is often glowingly figurative, and the tropes in *The Red Badge of Courage* form themselves into numerous patterns, as do James's. Dreiser rarely penned a simile or metaphor; often, when he did, the effort seems strained and the results painful, as in *Sister Carrie* (note some of its chapter titles, for example). *The Great Gatsby* by Fitzgerald is Jamesian in its figurative language, but the density of imagery is somewhat less, and the same may be said of his short stories. Hemingway is rarely figurative, and the few images are lonely and do not coalesce into patterns. Finally, Faulkner is challengingly imagistic, like James, and his figures elucidate much in the author's background, his unconscious mind, and—especially when in patterns—his characters and themes.

More to the point now than mere statistics and general comparisons, however, are functions of James's images. Some of the most charming figures in all of James are nothing more than elements of adornment in an elaborate prose. And, surprisingly, many are intriguing because of their homely diction. Others are more significant. Often an image having a certain gaucherie tells the reader that one of James's centers of revelation has received new information to ponder. And a vast number of the most effective figures challenge or forewarn the reader by a surprising or pleasant turn. The most important figures of this sort throw light—often ironic—upon character or situation by means of rhetorical effects. Now for some examples. The tropes contained in the following quotations are merely decorative: a certain Italian countess is "as subtle as a needlepoint" (xxv "DofM" 21); an old woman's "clicking needles . . . seemed as personal to her and as expressive as prolonged fingers" (X "Ch" 437); and an aristocratic lady's thin-legged deer remind an observer of "small pincushions

turned upside down" (XIV "SofL" 223).[6] More involved but
no more necessary to the novels and stories in which they
appear are many images like the following: "the atmosphere
of West Kensington, purified by the wind, was like a dirty
old coat that had been bettered by a dirty old brush" (X
SpofP 262); an independent young woman impresses an observer "as leaning, subject to any swing, so to speak, on the
easy gate of the house of life" (XIV "PB" 408-9); and a narrator praises fine conversation as "the gift of the gods themselves, the one starry spangle on the ragged cloak of humanity"
(XV "CF" 290). Often James surprisingly deflates characters
by the use of homely conceits: thus, one woman has "no more
prejudices than an old sausage-mill" (XVI "GF" 116), while
another whines "with a resentment as vain as a failure to
sneeze" (VIII *TM* II 309). Sometimes the comparison, while
still homely, is more complicated, as when a supercilious
character criticizes the flat lives of most people by saying,
" 'Their stories are like the underside of the carpet,—nothing
but the stringy grain of the tissue,—a muddle of figures without shape and flowers without colours' " (xxiv *WandW* 130);
or when James suggests the patronizing attitude of a son toward his admittedly inept father: ". . . poor Father [he thinks],
the fine damp plaster of whose composition, renewed from
week to week, can't be touched anywhere without letting your
finger in, without peril of its coming to pieces . . ." ("MS"
532). Scores of strange figures describe the flash of wisdom
into the minds of narrators and other central characters. Admittedly it is hard to describe such mental illumination in
literal terms, but James surely outdoes all rivals, very often

6. James has a surprising number of figures in his prefaces comparing himself to an embroiderer: see, for example, I vii-viii, IX xx, XIX
xiv. For a brief discussion of this pattern, see Robert L. Gale, "Henry
James's Imagistic Portrait of Henry James," *Forum* (University of
Houston), III (Summer, 1961), 34.

indeed with "light" imagery.[7] In one of the weirdest of such similes, he has John Marcher suddenly remember Miss Bartram:

As soon as he heard her voice . . . the gap was filled up and the missing link supplied. . . . Her face and her voice, all at his service now, worked the miracle—the impression operated like the torch of a lamp-lighter who touches into flame, one by one, a long row of gas-jets. Marcher flattered himself the illumination was brilliant. . . (XVII "BinJ" 64-65).[8]

Often truth suddenly appears on the fluid surface of reality, and occasionally revelation opens and spreads before one. Thus, one character "couldn't help almost seeing it as the spray of sea-nymphs, or hearing it as the sounded horn of tritons, emerging, to cast their spell, from the foam-flecked tides around, that he was regarded as a creature unnaturally 'quiet' . . ." (XXV *IT* 247),[9] while for another "Light broke

7. Further, as R. W. Short has pointed out, James indicates moral progress by having light dispel darkness. The heart of Short's excellent paragraph on this subject is worth quoting in full: "A complicated set of ambiguities is involved, which must be briefly summarized. For James, as for Milton, light together with height and air was good, and dark was bad. Moral progress is from dark to light. But the best people are often at their best, or nearing their best, in their darkest moments and environments; and conversely, bad people may be associated with light"; R. W. Short, "Henry James's World of Images," *PMLA*, LXVIII (December, 1953), 950. I must add, however, that in my opinion this article is marred by two flaws: Short does not explicitly define what he regards as an image (he treats as images title symbols [p. 955], meetings of characters [p. 952], and even meals—which, he says, "may be called images because they are time-pegs" [p. 952]); and in spite of his comprehensive title—"Henry James's World of Images"—he quotes or refers directly to imagery from only six of James's novels and only three of his short stories, and virtually all of his evidence—which he has selected, presented, and interpreted brilliantly—comes from *The Princess Casamassima, The Sacred Fount, The Wings of the Dove,* and *The Golden Bowl.*

8. Numerous images in James also concern "kindled trains"; see xxiv "IofC" 454, XIII "PP" 402, iii *Eurs* 167, for three examples.

9. I feel that the many sea-nymph images in James, of which this is representative, may have exerted an influence upon T. S. Eliot as he was writing the conclusion of "The Love Song of J. Alfred Prufrock."

. . . at last, indeed, quite as a consequence of the fear of breathing a chill upon this luxuriance of her spiritual garden. As at a turn of his labyrinth he saw his issue, which opened out so wide . . . that he held his breath with wonder" (XXIII *GB* II 207). James often is little short of grotesque in showing awareness dawning upon a person. "It was the click of a spring—he saw the truth" (XXI *Amb* I 220).[10] Or "there hung in his eye at the same time the lively truth, which fairly jerked out arms and legs like those of a toy harlequin worked by a spring, that manner was essentially and by an extraordinary law to be his constant retort and weapon" (XXVI *SeofP* 158). Finally, James lays bare essential character and foreshadows important circumstance by recourse to startling figures. For example, one young man, who manifestly wants nothing so much as to be walked on by others, is characterized by means of this typically Jamesian image:

He was coming in as they came out; and his "I *hoped* I might find you," an exhalation of cool candour that they took full in the face, had the effect, the next moment, of a great soft carpet, all flowers and figures, suddenly unrolled for them to walk upon and before which they felt a scruple (xxviii "Pap" 193).

The following justly celebrated simile suggests the tedious correctness of Owen Gereth of *The Spoils of Poynton*: " 'You don't think I'm hard or rough, do you?' he asked of Fleda, his impatience shining in his idle eyes as the dining-hour shines in club-windows" (X *SpofP* 47).[11] Finally, Maggie Verver's inevitable feeling of remoteness from the experience of the heady passion of resentful and vindictive jealousy is caught in the following extended conceit:

10. Pressed springs constitute a mannerism in James's style.
11. F. O. Matthiessen discusses this fine image briefly, in connection with comments on Eliot's theory of the objective correlative; see *American Renaissance: Art and Expression in the Age of Emerson and Whitman* (New York: Oxford University Press, 1941), p. 305 n. 10.

She might fairly . . . have missed it as a lost thing; have yearned for it . . . [as] a range of feelings which for many women would have meant so much, but which for *her* husband's wife, for her father's daughter, figured nothing nearer to experience than a wild eastern caravan, looming into view with crude colours against the sky, all a thrill, a natural joy to mingle with, but turning off short before it reached her and plunging into other defiles (XXIV *GB* II 236-37).[12]

The examples already quoted demonstrate that James's imagery is often comic and emphatic, is usually graphic and concrete—bringing abstract situations and almost indefinable traits of character down to tangible reality—and is regularly challenging to the would-be explicator. Reducing to complete order almost seventeen hundred images, written through half a century in eleven long novels and eleven short novels and twelve long short stories and a hundred and one short stories, is admittedly impossible. One might analyze them chronologically to show their development through the decades. One

---

12. For a very full explanation of the functions of imagery in James's fiction, see Alexander Holder-Barell, *The Development of Imagery and Its Functional Significance in Henry James's Novels*, The Cooper Monographs (Bern: Francke Verlag, 1959). Holder-Barell briefly discusses rhetorical images and then divides his subject into four main parts: expanding images (these emphasize facts, illustrate statements, clarify, and provide humor), characterizing images (these are used in dialogue, descriptions of physical appearance, and revelation of inner nature), images making abstractions concrete (these concern thoughts, ideas, and feelings), and constructive images (these contribute to the structure of a novel by building iterative patterns and by foreshadowing). In spite of the title of his monograph, Holder-Barell considers imagery in only six novels: *Roderick Hudson, The Portrait of a Lady, The Old Things* (better known by its revised title, *The Spoils of Poynton*), *The Ambassadors, The Wings of the Dove,* and *The Golden Bowl.* Further, I feel that Holder-Barell ought to have used the categorizing approach to imagery—which he disparages in his introduction—either considerably more or somewhat less: war and animal images, for example, are discussed only as characterizing, whereas they—as well as flower, religion, and other types of figures not considered—function in all four of the ways specified. For the best brief statement of the functions of imagery in James, see William M. Gibson, "Metaphor in the Plot of *The Ambassadors,*" *New England Quarterly,* XXIV (September, 1951), 292.

might demonstrate their different functions in the works. Or one might—as I shall do—follow Caroline F. E. Spurgeon's method with Shakespeare's imagery, and place the figures into major and minor categories according to the contents of their vehicles.[13] So handled, the figures in James's fiction fall into six major groups—water, flower, and animal (the non-human half), and war, art, and religion (the human half)—and into many minor ones, those, for example, involving fire, metals, sensations, children, James's personal loves—including America, money, travel, and wine—and the like. The dangers of Miss Spurgeon's approach are only too well known,[14] but I still feel that it provides the most reliable method of handling the bulk of James's similes and metaphors; and I shall be content if by following it I can lead general readers of James back to his fiction with new alertness and can provide other scholars with evidence for more specialized studies of aspects of James.

13. Caroline F. E. Spurgeon, *Shakespeare's Imagery and What It Tells Us* (New York: The Macmillan Company, 1936).

14. See in particular Mario Praz, review of Spurgeon, *Shakespeare's Imagery*, in *English Studies*, XVIII (August, 1936), 177-81; Lillian Herlands Hornstein, "Analysis of Imagery: A Critique of Literary Method," *PMLA*, LVII (September, 1942), 638-53; and Josephine Miles, "The Problem of Imagery," *Sewanee Review*, LVIII (Summer, 1950), 522-26. For a superb introduction to the whole problem of the analysis of figurative language, see René Wellek and Austin Warren, *Theory of Literature*, 2nd ed. (New York: Harcourt, Brace and Company, 1956), Ch. XV, "Image, Metaphor, Symbol, Myth," especially pp. 175-78, 196-201.

II · THE GREAT WAVE

. . . the effect of the occurrence of anything in particular was to make the sea submerge the island, the margin flood the text. The great wave now for a moment swept over (XIX *WofD* I 199).

Introduction

The more than thirteen hundred water images, about one-twelfth of the total number of figures, are spread rather evenly through the decades of James's fictional production. A slightly larger proportion appears in the fiction of 1900-1910 than elsewhere. Freud and Jung might have a word or two on their sources; but, as everyone knows, James loved the Hudson River and the beach at Newport and countless other water resorts, and he was an inveterate ocean-traveller. So it was natural that, like his own Maggie Verver, he "had images . . . that were drawn from steamers and trains, from a familiarity with 'lines,' . . . an experience of continents and seas" (XXIII GB I 15).[1] Whether the frequency of water imagery in James indicates any mythic pattern or unconscious return to the amniotic realm, it would take a daring psychologist or an irresponsible literary critic to say;[2] suffice it here to remark that James's works rarely seem to lend themselves to the sort of treatment either recommended by Maud Bodkin or practiced by Marie Bonaparte:[3] most of James's characters are sedentary and sophisticated, and to James water was something mainly to be looked at for aesthetic pleasure and ships were mainly means of transportation from one place to another. James displays no such intimacy with water as we find in Twain or Melville.

i. Water in Movement

Water in movement is extremely frequent in the imagery of James. Often, characters and elements are seen as simply floating or drifting on the current; almost as often, persons are imaged as passive at the water's edge watching others speed by. Thus, " 'To be young and ardent, in the midst of an Italian spring, and to believe in the moral perfection of a beautiful woman—what an admirable situation! Float with the

1. R. W. Short, making far too much of this passage, says that it "can be taken as an almost complete description of the thematic imagery of the . . . novel"; "Henry James's World of Images," *PMLA*, LXVIII (December, 1953), 956. Such a comment ignores all the art, war, and metal imagery, and figures of many other categories in addition, in *The Golden Bowl.*

2. For similar warnings, see Stanley Edgar Hyman, *The Armed Vision: A Study of Modern Literary Criticism* (New York: Alfred A. Knopf, 1948), p. 219; and Theodore Howard Banks, *Milton's Imagery* (New York: Columbia University Press, 1950), p. xiii.

3. Maud Bodkin, *Archetypal Patterns in Poetry: Psychological Studies of Imagination* (New York: Vintage Books, 1958), pp. 96, 110-11; and Marie Bonaparte, *The Life and Works of Edgar Allan Poe: A Psycho-Analytic Interpretation* (London: Imago Publishing, 1949), *passim.*

current; I'll stand on the brink and watch you'" (xxv "DofM" 30)—so a retired general advises his young friend half loftily and, as we sense at the end, half pathetically. Was celibate, observant James, thirty-six years of age when this story appeared, watching his youth go out to sea? And "Dora . . . hung back disinterestedly, as if not to challenge their discernment, while the current passed her, keeping her little sister in position on its brink meanwhile by the tenderest small gesture" (xxvi "MrsT" 293). Since it is always arduous to resist the current, most people are passive in the drift of things, and we read that Milly Theale's "sudden social adventure . . . had been favoured . . . by the simple spring-board of the scene, by one of those common caprices of the numberless foolish flock, gregarious movements as inscrutable as ocean-currents. The huddled herd had drifted to her blindly—it might as blindly have drifted away" (XX WofD II 43).

In James's imagistic seas, water moves in waves, in tides of all sorts, and in floods. With almost monotonous regularity, for example, James has knowledge come in breaking waves: ". . . even before I reached him it had rolled over me in a prodigious wave that I had lost nothing whatever" (xxix SF 175); "'The truth rolled over me in a stifling wave'" (XVII "FofF" 356).[4]

As for tides, they may rise, turn, or sadly ebb. Thus, a tourist in Washington opines optimistically that "a mighty tide is sweeping the world to democracy" (XIV "PofV" 599), while a witness of the Roman sea of light records in cadenced prose, "I would . . . strain my ear to the soft low silence, pity the dark dishonored plain, watch the heavens come rolling down in tides of light, and breaking in waves of fire against the massive stillness of temples and tombs" ("TC" 695). After an encounter with Mrs. Wix, Maisie's wayward mother seems "a

4. As though tired of this figure later in his writing career, James used it little in the revisions.

little besprinkled by such turns of the tide" (XI *WMK* 355), and the narrator of the story "Glasses," writing of his mother's death, says simply, "that high tide had ebbed" (xxvii "Gl" 243). More poignantly, since he deplores waste, James has the procrastinating painter of "The Madonna of the Future" finally conclude that "one by one, the noiseless years had ebbed away and left him brooding in charmed inaction, for ever preparing for a work for ever deferred" (XIII "MofF" 472).[5]

Water moving out to sea serves James's imagination well, whether in description of loss or of release. Thus, thinking of her recently dead husband, Mrs. Warren Hope in "The Abasement of the Northmores" "had much of the time the sense of walking by some swift stream on which an object dear to her was floating out to sea. All her instinct was to keep up with it. . . . Alas it only floated and floated. . . . She ran, she watched, she lived with her great fear; and all the while, as the distance to the sea diminished, the current visibly increased" (XVI "AofN" 200). For relief, we may turn to *The Sacred Fount* and its narrator's comments, which are perhaps sexually loaded: May Server is "the acrid channel forsaken by the stream," and Mrs. Brissenden, "the full-fed river sweeping to the sea, the volume of water, the stately current, the flooded banks into which the source had swelled" (xxix *SF* 191).[6] Melodramatically, the clandestine embrace of Char-

5. The cadence of the line is faintly Keatsian—"For ever piping songs for ever new . . ." Keats was one of James's favorite poets. See pp. 111-12 below. The moral of James's line seems to echo that of Emerson's "Days."

6. James may have tapped the same source as this image had when seven years later he penned another one, even more bizarre, to describe a hurriedly clad woman in the episode called "The Married Son," James's contribution to the round-robin novel *The Whole Family:* "The powder on the massive lady's face indeed transcended . . . the bounds of prose, did much to refer her to the realms of fantasy, some fairyland forlorn [Keats again], an effect the more marked as the wrapper she appeared hastily to have caught up, and which was somehow both volu-

lotte and the Prince in *The Golden Bowl* is depicted in a fluid image worthy of D. H. Lawrence: "They vowed it, gave it out and took it in, drawn, by their intensity, more closely together. Then of a sudden, through this tightened circle, as at the issue of a narrow strait into the sea beyond, everything broke up, broke down, gave way, melted and mingled" (XXIII *GB* I 312).

James frequently images time as a flux. In doing so, he is in the company of many illustrious writers, from Heraclitus to Bergson. The process of reminiscence James often—especially after he was fifty—pictured as "remounting the stream of time." In its simplest form, James once used the image merely as follows: "Mrs. Mulville had to remount the stream" (XV "CF" 324). More elaborately, "they went over the whole thing, remounted the dwindling stream, reconstructed, explained, understood. . ." (XVI "BW" 162). Most fully—"She might have been wishing, under this renewed, this still more suggestive visitation, to keep him with her for remounting the stream of time and dipping again, for the softness of the water, into the contracted basin of the past" (XXIV *GB* II 258). Perhaps the most appropriate use of this little image comes in *The Sense of the Past,* in which Ralph Pendrel surveys his situation in London with his time-redolent house and then concludes that "It was to this he had been brought by his desire to remount the stream of time, really to bathe in its upper and more natural waters, to risk even, as he might say, drinking of them" (XXVI *SeofP* 48).[7]

minous and tense (flowing like a cataract in some places, yet in others exposing, or at least defining, the ample bed of the stream) reminded me of the big cloth spread in a room when any mess is to be made" ("MS" 542). For details of *The Whole Family,* see B. R. McElderry, Jr., "Henry James and *The Whole Family," Pacific Spectator,* IV (Summer, 1950), 352-60.

7. In his prefaces, James also likened his revisionary process to remounting the stream: see II xii, X xx, XIII vii, XVII ix, XIX xiii.

ii. Travel by Water

Imagery concerning travel by water varies from numerous conventionally romantic sailing figures to a very few which use modern vessels. Chronologically the earliest of the many old-fashioned sailing images in James is also one of the most dreadfully romantic. It might have come from Gothic fiction of the previous century. "What bliss to gaze upon the smooth gurgling wake of a good deed, while the comely bark sails on with floating pennon! What horror to look into the muddy sediment which floats round the piratic keel!" ("SofY" 271).[8] Just as traditional are the too-numerous uses of the wind-in-the-sails theme, which James plays upon from *The Europeans* to *The Sense of the Past*. Thus, "Felix . . . rejoined with the alacrity of a maritime adventurer who feels a puff of wind in his sail" (iii *Eurs* 166). But Ralph Pendrel does not "feel it as wind in his sails" (XXVI *SeofP* 161) when he can inspire dull Perry; until Nan Midmore is mentioned, Ralph's "sail had done nothing but swell in the breeze," but thereafter it "indulge[d] in its first, its single flap" (161). Lastly, the young man explains to Sir Cantopher his impatience to visit Molly by saying, " 'You'll understand how with such a wind in my sails I couldn't be slow to get into port' " (223).[9]

The romantic in James seems to have been responsible for the following reactionary remark by the retired sea-captain in "A Landscape Painter": " 'A tavern is only half a house, just as one of these new fashioned screw-propellers is only half a

8. Note that this figure contains the words "wake" and "float," both of which James overused for fifty years. Since for centuries the various originally figurative connotations of "float" and "wake" have been denotative and hence literal, I do not regard as figurative James's usages involving them unless they are elaborated imagistically with such words as "bubbles," "waves," and "glide."

9. The whole passage has vague unconscious sexual overtones, too faint, however, to be caught well. It is appropriate for Ralph to use sailing imagery, since he has just crossed the Atlantic and since he is also rather romantic in temperament.

ship' " (xxv "LaP" 350). At any rate, James rarely created an image dealing with a thoroughly admirable modern ship. Note that when Mrs. Susan Stringham of *The Wings of the Dove* considers the strange, old-world elements of Maud Lowder's life, she suggests that no modern ship could bear their weight if an attempt were made to export them to the new world. "They represented, she believed, the world, the world that, as a consequence of the cold shoulder turned to it by the Pilgrim Fathers, had never yet boldly crossed to Boston—it would surely have sunk the stoutest Cunarder . . ." (XIX *WofD* I 170). It may be that since modern ocean-travel was prosaic to James because of its very frequency, he preferred to use romantic sailing images or—when employing more modern vessels—to avoid any imagistic use of technicalities and instead to strive for comic effects. Many of the characters in James's fiction who employ or inspire sailing imagery are surely well-travelled enough for their author to have used serious imagery having to do with ships, if his main purpose had been to characterize them. But instead, the purpose of much of James's boat imagery, even in serious contexts, seems to me humorous.[10] Thus, we find Maxime de Cliché's wife to be a woman "whose cheeks were like decks in a high sea" (XIII *Re* 94) and who, when reduced to tears, "mopped the decks" (96). Again, Mrs. Stringham regards Milly as "a boat that she more and more estimated as, humanly speaking, of the biggest" (XIX *WofD* I 104) and beside which she herself "floated off with the sense of rocking violently at her side" (113). Mrs. Stringham's old school friend is pictured even more comically: "Mrs. Lowder . . . steer[ed] in the other quarter a course in which she called at subjects as if they were islets in an archipelago"

10. William M. Gibson speaks—rightly, I feel—of the "rather mechanical boat-images" contained in *The Ambassadors*; "Metaphor in the Plot of *The Ambassadors*," *New England Quarterly*, XXIV (September, 1951), 295 n. 16. The images in question may be found in XXII *Amb* II 64-65, 94, 111, 130.

(161-62). Finally, to return to the days of the romantic clippers, we can note that Rosanna Gaw of *The Ivory Tower* suggests a ship to James, and that the gigantic girl's "draperies, white and voluminous, yielded to the mild breeze in the manner of those of a ship held back from speed and yet with its canvas expanded" (XXV *IT* 1); further, when the girl waits for her tiny, aged father, the two "resemble . . . a big ship staying its course to allow its belittled tender to keep near" (15).

With one minor exception, James saw his shipboard images from deck or pilot-house, not from galley, hold, or engine-room. Exceptionally, we find Roderick Hudson answering his patron's challenge as follows: "'Well then, haven't I got up steam enough? It won't have been for want of your being a first-class stoker . . .'" (I *RH* 85). That slight figure is forgotten when one considers the dozens of images which put James back on deck, often quietly watching the bustle of others. Thus, servants in *The Awkward Age* are likened to "'hands' mustered by a whistle on the deck of a ship" (IX *AA* 234); a quietly efficient Venetian *domestico* is compared to "a barefooted seaman on the deck of a ship" (XX *WofD* II 167); and Straith of "Broken Wings" "might at her arrival [Mrs. Harvey's] have reminded her of the master of a neat bare ship on his deck and awaiting a cargo" (XVI "BW" 155).

iii. Danger in Water

Danger in the water—somewhat more frequent and certainly more fraught with drama than mere pleasure there—takes two forms in James's imagery: often a vessel is seen endangered or wrecked; less often a person is pictured as wallowing in the engulfing flood. If aboard ship, James's figuratively endangered person may be a lonely sailor (Basil Ransom in New York reminds himself oddly of "a man in an open boat, at sea, who should just have parted with his last rag of canvas" [viii *Bo* I 228]), or a frightened passenger of a liner ("She had the impression known to the passengers on a great steamer when, in the middle of the night, they feel the engine stop"[11] [XVIII "Ma" 279]); but that person is never a stoker before an overheated boiler or anything similarly lowly. Too often for me to want to demonstrate the fact, we find the embattled figure limned no better than this: "he was by this time quite at sea and could recognise no shores" (VI *PC* II 27).[12] As for the many victims of shipwreck who are thrown into the deadly waters, James's first water image—in the anonymously published "A Tragedy of Error,"[13] 1864—shows us a representative group: "'When a ship goes to pieces on those rocks out at sea, the poor devils who are pushing their way to land on a floating spar, don't bestow many glances on those who are battling with the waves beside them'" ("TofE" 205).

James occasionally uses hackneyed idioms concerning water and elaborates them into imagery of moderate interest. Thus, Adam Verver burns his ships behind him, which action signals his proposal to Charlotte, and the train of images runs thinly through the next several pages: seeking "a lurid grandeur" (XXIII *GB* I 216), he "applied his torch" (217) with

11. This image—like a similar one from *The Princess Casamassima* ("the cabinet-maker . . . restor[ed] his pipe to his lips after an interval almost as momentous as the stoppage of a steamer in mid-ocean" [V *PC* I 348])—tells more about James's probable personal experiences than about the heroine of "The Marriages," Adela Chart, whose personal point of view is, however, probably reflected when earlier James says that her father's hated lady friend has a voice which "resembled the bell of a steamboat" (XVIII "Ma" 257).

12. Here we have Hyacinth Robinson endangered because of his promise to serve Hoffendahl; the image is partly prepared for when earlier we read that Hyacinth's "imagination . . . had launched itself into possible perils" (V *PC* I 355).

13. For details of this story, see Leon Edel, *Henry James: The Untried Years* (Philadelphia and New York: J. B. Lippincott Company, 1953), pp. 215-18; for a demonstration that the imagery of this anonymously published short story is clearly Jamesian, see Robert L. Gale, "A Note on Henry James's First Short Story," *Modern Language Notes*, LXXII (February, 1957), 103-7.

a "redoubled thrust of flame" (218) and then enjoyed "the fine pink glow . . . of his ships . . . definitely blazing and crackling" (221).[14] Figurative ships when in distress are often lightened, once extravagantly: "There was a fearful amount of concession in it, but what you kept had a rare intensity. You were perpetually throwing over the cargo to save the ship, but what a motion you gave her when you made her ride the waves—a motion as rhythmic as the dance of a goddess!" (xxvi "NV" 452).[15] Two other water idioms—leading a horse to water and washing one's hands of something—are frequent in James but are rarely elaborated into imagery. One notable exception: "if, as she declared, she had washed her hands of him, she had carefully preserved the water of this ablution, which she handed about for analysis" (XV "CF" 301).

The fiction is a welter of ships in storms, colliding, leaking, sending up rockets, dropping lifeboats, and smashed to mere floating planks. For example, "The Pupil" has a steady undertow of danger at sea: hatches are closed for the impending blow, glassy eyes scan the horizon for the nearest port, Pemberton wonders why nobody is "pitching Morgan into some sort of lifeboat" (XI "Pu" 569). Such imagery is beautifully apt in a short story cast in watery Venice, in Nice by the sea, and in occasionally rain-swept Paris; further, the plot concerns the break-up of a selfish and drifting family whose motto in times of storm is "a frightened *sauve qui peut*"

14. Adeline R. Tintner perceptively relates Adam Verver's seeing himself as the Cortez of Keats's sonnet on Chapman's Homer to this sequence of ship-burning figures, which show Adam "subsconsciously using the legend of Cortez' burning of his ships, when he proposes to Charlotte"; "The Spoils of Henry James," *PMLA*, LXI (March, 1946), 250. Also see p. 111 below.

15. Here James is discussing the need of a dramatist to compress his material into scenic ideas; the ecstatic image reflects James's joy during 1892, one of his early *années dramatiques*. For other images having to do with lightening endangered vessels, see "GuC" 570, I *RH* 296, X *SpofP* 57.

(572); and finally, the name "Morgan" means "one who lives by the sea."[16] Ultimately the wreck of the Moreens is all too real. Vivid images picture the distress of Lady Agnes in *The Tragic Muse* at learning that her son Nick has given up politics for painting: "her face was like that of a passenger on a ship who sees the huge bows of another vessel towering close out of the fog" (VIII *TM* II 181); though she fights back "after her first drowning gasp" (181), she soon knows that Nick's "behaviour had sprung a dreadful leak in the great vessel of their hopes" (226). A warning in James's fiction may take the form of "a rocket or two . . . sent up" (XI *WMK* 303), "wild signals and rocket-flights" (XI "InC" 390),[17] or "a shipwrecked signal to a sail on the horizon" (*Ou* 41).

James, who evidently hated streetcars, on two occasions thirty years apart used precisely the same mocking life-boat figure deriving from them: "the people . . . projected themselves upon it [a streetcar] in . . . a movement suggesting the scramble for places in a life-boat at sea—and were engulfed in its large interior" (iii *Eurs* 2-3); and "She made use of . . . the terrible things [streetcars] that people scrambled for as the panic-stricken at sea scramble for the boats" (XVII "JC" 439).[18]

Flotsam from smash-ups also occasionally aids characters

16. See Terence Martin, "James's 'The Pupil': The Art of Seeing Through," *Modern Fiction Studies*, IV (Winter, 1958-59), 338. For other water images in "The Pupil," see XI "Pu" 548, 570, 574, 575.

17. It is possible that James composed these two images, which appear in the original texts exactly as in the quoted revised editions, at about the same time: *What Maisie Knew* was first published in 1897, "In the Cage" in 1898.

18. *The Europeans* was first published in 1878, "The Jolly Corner" in 1908. For similar comments on streetcars, see also xxv "NEW" 107-8, viii *Bo* I 257-59, xxviii "RofV" 383-84. T. W. Higginson accused James of "exhibiting horsecars in the streets of Boston nearly ten years before their introduction" when he wrote *The Europeans*; "Henry James, Jr.," in *The Question of Henry James*, ed. F. W. Dupee (New York: Henry Holt and Company, 1945), p. 3.

jeopardized by circumstance. Thus, Christina Light's mother sees Rowland Mallet as "her single floating spar" (I *RH* 396); Maggie's one word "Wait!" to her Prince is "their plank now on the great sea" (XXIV *GB* II 352-53); and the narrator of "The Tone of Time" is like a person "clinging to a plank" (xxvi "TofT" 456).[19]

Most of James's often tiresomely frequent and mannered images involving light are simple and unrewarding;[20] sometimes, however, as in the case of figures concerning danger and lights at sea, they are exciting. Thus, Dr. Sloper of *Washington Square* says that his unbalanced sister Mrs. Penniman "'is like a revolving lighthouse; pitch darkness alternating with a dazzling brilliancy!'" (v *WS* 39); in the eyes of the pathetic little clerk in the story "In the Cage" the romantic Captain Everard "shone . . . like a tall lighthouse" (XI "InC" 484);[21] and the narrator of "Sir Edmund Orme," hoping to see the noble apparition again, confides to us, "I was on the look-out for it as a pilot for the flash of a revolving light" (XVII "SirE" 390). Lights, the sea, and danger coalesce several times in James's imagery, to make an almost archetypal pattern, when the literal subject is human eyes, which we might call James's favorite human organ (with the voice close behind). For example, the narrator of "The Coxon Fund" pronounces Saltram's beaux yeux "tragic and splendid—lights on a dangerous coast" (XV "CF" 297),[22] while the eye-glasses

19. See also XVII "JB" 534, 536; *OH* 145.
20. In *The Wings of the Dove*, *The Ambassadors*, and *The Golden Bowl* alone, the word "light" appears more than 250 times in imagistic or at least highly imaginative contexts.
21. Jean Frantz Blackall valuably analyzes images of light in this short story; see her "James's *In the Cage*: An Approach through the Figurative Language," *University of Toronto Quarterly*, XXXI (January, 1962), 170-71. However, Mrs. Blackall considers as figurative several passages involving "light" which I regard as literal and/or symbolic but not figurative.
22. Samuel Taylor Coleridge, prototype of Saltram in "The Coxon Fund," also had fine eyes.

of the unpleasant critic Mr. Morrow in "The Death of the Lion" suggest to the narrator "the electric headlights on some monstrous modern ship, and I felt as if Paraday and I were tossing terrified under his bows" (XV "DofL" 112).[23]

Notable are the numerous but rarely developed figures showing persons not aboard ship and yet in dangerous waters. At one point, Graham Fielder of *The Ivory Tower* "had . . . the gasp and upward shake of the head of a man in too deep water" (XXV *IT* 116). Jean Martle of *The Other House* is once pictured in an even more violent way—"Unguardedly stepping into water that she had believed shallow, she found herself caught up in a current of fast-moving depths —a cold, full tide that set straight out to sea" (*OH* 161). Hyacinth Robinson's fate will probably be, we read once, "to be submerged in bottomless depths or dashed to pieces on immoveable rocks" (VI *PC* II 263). Finally, indeed, "the waters . . . closed over him [Warren Hope] as over Lord Northmore" (XVI "AofN" 200). In general, warm and sunny heights to James represent positions of safety; but progress in life involves coming down—as in their individual ways Hawthorne's Hilda, Melville's White Jacket, James's Milly, Fitzgerald's Daisy Buchanan, and Salinger's Holden Caulfield all do—and being caught in the swirl of dark, cold, wet life. With James the outcome far more often than otherwise is submersion, despair, and ruin.[24]

iv. Pleasure in Water

If danger often lurks for the traveller or the swimmer, extreme pleasure almost as often comes to other persons passively bathing in blandness, in fragrant and even tinted

23. Is a non-phonemic optometric pun intended with "bows"?
24. See also "GuC" 567, iii *Eurs* 155, I *RH* 435, xxviii "Pap" 127-28, XVI "GGP" 243. Note that George Dane of "The Great Good Place" and Spencer Brydon of "The Jolly Corner" emerge after their descent spiritually rejuvenated, even reborn, like White Jacket after his plunge.

waters, in tepid baths, and in refreshingly cool waters. For a few examples, the "great conditions" governing a lovely house party positively "bathed the house . . . in a universal blandness, . . . a happy solvent for awkward relations" (XVI "BW" 139); and English life to rejected Christopher Newman may seem dull, "but the dulness was as grateful as a warm, fragrant bath" (II *Ame* 524). The Prince regards a remark by Maggie as "sweeten[ing] . . . the waters in which he now floated . . . as by the action of some essence [comprised of 'exquisite colouring drops'], poured from a gold-topped phial, for making one's bath aromatic" (XXIII *GB* I 10). As if in compensation, the Prince, with Charlotte's aid, later fashions "a bath of benevolence" for Maggie, "over the brim of which she could but just manage to see by stretching her neck"; but the oppressed young woman objects, since "unless one were a patient of some sort, a nervous eccentric or a lost child, one usually wasn't so immersed save by one's request" (XXIV *GB* II 44). George Dane's ecstatic condition while he visits "the great good place" is suggested by several images deriving from the pleasure of "the broad deep bath of stillness" (XVI "GGP" 234)—"Oh the deep deep bath" (251)—with its "soft cool plash" (251) and "hushed depths" (252).[25] Passive persons are often imaged as enjoying pleasant movement on or temporarily beneath the waves: for example, George Stransom from "The Altar of the Dead," which swirls with a dozen mythopoeic water figures,[26] wishes that "he could sink . . . to the very bottom [in prayer]"

25. Here, it would seem, James is offering evidence in support of Bodkin; see *Archetypal Patterns in Poetry*, p. 110. The water imagery in "The Great Good Place" also supports John W. Schroeder's interesting interpretation of Dane's action as a "relapsing into a condition of what we might describe as foetal dependency"; "The Mothers of Henry James," *American Literature*, XXII (January, 1951), 427.

26. Northrop Frye, *Anatomy of Criticism: Four Essays* (Princeton: Princeton University Press, 1957), p. 43, suggests that we read "The Altar of the Dead" "as ironic myth."

and "float . . . away on the sea of light" (XVII "AofD" 14).[27] Milly Theale and Hyacinth Robinson are similarly passive. Of the almost ninety water images in *The Wings of the Dove,* several—and all of them significantly in the first volume—show Milly unsuspectingly surrendering herself to the buoyant social medium. "She couldn't stop for the joy, but she could go on for it, and with the pulse of her going on she floated again, was restored to her great spaces" (XIX *WofD* I 132). And "The sense was constant for her that their relation might have been afloat, like some island of the south, in a great warm sea that represented, for every conceivable chance, a margin, an outer sphere, of general emotion . . ." (199). Before Lord Mark shows the poor girl the Bronzino, in presence of the Matcham gathering, "they were all swimming together in the blue" (213). But after the Bronzino episode,[28] Milly's waters become troubled, their colors darken, and other types of imagery become more frequent. Hyacinth is similarly caught at last by the undertow of fate. Although he accuses Paul Muniment of being " 'fond of still waters' " (VI *PC* II 212), it is really Hyacinth who is at first the fatally inactive of the two; we read that, returning from splendid Paris, "he lingered on the brink before he plunged again into Soho" (147), and, some time before the inky, chilling end, he recognizes in an image of exquisite beauty that "there was joy and exultation in the thought of surrendering one's self to the wash of the wave, of being carried higher on the sun-drenched crests of wild billows than one could ever be by a dry lonely effort of one's own" (263). Also, many of the nearly one hundred water similes and metaphors in *The Golden Bowl* flow together to form a pattern catching up

27. See also XVII "AofD" 3, 14, 17, 22, 29, 34, 43, 44, 46, 51, 55.
28. Best analyzed, I think, by Miriam Allott, "Symbol and Image in the Later Work of Henry James," *Essays in Criticism*, III (July, 1953), 326-28.

Maggie. At first she would like to escape with her father and loll passively: "it was wonderfully like their having got together into some boat and paddled off from the shore where . . . complications . . . made the air too tropical. . . . Why . . . couldn't they always live . . . in a boat?" (XXIV *GB* II 255).[29] Then Maggie sees herself naïvely as "a creature consciously floating and shining in a warm summer sea, some element of dazzling sapphire and silver, a creature cradled upon depths, buoyant among dangers, in which fear or folly or sinking otherwise than in play was impossible" (263). Once she even feels "as if she had somehow been lifted aloft, were floated and carried on some warm high tide beneath which stumbling-blocks had sunk out of sight" (24-25). But currents come to muddy Maggie's twinkling summer sea. Between the innocence and the recovery, the young woman has little time for idle drifting—yet she does nothing to control the movement of others. Her reward, at the end of decisive inaction, is to feel that the Prince is at last again "hers in a degree and on a scale, with an intensity and an intimacy, that were a new and a strange quantity, that were the irruption of a tide loosening them where they had stuck and making them feel they floated" (339-40). Finally, the less elaborately imaged Isabel Archer finds herself "afloat on a sea of wonder and pain" (IV *PofL* II 376) and is horribly made to envy Ralph his privilege of dying: she longs "To cease utterly, to give it up and not know anything more—this idea was as sweet as the vision of a cool bath in a marble tank, in a darkened chamber, in a hot land" (391).

If James enjoyed watching the pleasantly spraying fountains of the various gardens he knew, the fact comes out very little in

29. Gibson comments incidentally on the "remarkable sustained marriage-boat imagery of *The Golden Bowl* and the closely related set of equilibrium figures"; "Metaphor in the Plot of *The Ambassadors*," p. 295 n. 16.

his imagery, even though one might have predicted more fountain similes in the works of an author so devoted to Hawthorne's fiction as James was. We hear Roderick Hudson, who is a little like Roderick Elliston, romantically explaining, "'I shall disappear, dissolve, be carried off in a something as pretty, let us hope, as the drifted spray of a fountain'" (I *RH* 231). Later, Mrs. Light laments to Mallet, the sympathetic outsider, that her wayward daughter Christina will "'not heed *us*, no more than if we were a pair of running fountains'" (397). And we have Mrs. Alsager, inspiration of the dramatist in the short story "Nona Vincent," seriously compared to "the nymph of a fountain in the plash of the marble basin" (xxvi "NV" 448). But there is almost nothing in addition.

Occasionally Jamesian characters may be seen in imagery buffeting the watery elements with relish; but the similes and metaphors thus conjured up are never interesting, and one is led to suspect that James was here writing with little interest and from almost no direct experience.[30]

v. Fishing

James's metaphorical fishermen seem also to be having so little fun that one must conclude that their creator neither enjoyed nor understood the intricacies of angling. James was always anxious to avoid the general in his preference for the specific; yet in all the water figures only two types of living fish are named—trout and gold-fish.[31] However, three times with great success James uses fish imagery to portray what

30. See for example II *Ame* 243, VII *TM* I 252, VIII *TM* II 117, XIII "PP" 428, XVII "Bi" 140, XVIII "Ma" 283. There are no such figures, oddly enough, in the fiction not in the New York Edition.

31. V *PC* I 123, XXIV *GB* II 288. Carp may be added, if we wish to accept the idiom concerning *les yeux de carpe* as elaborated into an image (xxviii "Pap" 85). James's imagistic herrings and sardines are dead: see IX *AA* 414; XVIII "BH" 384; xxviii "Pap" 185; xxix *SF* 86, 87.

F. O. Matthiessen has called "the denseness of experience, the way in which the Jamesian individual feels that he is held in close contact with his special group, the slowly circulating motion of their existence all open to the observing eye."[32] The three figures come from the three major-phase novels, in which, certainly, the social medium and the individual's restricted movements within it are subject to close scrutiny. Maggie regards visitors at Fawns as "a kind of renewed water-supply for the tank in which, like a party of panting gold-fish, they kept afloat" (XXIV GB II 288). In a lengthy passage, Waymarsh is pictured as "drawn into the eddy" where "Strether seemed to bump against him as a sinking swimmer might brush a submarine object"; all the while, "the fathomless medium held them—Chad's manner was the fathomless medium; and our friend felt as if they passed each other, in their deep immersion, with the round impersonal eye of silent fish" (XXI Amb I 172).[33] And Merton Densher also feels immersed—but for him it is often "in an element rather more strangely than agreeably warm" (XX WofD II 212), in which "he floated, he noiselessly swam . . . and they were all together . . . like fishes in a crystal pool" (213).[34]

vi. Ice

When an ice image is used to describe a Jamesian character, he is without exception an American—and almost always in America. It is possible that James's memories of winters in New York and New England came to mind in figurative language only in connection with his American per-

32. *Henry James: The Major Phase* (New York: Oxford University Press, 1944), p. 63.

33. Vernon Lee calls this image from *The Ambassadors* "a masterstroke"; "The Handling of Words: Meredith, James," *English Review*, V (June, 1910), 439.

34. Thomas Beer in an unfavorable article compares James himself to a "gleaming fish" gliding "through the shades of his aquarium"; "The Princess Far Away," *Saturday Review of Literature*, I (April, 1925), 702.

sonae. Perhaps he regarded Americans as essentially chillier types than their European counterparts; consider, for example, the Wentworths in the only extended piece of fiction James ever cast in New England, and note further the title "A New England Winter" and the town of Grimwinter in "Four Meetings."[35] At any rate, the following characters are thoroughly indigenous Americans: Roger Lawrence, who is "like a polar ice-block in the summer sea" (xxiv *WandW* 98); Mary Garland, of "a serenity with a surface like slippery ice and from which any vain remark rebounded with its heels in the air" (I *RH* 413); Catherine Sloper, who not only resembles "a lump of ice" but also "a red-hot coal" (v *WS* 180); Mr. Wentworth, who has "a light in his face that might have been flashed from an iceberg" (iii *Eurs* 191); Olive Chancellor, whose eyes have "the glitter of green ice" (viii *Bo* I 21); Mrs. Newsome, who marvelously resembles "some particularly large iceberg in a cool blue northern sea" (XXII *Amb* II 223);[36] and finally Davey Bradham, whose worldly face is "lined and scratched and hacked across much in the manner of the hard ice of a large pond at the end of a long day's skating" (XXV *IT* 27). The conclusion is inescapable that here James unconsciously implies that many Americans are cold and passive in the grip of reality. One cannot conceive of James's using ice imagery to suggest the nature of Christina Light, Kate Croy, or Madame de Vionnet, or indeed of Isabel Archer once she got to Europe. Many of the other ice images are limited to extensions of idioms like those about breaking the ice and skating on thin ice.[37]

35. James only made his satire less obvious when in the revised version of "Four Meetings" he renamed the little New England town North Verona.

36. This image, one of the most famous in all of James, Gibson analyzes especially well; "Metaphor in the Plot of *The Ambassadors*," p. 294.

37. See I *RH* 446, XII "TofS" 149, for examples.

vii. Miscellaneous

A few images have to do with sea shells and the roar of the sea which rewards the patient, sensitive ear placed at their opening. Interestingly, the murmur James has his characters hear is usually a steady echo from the past. Thus, Marco Valerio waits spellbound in the little pantheon in his villa grounds: "The huge dusky dome seems to the spiritual ear to hold a vague reverberation of pagan worship, as a shell picked up on the beach holds the rumour of the sea" (xxvi "LofV" 26). Similarly, when Isabel is captivated by the antiquity of her aunt's Florentine *palazzo*, she thinks that "To live in such a place was . . . to hold to her ear all day a shell of the sea of the past. This vague eternal rumour kept her imagination awake" (III *PofL* I 355).

The pearl came to symbolize for James priceless knowledge to be found in the depths of life's experience; oddly, it rarely stood for mere material wealth, as gold did.[38]

Dropped plummets figure manneristically in James, who uses them often to suggest penetrating glances and perspicacious thoughts: thus "she fathomed . . . old pools with bright plummet glances" ("SofY" 264);[39] and "the current of her growth would soon begin to flow deeper than the plummet of a man's wit" (xxiv *WandW* 32).[40]

Water in the desolation of deserts was an hallucinatory desire which teased James's imagination. More than fifty desert images appear in his fiction—enough to make one wonder if his writing were an influence upon T. S. Eliot's *The*

38. For pearl images, see IX *AA* 192; X *SpofP* 66; XX *WofD* II 396; XV "FinC" 241, 274; XXVI *SeofP* 211-12. For a discussion of gold imagery, see pp. 171-73 below.

39. See also VI *PC* II 231, XII "Li" 348.

40. See also IX *AA* 119, xxvii "LoB" 34, XI *WMK* 252-53, and xxix *SF* 15. These images again demonstrate that James takes pains to avoid the literal, with the result that he achieves yet another distinctive little pattern of tropes with simple plummets.

Waste Land. Imagined water in James's waste land suggests
promised if specious bliss amid sandy tracts, as when the
estate of Matcham beckons the illicit lovers, Charlotte and
the Prince, for whom their chance there "told them, with an
hourly voice, that it had a meaning—a meaning that their associated sense was to drain even as thirsty lips, after the
plough through the sands and the sight, afar, of the palm-
cluster, might drink in at last the promised well in the desert"
(XXIII *GB* I 346). The love affair of Charlotte and the
Prince stands half way between the affairs which form the
foreground and the background of *The Waste Land.* It has
the emotional intensity of some of the unholy loves from the
past; yet it is essentially as sterile as the "modern" liaisons
Eliot ridicules and deplores. James anticipates Eliot again, I
think, when later in *The Golden Bowl,* implying that the
Prince's imagined oasis in Charlotte is but a mirage and that
his duty is but an acceptance of dry sand, he balances the
image quoted above from the first volume with the following
bitter one in the second:

As regards herself Maggie had become more conscious from
week to week of ingenuities of intention [in the Prince] to
make up to her for their forfeiture, in so dire a degree, of any
reality of frankness—a privation that had left on his lips perhaps a little of the same thirst with which she fairly felt her
own distorted, the torment of the lost pilgrim who listens in
desert sands for the possible, the impossible plash of water
(XXIV *GB* II 281).

Notable also is the image which suggests the allurement of
English place names for the pathetic clerk—an Eliotesque
office worker, surely—of "In the Cage": the names "tormented
her with something of the sound of the plash of water that
haunts the traveller in the desert" (XI "InC" 428).

Finally, the sacred-fount image, which finds its fullest expression in the novel entitled *The Sacred Fount*,[41] has its beginnings in the little-read vampire story "De Grey, A Romance." In it, contact with Paul De Grey's vitality causes Margaret Aldis to burgeon. "He bent to pluck this pallid flower of sunless household growth; he had dipped its slender stem in the living waters of his love, and lo! it had lifted its head, and spread its petals, and brightened into splendid purple and green" ("DeG" 73). In terms of unconscious sexual symbolism, the following somewhat similar figure from "The Lesson of the Master," twenty years later, is more accurate: when Paul Overt meets Marian, who is sympathetic to his literary ambitions, "He couldn't get used to her interest in the arts he cared for; it seemed too good to be real—it was so unlike an adventure to tumble into such a well of sympathy. One might stray into the desert easily—that was on the cards and that was the law of life; but it was too rare an accident to stumble on a crystal well" (XV "LofM" 55). From a survey of all of the sacred-fount imagery, one should conclude that James regarded people as capable of drawing upon the intellectual and aesthetic reservoirs of others without danger to either side but that figuratively tapping another's fount for amatory purposes could reduce the one vampirized to the condition of "a sponge wrung dry and with fine pores agape" (xxix *SF* 107).

Conclusion

Such, then, are the water images in James's fiction. Water in movement is frequent: persons and objects float or drift before the observation of others; there are waves, tides, and floods; and time is often a remountable stream. Figures concerning travel by water are numerous, with romantic sailing

41. See xxix *SF* 24, 32, 38, 155; "OR" 18; XXII *Amb* II 48. For an excellent summary of the sacred-fount motif in James's fiction, see Leon Edel, "Introduction" to Henry James, *The Sacred Fount* (New York: Grove Press, 1953), pp. xxv-ix.

images in the numerical lead if usually unimpressive in quality; imagistic sailing folk in James regularly enjoy the position —occasionally a trifle comic—of opulent passenger rather than that of grimy seaman or stoker. Dramatic danger lurks in James's figurative seas, and wrecks are more often the outcome than escapes. Pleasure for passive bathers may be frequent, but when they plunge into the dark depths, as they usually are forced to do, misery follows, or worse. If his imagery is any guide, James experienced but scant pleasure either in fountains or in fishing; occasionally, however, he brilliantly images gregarious persons as items in an aquarium readily accessible to the observer. The only figuratively icy characters in James's works are Americans, but the "rumour" of the past can penetrate the ear of a person of any nationality if he will only listen to the figurative seashell which has captured it. Finally, James skilfully used images concerned both with imagined water in the thirsty desert and with sacred founts—to portray frustration and exploitation.

The water images cluster into iterative patterns in *Roderick Hudson, The Bostonians,* "The Pupil," *The Reverberator,* "The Great Good Place," *The Other House,* "The Altar of the Dead," "Julia Bride," *The Wings of the Dove, The Ambassadors,* and *The Golden Bowl,* and to a lesser degree in other works as well. Like most of the water figures quoted above, those forming into patterns accomplish three main purposes: to show the meaningless drift of the sociable masses, as in *The Bostonians* and *The Wings of the Dove*; to suggest the peril of imminent ruin, as in *The Other House* and "Julia Bride"; and to indicate promised or anticipated bliss, as in "The Great Good Place" and "The Altar of the Dead." It is unsafe to do more than suggest that the slightly greater proportion of water imagery which James produced before 1885 and then the slight rise again just after 1900 may be partly owing to his many voyages in early maturity and then his plans to return to America in 1904. Also, the plots of *Roderick Hudson, The Reverberator,* and *The Wings of the Dove* include ocean crossings or describe persons having just completed them, while *The Other House* has as its melodramatic climax a murder by drowning, all of which facts may in part account for the presence of much of the water imagery. However, it should be added at once that the level of water metaphors and similes running through all the fiction and from decade to decade varies almost imperceptibly: from first to last, seven to nine per cent of the imagery concerns water, in movement, affording means for travel, or providing pleasure or terror. Through it, James seems to be whispering two messages to the attentive reader: that a basic social ambience may be large or small, but it is encompassing and individuals within it are inevitably interrelated; and further, that those who seek to escape from one area—a certain confining shore, for example—only run the greater risk of being engulfed by danger elsewhere at the very moment when they seem secure and gay.

III · FIERY-HEARTED ROSE

The reason was simply that they had not seen yet
"The Major Key," that fiery-hearted rose as to
which we watched in private the formation of
petal after petal and flame after flame (XV "NT"
175).

Introduction

All his life James loved gardens. Among the memories he first writes of in his autobiography is one of long summer afternoons in Albany, "occasions . . . tasting of accessible garden peaches in a liberal backward territory that was still almost part of a country town."[1] And close to the end of his career, writing a letter at Lamb House in August of 1914, he remarked that

1. Henry James, "A Small Boy and Others," in *Autobiography*, ed. by Frederick W. Dupee (New York: Criterion Books, 1956), pp. 4-5.

The country and the season here are of a beauty of peace, and loveliness of light, and summer grace, that make it inconceivable that just across the Channel . . . the fields of France and Belgium are being . . . given up to unthinkable massacre and misery. One is ashamed to admire, to enjoy, to take any of the normal pleasure, and the huge shining indifference of Nature strikes a chill to the heart and makes me wonder of what abysmal mystery, or villainy indeed, such a cruel smile is the expression.[2]

So many crucial or at least transitional scenes in his fiction are laid in gardens that one is tempted to wonder, with William Troy,[3] at their possible significance. Images drawn from flowers, fruits, and gardens, while less frequent than those of water, come to more than six hundred in number—almost four per cent of the whole—appearing slightly more often in the works before 1890 than after. In imagery, James's favorite flowers are the rose, which appears more often than all other specific flowers combined, and then the lily, the daisy, and the violet. His favorite imagistic fruits are the plum, the peach, and the apple.[4] The absence of such rarer flowers as mark the

2. *The Letters of Henry James,* ed. by Percy Lubbock, 2 vols. (New York: Charles Scribner's Sons, 1920), II, 389-90.

3. William Troy, "The Altar of Henry James," in *The Question of Henry James: A Collection of Critical Essays,* ed. by F. W. Dupee (New York: Henry Holt and Company, 1945), pp. 268-70. See also Louise Dauner, "Henry James and the Garden of Death," *University of Kansas City Review,* XIX (Winter, 1952), 137-43, and William M. Gibson, "Metaphor in the Plot of *The Ambassadors,*" *New England Quarterly,* XXIV (September, 1951), 302-5. But for a contrary opinion—rather rancorously expressed, I must add—see Robert Wooster Stallman, *The Houses That James Built and Other Literary Studies* ([East Lansing]: Michigan State University Press, 1961), pp. 16, 24, 33. In an effort to mediate between those who think that crucial decisions are made in Jamesian gardens and those who think that only evasive thinking is accomplished in them, I should like to refer all interested readers to the charming old garden of odd Miss Wenham in "Flickerbridge," in the fourth section of which Frank Granger avoids making a decision and in the fifth section of which he makes it—and at both times he is sitting in the garden! See XVIII "Fl" 458-62.

4. Other flowers and fruits specified in the imagery are, in order of

imagery of Shakespeare, Milton, and Arnold, for example, can be easily explained. In the first place, cosmopolite James did not ramble through American or European woods to any great extent, and in the second he would surely have been open to criticism if he had dotted his realistic prose with comparisons involving "the tufted crow-toe," "the azured harebell," or the "pale pink convolvulus." So he usually employs the general terms "flower" and "blossom"; when he is more specific, it is for a particular purpose. Thus, Linda Pallant "struck you . . . as a felicitous *final* product—after the fashion of some plant or some fruit, some waxen orchid or some perfect peach" (XIII "LoP" 503); and Gertrude Whittaker seems to exhale "a certain latent suggestion of heroic possibilities which he who had once become sensible of them . . . would linger about her hoping to elicit, as you might stand and inhale a florid and vigorous dahlia which . . . should have proved delightfully fragrant" (xxv "PR" 426).

i. Wind in Flowers

Winds which stir the flowers, and gather their fragrance, are often found in James's imagery. The winds are usually gentle: "she had headshakes whose impulse seemed to come from as far away as the breeze that stirs a flower" (XVII "FofF" 335); "she had an individual patience and a lovely frock, together with an expression that played among her pretty features like a breeze amid flowers" (XV "DofL" 126);[5] and the murmur of Paris entering a pleasantly fur-

---

frequency, as follows: heliotrope, buttercup, dahlia, geranium, and orchid; and grape, pear, melon, and blackberry. Grains and vegetables are extremely rare in the imagery. The abundance of rose imagery is due in part to some half-dozen uses of unimportant though curious rose-leaf figures, such as "he found his rest troubled by this folded rose-leaf of doubt" (xxiv *WandW* 127) and "she . . . made him stretch himself on cushions and rose-leaves" (xxvi "NV" 466). Both of these usages reflect James's memory of children's literature.

5. James had used precisely the same image in I *RH* 23.

nished salon "strays among scattered objects even as a summer air idles in a lonely garden" (XXII *Amb* II 143).

People are occasionally likened to flowers caught by the wind, and the conclusion emerges that if one is pliant there is no permanent damage. Thus, Felix Young, the well-named and likable enough opportunist in *The Europeans,* always tries "to put Adversity off her guard, dodging and evading her with the easy, natural motion of a wind-shifted flower" (iii *Eurs* 60).[6] But in "The Siege of London," Mrs. Headway, as her name implies, is more obstinate; and we read that on one occasion "her pretty head was tossed back like a flower in the wind" (XIV "SofL" 202). Once, in *The Portrait of a Lady,* which has more than forty flower images,[7] a violent wind silences all zephyrs: Caspar Goodwood's insistent questioning of oppressed Isabel "was the hot wind of the desert, at the approach of which the others dropped dead, like mere sweet airs of the garden" (IV *PofL* II 434). This brief image has tremendous force: it evokes a sense of Goodwood's powerful singleness of aim, his physical superiority to the other men about Isabel, the sterility of the poor girl's life, and also her delicacy.

James must have enjoyed inhaling odor-laden winds passing through flowers and the blossoms of fruit trees. Since with him, as with John Donne and others, sensations and thoughts were intimately interlaced, often a thought may have a fragrance for him: thus, Fanny Assingham "drew in" relief at the absence of criticism by Maggie "as if it had been the

6. This is a rare figure comparing a man to a flower. See pp. 50-51 below, for other examples.

7. I cannot imagine why Miriam Allott would say of *The Portrait of a Lady* that "The method [of characterizing through images] is recognizably that of *The Golden Bowl,* but is naturally less effective since imagery is not an organic part of the book"; "Symbol and Image in the Later Work of Henry James," *Essays in Criticism,* III (July, 1953), 324. It is obvious that flower, war, art, motion, and animal imagery in patterns vivifies the entire novel.

warm summer scent of a flower" (XXIV *GB* II 160). Further, Amerigo's intellectual awareness of Charlotte's "easy command . . . of her crisis" at the big social gathering without Adam Verver is imaged "as the strong-scented flower of the total sweetness" (XXIII *GB* I 246).[8] Aesthetic and religious devotion may suggest similar imagery: Raphael's "Madonna of the Chair," for example, is said in the short story "The Madonna of the Future" to have about it "the fragrance of the tenderest blossom of maternity that ever bloomed among men" (XIII "MofF" 448).[9]

ii. Thriving Gardens

Productive activity in a given field James often compares to a thriving garden. The "happy salon" of Oliver Offord in "Brooksmith" is described thus: "Mr. Offord's drawing-room was indeed Brooksmith's garden, his pruned and tended human parterre, and if we all flourished there and grew well in our places it was largely owing to his supervision" (XVIII "Br" 350). Less inviting, ultimately, is Lord Theign's noble offensiveness in *The Outcry*; it is a painstaking and detailed creation, for the man is said to have "establish[ed] in the formal garden of his suffered greatness such easy seats and short perspectives, such winding paths and natural-looking waters as would mercifully break up the scale" (*Ou* 65). After much thought, Maggie fixes upon a plan; and then as the Prince enters, we read that "she had been . . . in the act of plucking it out of the heart of her earnestness—plucking it, in the garden of thought, as if it had been some full-blown flower that she could present to him on the spot" (XXIV *GB* II 25-26). Artistic endeavor is also imaged horticulturally: an English art-critic, for example, patriotically asserts that " 'We grew some of the loveliest flowers . . . Great Gains-

9. See also iv *Con* 96, XXVI *SeofP* 121.
8. For another phase of this pattern, see XXIII *GB* I 322.

boroughs and Sir Joshuas and Romneys and Sargents, great
Turners and Constables and old Cromes and Brabazons, form
. . . a vast garden' " (*Ou* 45), while a French poet compares art
to a boundless garden in which nationalism, however, unfortunately threatens " 'to crush to death . . . all the flowers
. . . , to shut out all the light' " (xxvii "Col" 177).

James's adoration of the natural beauty of the Italian scene
inspired him to evoke it often in lovely garden imagery. For
example, he conveys as follows a notion of the charm of Gilbert Osmond's Florentine "hill-top" when Isabel first sees it:
"The air was almost solemnly still, and the large expanse of
the landscape, with its gardenlike culture and nobleness of
outline, its teeming valley and delicately-fretted hills, its
peculiarly human-looking touches of habitation, lay there in
splendid harmony and classic grace" (III *PofL* I 380). The
lovely scene so impresses Isabel that when she later muses
upon the career of Osmond, soon to become her vicious husband, it seems to stretch beneath him like "the disposed vistas
and with the ranges of steps of a formal Italian garden"
(400).[10] Further, since devotion to art was virtually spiritual
in James, he naturally enough thought of gardens—particularly
the Italian ones he so adored—when he wished in "The Madonna of the Future" to express the deep joy attending time
spent in the presence of Florentine religious art: "We stood
more than once in the little convent chambers where Fra
Angelico wrought as if an angel indeed had held his hand,
and gathered that sense of scattered dews and bird-notes
which makes an hour among his relics resemble a morning
stroll in some monkish garden" (XIII "MofF" 455).[11]

10. It is significant that the first volume of *The Portrait of a Lady*
contains most of the pleasant garden images in the novel, while the
second volume has all of the unpleasant ones—which facts precisely
reflect the organic changes in the plot.

11. This figure uniquely combines elements drawn from gardens,
Italy, painting, and the medieval church. It will be seen that the love

More lightly, gardens can advance pleasantry and suggest the romantic faraway. For example, when a sudden opportunity to make a decision comes into the dull life of a certain governess, "She bloomed with alternatives—she resembled some dull garden-path which under a copious downpour has begun to flaunt with colour" (XVIII "Ma" 295). A humorously suggestive image describes the expression of Maisie's mother when, appropriately enough in Kensington Gardens, she turns her strong features back toward her temporarily deserted escort: "She directed to him the face that was like an illuminated garden, turnstile and all, for the frequentation of which he had his season-ticket[!]" (XI *WMK* 144). More innocently, little Maisie concludes at one point that the partly true, partly fictitious fairy tales which her friend Mrs. Wix spins are "a great garden of romance, with sudden vistas into her own life and gushing fountains of homeliness" (27).[12]

iii. Flower-like Women

James often compares women to flowers. Some have vernal delicacy, like Pansy Osmond, Duchess Jane's niece Aggie, and little Jeanne de Vionnet, who are all guarded *jeunes filles en fleurs*.[13] Many girls ready for engagement are compared to flowers. The list includes Francie Dosson ("'a perfect flower of plasticity'" [XIII *Re* 206]), Mamie Pocock ("a flower of expansion" [XXII *Amb* II 147]), and Cora Prodmore ("'the rose on its stem'" ["CE" 258]). Two blooming young women,

---

of art was akin to a religion in James. See Richard P. Blackmur, ed., *Henry James, The Art of the Novel: Critical Prefaces* (New York: Charles Scribner's Sons, 1934), p. xxxix; W. H. Auden, "Henry James and the Artist in America," *Harper's Magazine*, CXCVII (July, 1948), 36; Leon Edel, "The James Revival," *Atlantic Monthly*, CLXXXII (September, 1948), 98. See also pp. 165-66 below.

12. See also XII "TofS" 173-74, xxvi "NV" 481. James satirically used romantic flower figures on occasion; see ix *Bo* II 56, 57; xxviii "VG" 222, for representative examples.

13. III *PofL* I 369; IV *PofL* II 162; IX *AA* 93, 428; XXI *Amb* I 221.

who seem not likely to be picked, are similarly imaged: Felix of *The Europeans* pictures Gertrude to her sister as " 'a folded flower. Let me [he adds] pluck her from the parent tree and you will see her expand' " (iii *Eurs* 186); and to her ill-judging father, Catherine Sloper is "a rather mature blossom, such as could be plucked from the stem only by a vigorous jerk" (v *WS* 43).[14] To the solar radiance of love, still other women are sensitive, often fatally so. Thus, Charlotte Stant, whose hair incidentally has "a shade of the tawny autumn leaf" (XXIII *GB* I 46), has a waist which is "the stem of an expanded flower" (47). Jeanne de Vionnet has "pale pink petals . . . folded up . . . for some wondrous efflorescence in time; to open, that is, to some great golden sun" (XXI *Amb* I 277). Finally, in an image even more blatant in its unconscious sexual overtones, James suggests that Nora Lambert may one day find her "petals . . . playfully forced apart, [which] would leave the golden heart of the flower but the more accessible to . . . vertical rays" (xxiv *WandW* 58).[15]

14. James, not given to punning, intends no pun here in derogation of Morris Townsend.

15. I agree completely with F. W. Dupee when he says that "Like all the early stories, *Watch and Ward* is strewn with images so palpably and irresistibly erotic as to imply a whole resonant domain of meaning beyond anything he [James] could have intended"; *Henry James*, American Men of Letters Series ([New York]: William Sloane Associates, 1951), p. 61. Here is a comparable image from "The Ghostly Rental" of 1876: "I confess, moreover, that I felt the inclination to coquet a little, as it were, with my discovery—to pull apart the petals of the flower one by one. I continued to smell the flower, from time to time, for its oddity of perfume had fascinated me" ("GhR" 667). The following from "The Passionate Pilgrim" also seems too suggestive to have been intentional: "Something assured me that her heart was virgin-soil, that the flower of romantic affection had never bloomed there. If I might just sow the seed!" (XIII "PP" 377). For a contrary opinion on James's "revelation of meaning," see Oscar Cargill, *The Novels of Henry James* (New York: The Macmillan Company, 1961), p. 17 n. 36. Then if you please read the image by which James suggests that Gilbert Osmond wishes to be possessive with respect to Isabel Archer: "Her mind was to be his—attached to his own like a small garden-plot to a deer-park. He would rake the soil gently and water the flowers; he

James sometimes mockingly pictures the too-frequent artificiality and floridity of middle-aged women. Mildly enough, he describes Mrs. Ambient, the wife of the titular hero of "The Author of Beltraffio," as "a wonderfully cultivated human plant . . . delicately tinted and petalled" (XVI "AofB" 49). Lady Barbarina is handled as briefly but with less sympathy: she is "a flower . . . of the social hot-house" (XIV "LaB" 86). And Duchess Jane, we read, "had bloomed in the hot-house of her widowhood" (IX AA 15). James seems to be saying to these and other such women, all of whom ignore love, that to submit would be natural—if perhaps fatal.[16]

Finally, frail and aging women are without exception sparingly handled. Milly Theale is "the final flower" of a once "luxuriant tribe" (XIX WofD I 111) and is also an "imported" flower belonging to a group of "few varieties and thin development" (166). Alice Staverton of "The Jolly Corner" is "as exquisite . . . as some pale pressed flower" (XVII "JC" 440). And patient, china-fragile May Bartram "was a sphinx, yet with her white petals and green fronds she might have been a lily too—only an artificial lily, wonderfully imitated and constantly kept, without dust or stain, though not exempt from a slight droop and a complexity of faint creases, under some clear glass" (XVII "BinJ" 98-99). In this supremely fine little image, James suggests Miss Bartram's purity, fragility, forced unnaturalness, and progressive desiccation and aging, as well as her essential openness and potential attractiveness for Marcher.

Flower figures having the general purpose of lighting up feminine nature constitute iterative patterns in *Watch and Ward* and "The Siege of London." In the first, having ap-

---

would weed the beds and gather an occasional nosegay" (IV *PofL* II 200). Osmond is patently not a sensualist, and therefore the Freudian overtones of this image are inappropriate, and in my view unintentional.

16. See ix *Bo* II 229; IX *AA* 15, 390; "CCon" 570.

parently "sprung from a horribly vulgar soil" (xxiv WandW 24), Nora Lambert is a "poor little uprooted germ of womanhood" (18). Roger Lawrence is nonetheless anxious to have her fall in love with him, and so he "watched patiently, as a wandering botanist for the first woodland violets for the year, for the shy field-flower of spontaneous affection" (28). But Nora's cousin Fenton comes along; he cocks a cynical eye at womanhood generally, for "Women, to him, had seemed mostly as cut flowers, blooming awhile in the waters of occasion, but yielding no second or rarer satisfaction" (60). And James adds that "Nora was expanding in the sunshine of her cousin's gallantry" (60). Becoming interested, Fenton soon may be seen greedily appraising the girl's financial prospects and deciding that "it would surely take a great fool not to pluck the rose from so thornless a tree" (59). But when he fails to trick Lawrence, the scheming young man feels "a certain angry impulse to break a window, as it were, in Roger's hothouse" (61). Almost fatally, a quarrel then splits ward and watcher: "It had scattered its seed; they were left lying, to be absorbed in the conscious soil or dispersed by some benignant breeze of accident, as destiny might appoint" (77). Hubert, the mildly libidinous parson, advises Lawrence on this secular matter: " 'Don't sow for others to reap [he says]. If you think the harvest is not ripe, let it ripen in milder sunbeams than these vigorous hand-kisses' " (84) which Lawrence has just tried on the hand of Nora, whose subsequent visit to Europe causes her to bloom, we read, "into ripeness in the sunshine of a great continent" (114). Finally, toward the end, Lawrence is thoroughly in love with the now more beautiful, mature creature, for "the flower of her beauty had bloomed in a night, that of his passion in a day" (144).

Similarly, "The Siege of London" has a little pattern of half a dozen flower figures. Mrs. Headway's "complexion had the bloom of a white flower" (XIV "SofL" 155). We have a new light upon this rather rank "flower of the Pacific slope . . . transplanted at an hour's notice" (159) to London, when we read that Littlemore, who knows much about her, "occasionally spoke of her as a full-blown flower of the West, still very pretty, but of not at all orthodox salon scent" (185). Finally, infatuated Sir Arthur, pondering over her western past, concludes romantically enough that "she had been a lily among thistles" (189).[17]

iv. Flower-like Men

Only a few words need be said of James's somewhat infrequent and usually disparaging comparisons of men to flowers. Such images often show character as weakened by sheltered living or decadent traditions. Thus, the mother in "Master Eustace" appears to be cultivating trouble by pampering her boy Eustace, and the narrator tells her "that there was never an easier child to spoil, and that those fondling hands of hers would sow a crop of formidable problems for future years" (xxvi "MEu" 46).[18] Similarly, Eugene Pickering has been dangerously sheltered, but one feels that his sense of humor will save him. As he describes his over-protective father, Eugene is obviously no Eustace: " 'he thought . . . that children were not to grow up like dusty thorns by the wayside. So you see . . . I am a regular garden plant. I have been watched and watered and pruned, and if there is any virtue in tending I ought to take the prize at a flower-show' " (xxiv "EP" 251). Richard de Mauves, we read, might "have exhaled the natural fragrance of a late-blooming flower of hereditary honour" (XIII "MdeM" 234), but for an extravagance of will and temper; so he can later be dismissed as

17. Again, I doubt that the sexual overtones of lily and thistles are conscious, but they are certainly there for many modern readers.
18. Other figures in the story reinforce the basic metaphor likening Eustace to uncontrollable vegetation; see 55, 74.

merely "the ripest fruit of time" (261). Finally, the most vicious image of this type is reserved for the effete Gilbert Osmond, James's least pardonable sinner. Ralph complains to Isabel of her engagement to Gilbert in these terms: " 'You seemed to me to be soaring far up in the blue. . . . Suddenly some one tosses up a faded rosebud—a missile that should never have reached you—and straight you drop to the ground' " (IV *PofL* II 69-70).

There are only two men in James compared with some compliment to blossoms, but in both cases the men are deficient in masculinity. Thus, Mr. Vetch tells Pinnie that her beloved Hyacinth (note the flowery name) " 'thinks himself the flower of creation' " (V *PC* I 33); but he mitigates his criticism by adding that " 'a fine, blooming, odoriferous conceit is a natural appendage of youth and intelligence' " (33-34). And Nick Dormer similarly praises with slightly damning flowery language his odd friend Gabriel Nash: " '. . . in dealing with him you know what you've got hold of. With most men you don't; to pick the flower you must break off the whole dusty thorny worldly branch. . . . Poor Nash has none of these encumbrances: he's the solitary fragrant blossom' " (VII *TM* I 81).[19] Note that with both Hyacinth and Gabriel, the flower images appear early and are not developed later; it would seem that James saw at once that there was little to the comparisons.

v. Fruits

In general, fruit images, less interesting than flower images, are used similarly. The best of them reveal a delight in savor and appearance; hardly any show technical awareness of such labor problems as planting, irrigating, and pruning.

19. For an excellent summary of Oscar Cargill's theory that Oscar Wilde is the model of James's Gabriel Nash, see his *The Novels of Henry James*, pp. 191-93; see also pp. 200-1 n. 36 for further bibliographical aid apropos of this identification.

James emerges once again as a taster and an onlooker, not a doer.[20] From the rather frequent plum and peach imagery, we may draw the conclusion that James was intimate with prepared and served plums but with peaches nearer the branch. Thus, one character is made to complain: "But now! has the sweetness really passed out of life? Have I eaten the plums and left nothing but the bread and milk and cornstarch . . . ?" (xxv "LiM" 212). Another person suspects a certain Italian villa grounds of being "as full of buried treasures as a bridal cake of plums" (xxvi "LofV" 12). One question too many from a curious person is "another plum in the pie" (XXIII *GB* I 399), while the soft voice of a considerate person "always drew the sting from a reproach, and enabled you to swallow it as you would a cooked plum, without the stone" (xxvi "MrsT" 261). On the other hand, peach imagery almost always has to do with fresh, natural young ladies. Thus, the passive but gently responsive Pansy Osmond is charmingly imaged: "If he [Ned Rosier] had not spoken she would have waited for ever; but when the word came she dropped like the peach from the shaken tree" (IV *PofL* II 112). Of the protected upbringing of Aggie we read that "Since to create a particular little rounded and tinted innocence had been aimed at, the fruit had been grown to the perfection of a peach on a sheltered wall" (IX *AA* 238).[21]

vi. Flower Patterns

In two novels, iterative patterns concerning the blight and destruction of flowers are excellently developed. Rather early in *The Portrait of a Lady* we read that Isabel's "nature had . . . a certain garden-like quality, a suggestion of perfume and murmuring boughs, of shady bowers and lengthening vistas"

20. We do have one lawn-irrigator (XV "NT" 201). The little imagery concerned with vegetables and grains is also from the point of view of the idle watcher or grateful eater.
21. See also II *Ame* 439, XIV "PB" 472, xxviii "BofD" 419.

(III *PofL* I 72).[22] All the more sinister, therefore, is snake-like Gilbert, who has a "faculty for making everything wither that he touched . . . as if his presence were a blight" (IV *PofL* II 188-89). In the course of time, his presence threatens to stupefy Isabel, for whom, as we read close to the end of the novel, "action had been suddenly changed to slow renunciation, transformed by the blight of Osmond's touch" (357).

The other novel containing a similar if slighter pattern is *The Tragic Muse*. Nick remarks of his talent, " 'I've plucked it up; it's too late for it to flower' " (VIII *TM* II 70). Next, we learn of Peter and Miriam that "he was deeply occupied with plucking up the feeling that attached him to her, and he had already, by various little ingenuities, loosened some of its roots" (89). And at last, poor "Biddy's prospects had withered to the finest dreariest dust" (371).

vii. Miscellaneous

Very few clusters of flower imagery remain for mention. James aptly compares the untrue, the inexact, and the unreal to artificial flowers. Thus, Countess Gemini says, " 'I don't make professions any more than I make paper flowers or flouncey lampshades—I don't know how. My lampshades would be sure to take fire, my roses and my fibs to be larger than life' " (IV *PofL* II 87). We learn that Prince Casamassima's "English was far from perfect, but his errors were like artificial flowers of accent" (VI *PC* II 318). Fleda Vetch at one point "found herself tricking out the situation with artificial flowers, trying to talk even herself into the fancy that Owen . . . might come in" (X *SpofP* 216). Two women do their hair so artificially that James must take imagistic exception: Mrs. Ruck of "The Pension Beaurepas" employs "an arrangement of hair, with forehead tendrils, water-waves and other

22. Irrelevantly, old Mr. Touchett is said to have the quality even in old age of "unthumbed fruit" (III *PofL* I 51).

complications," all of which reminds the narrator "of those framed 'capillary' tributes to the dead which used long ago to hang over artless mantel-shelves between the pair of glass domes protecting wax flowers" (XIV "PB" 406); meanwhile, the central character in "Fordham Castle" observes at the Pension Massin "the American lady with the mathematical hair which reminded him . . . of the old-fashioned 'work,' the weeping willows and mortuary urns represented by the little glazed-over flaxen or auburn or sable or silvered convolutions and tendrils, the capillary flowers, that he had admired in the days of his innocence" (XVI "FC" 398-99).

James occasionally compares hair with elements from real gardens, but in a uniformly grotesque fashion and always with women whom he does not greatly admire. Thus, Mrs. Luna from *The Bostonians* has "hair . . . in clusters of curls, like bunches of grapes" (viii *Bo* I 6); Lady Agnes of *The Tragic Muse* has a "white, triangular forehead, over which her close-crinkled flaxen hair . . . made a looped silken canopy like the marquee at a garden-party" (VIII *TM* I 5-6); and the hair of Julia Bride's aging but still amorous mother has "arranged silver tendrils which were so like some rare bird's-nest in a morning frost" (XVII "JB" 498).[23]

Finally, an odd little set of figures has to do with garden walls. One such image simply enough suggests that the family in "The Married Son" is sheltered, limited, and stuffy: as the narrator puts it, "indeed we grow about as many cheap illusions and easy comforts in the faintly fenced garden of our life as could very well be crammed into the space" ("MS" 534). But the other garden-wall figures are apt to be more puzzling. Henrietta Stackpole tells Mr. Bantling, "'I always feel as if I were talking to *you* over something with a neat top-finish of broken glass'" (IV *PofL* II 5). In her eyes, it

23. Had James been recently reading *Romeo and Juliet*, II, v, 76?

is clearly his conservatism which hedges them apart; yet these questions remain: whose estate is threatened, and by whom, what does the broken glass signify, and are the walls seriously defended? More suggestive are the implications of the image making of Madame Merle a very private garden. Toward the end of the first volume of *The Portrait of a Lady* we read of Isabel that "Our heroine had always passed for a person of resources and had taken a certain pride in being one; but she wandered, as by the wrong side of the wall of a private garden, round the enclosed talents, accomplishments, aptitudes of Madame Merle" (III *PofL* I 270). The second volume is in large part an illumination of that sinister garden. Also, when Kate Croy and Merton Densher first meet at a large party, each tries to see into the garden of the other's private personality; James pictures those efforts in the following splendid image:

She had observed a ladder against a garden-wall and had trusted herself so to climb it as to be able to see over into the probable garden on the other side. On reaching the top she had found herself face to face with a gentleman engaged in a like calculation at the same moment, and the two enquirers had remained confronted on their ladders. The great point was that for the rest of that evening they had been perched—they had not climbed down; and indeed during the time that followed Kate at least had had the perched feeling—it was as if she were there aloft without a retreat (XIX *WofD* I 53).[24]

24. Alexander Holder-Barell charmingly analyzes the implications of this image and shows that it may have had "its origin in a real happening in his [James's] life," namely, seeing his direct brother William trying when at Lamb House in Rye to climb a garden wall with a ladder to spy on G. K. Chesterton, supposedly on the other side; *The Development of Imagery and Its Functional Significance in Henry James's Novels*, The Cooper Monographs (Bern: Francke Verlag, 1959), pp. 95, 179. For images slightly similar to the one just quoted from *The Wings of the Dove*, see "CE" 238, XXIV *GB* II 295.

The elements of allurement, mystery, and exposure are all focused in this single extended metaphor.

Many other figures belong in this luxuriant floral category. They do not easily find a place, however, in any of the patterns discussed above. Nonetheless, several stand out as isolated examples of remarkable rhetoric and hence deserve passing notice. Two may be uprooted from their contexts to serve as examples. Concerning Ralph Touchett's calm after an unlasting return to health, we read that "His serenity was but the array of wild flowers niched in his ruin" (III *PofL* I 54). And by a very early sacred-fount image Henrietta Congreve is erroneously pictured in "Osborne's Revenge"—"She drained honest men's hearts to the last drop, and bloomed white upon the monstrous diet" ("OR" 18).

Conclusion

Our saunter through the Jamesian garden must now draw to a conclusion. James enjoyed innumerable hours of conversation and contemplation in gardens adjacent to various English country estates—including his own at Lamb House, in Rye—and French and Italian villas, and he therefore inevitably cast many fictional scenes in similar floral locales. Accordingly, his flower imagery blossomed naturally, given the circumstances of his life and the settings of his novels and stories. Such similes and metaphors have to do with blossoms, fragrances, and fruits by the garden wall. Often they are pleasantly delicate and feminine, less frequently acrid, withered, and painful. When he compares men to flowers, James is usually disparaging; but he almost never is so when he likens lithe and fragile women to roses, lilies, daisies, and violets. (Note the characteristics of Rose Tramore ["Ch"], Lily Gunton ["MG"], Daisy Miller ["DM"], and Violet Grey ["NV"].) Aged women are treated with special care in flower imagery, which, however, can turn comic or ironic when its target is artificiality or feminine ornateness. In the main, it might reasonably be said that a typical Jamesian heroine or even hero, sensitive, delicate, and embattled, could be master-metaphored as a flower in a jungle.

James writes of troubled, gentle Adela Chart, heroine of "The Marriages," when she wanders in her adored dead mother's lovely garden: "there was in her passion for flowers something of the respect of a religion" (XVIII "Ma" 295).[25] So too, perhaps, with James's probably similar passion. It certainly could be readily shown that in his critical prefaces, when James wishes to describe artistic inspiration and tenderly cultivated productivity, he uses seed, flower, and garden tropes.[26]

25. For other instances of James's juxtaposing gardens and religion, see I *RH* 413, II *Ame* 422, XIII "MofF" 455.
26. See, for examples, V v; X xviii; XI v, xxii; XIV xii; XVI viii; XVIII xxiii; XXI v.

IV THE UNIVERSAL MENAGERIE

London closed the parenthesis and exhibited him in relations; one of the most inevitable of these being that in which he found himself to Mrs. Weeks Wimbush, wife of the boundless brewer and proprietress of the universal menagerie (XV "DofL" 123).

Introduction

From the vast world of animals, birds, insects, fish, and reptiles come nearly a thousand figures of speech in James's fiction. Over one-half of this total is animal imagery, and nearly one-third bird imagery. Specifically named are thirty-three different kinds of animals, twenty-six birds, eleven fish and amphibians, thirteen insects, and a pair of snakes. In order of frequency the animals specified are as follows: horse, sheep, dog, and cat (more than thirty times each); lion (more than twenty times); rabbit, cow, donkey, tiger, deer, bear, wolf, monkey, and mouse (five to ten times each); and ox, leopard, panther, antelope, guinea pig, porcupine, zebra, buffalo, camel, catamount, elephant, fox, gazelle, giraffe, goat, hippopotamas, kangaroo, squirrel, and weasel (fewer than five times each). The birds in imagery are as follows: dove (more than fifteen times); eagle and goose (more than five times each); chicken, parrot, swan, bat, nightingale, vulture, canary, hawk, magpie, ostrich, peacock, skylark, swallow, turkey, cormorant, crane, falcon, hummingbird, owl, parakeet, phoenix, popinjay, and sandpiper (fewer than five times each). The aquatic creatures, none of which is named as often as five times, are as follows: herring, toad, carp, goldfish, sardine, sucker, trout, whale, frog, salamander, and tadpole. The insects are as follows: grasshopper and fly (five or more times each); beetle, firefly, butterfly, ant, bee, caterpillar, ephemera, flea, leech, locust, and mosquito (fewer than five times each). The list will surely be complete enough when I add to it an anaconda and a viper, half a dozen vague Thurberesque dragons, and two insignificant worms.[1]

It is needless to document any author's observance and knowledge of animals. James certainly had the normal access to barnyards and pastures and circuses. Still, it will surprise some to learn that the New York City of his boyhood was pleasantly rural in what are now violently urban areas. James tells in his autobiography about his joy at going indirectly home to Washington Square by way of Eighteenth Street and

1. When it simplifies matters to do so, I use the generic term; thus sheep, lamb, and ram are considered one group, the many varieties of dog one, ape and monkey one, cow and bull one, etc. If no animal is named in the image, I have not counted the usage in this tabulation; thus harness, shepherd, tail-wagging, wing, and fang figures, for example, are not reflected in this listing.

Broadway, where he delighted in peering through rails enclosing

. . . "grounds" peopled with animal life, which, little as its site may appear to know it to-day, lingered on into considerably later years. I have but to close my eyes in order to open them inwardly again . . . to a romantic view of browsing and pecking and parading creatures, not numerous but all of distinguished appearance: two or three elegant little cows of refined form and colour, two or three nibbling fawns and a larger company, above all, of peacocks and guineafowl, with, doubtless—though as to this I am vague—some of the commoner ornaments of the barnyard.[2]

The even uncommoner sorts of animals were on display during these same early days at Mr. Barnum's Great American Museum, which the young James boys visited regularly "on the non-dental Saturdays."[3] A third source of the animal imagery certainly lies in James's reading: the winged horse, Faust's dog, and the phoenix, for three examples among many other possible ones; and undoubtedly such others as the vulture and the anaconda owe more to books than to direct observation.

In spite of the fact that the sources of James's animal figures should seem to lie in his youthful experiences, it is true that these figures appear somewhat more often in the latter half of James's career, particularly in the production of the 1890's. I suggest that as James grew older and as his dream of conquering the London stage turned to a nightmare, he unconsciously thought of even his own fictional dramatis personae as increasingly bestial. He certainly regarded the jeering audience at the first night of his play *Guy Domville* as such, for in his words it "kicked up an infernal row at the fall of the curtain. There followed an abominable quarter of

2. Henry James, "A Small Boy and Others," in *Autobiography*, ed. Frederick W. Dupee (New York: Criterion Books, 1956), p. 16.
3. *Ibid.*, p. 89.

an hour during which all the forces of civilization in the house waged a battle of the most gallant, prolonged and sustained applause, with the hoots and jeers and catcalls of the roughs, whose *roars* (like those of a cage of beasts at some infernal 'zoo') were only exacerbated (as it were) by the conflict. It was a cheering scene . . . for a nervous, sensitive, exhausted author face to face . . ."[4] Further, naturalism came more to the fore in the 1890's and also helped lower man in the scale of creation; and James, while opposed to the philosophical and critical bases of naturalism, could not have remained uninfluenced by all of its tenets.

i. Animals

At any rate, back to the menagerie. The noble grace of the horse is cited in James's imagery much less than its speed, strength, and utility, a fact which suggests that the increasingly sedentary James considered the horse mainly useful and not often magnificent. For example, when Roderick Hudson abruptly doubts his own ability, his sponsor Rowland Mallet finds himself "in the situation of a man who had been riding a blood-horse at a steady gallop and of a sudden felt him stumble and shy" (I *RH* 126). James almost always avoids using the horse figure in any sexually symbolic sense, but we do find the impetuous countess in the short story "Benvolio" unwilling to submit suddenly to the titular hero's mastery before first enjoying her freedom in travel. James writes with probable innocence: "They say the world likes its master— that a horse of high spirit likes being well ridden. This may be true in the long run; but the Countess, who was essentially a woman of the world, was not yet prepared to pay our young man the tribute of her luxurious liberty" (xxiv "Be" 349-50). The mettle of high-stepping horses is as often ridiculed as

4. *The Letters of Henry James*, ed. Percy Lubbock, 2 vols. (New York: Charles Scribner's Sons, 1920), I, 227.

praised by James. Newman, for example, hates the degradation of putting pressure on the Bellegardes, feeling that such "curveting and prancing were exclusively reserved for quadrupeds and foreigners" (II *Ame* 487), while Mitchy feels that to make any effort to strike a pose before Nanda's eyes would be to "prance and caracole and sufficiently kick up the dust" (IX *AA* 352). War-horse figures are simple and infrequent in James; thus, an old play is called a "lame war-horse . . . who had been ridden to death and had saved a thousand desperate fields" (VIII *TM* II 123), while the editor of a grossly successful magazine is seen " 'mainly in the saddle and in the charge—at the head of his hundreds of thousands [of readers]' " (xxvi "JD" 369). Further, sport images concerning horses, though more numerous than war-horse figures, are no less commonplace; thus, "they followed the chase for which I myself had sounded the horn" (XV "FinC" 243), and "he had never known a difficulty; he had taken all his fences" (X *SpofP* 86).[5] Images concerning the care of horses show still less freshness.[6] Only one carries provocative implications; the Prince Casamassima tells a confidante of his humiliation at being obliged to spy from across the street while Paul Muniment visits the Princess in her house: " 'I arrived in London only this morning, and this evening I spent two hours walking up and down opposite there, like a groom waiting for his master to come back from a ride' " (VI *PC* II 306). The Prince clearly feels reduced in status, his wife is a highstepper, and Paul probably has replaced him.[7]

5. See also IX *AA* 292, xxvi "So" 368, VIII *TM* II 109. It is a little surprising to learn that James in the early 1870's was not a bad horseman himself; see Leon Edel, "Roman Rides," *Henry James: The Conquest of London: 1870-1881* (Philadelphia and New York: J. B. Lippincott Company, 1962), pp. 97-102.

6. For examples, see XIV "PofV" 589-90, XXI *Amb* II 109.

7. See F. Dupee, *Henry James*, American Men of Letters ([New York]: William Sloane Associates, 1951), p. 160.

Images involving horses in harness are rather numerous: they are used to show persons confined to a routine, a career, or a way of life, but with only one exception they lack detail and development. The narrator of "The Death of the Lion" pictures the condition of Paraday, "promptly caught and saddled" for the painter Rumble's "circus"; and the narrator adds, " 'I positively feel my own flesh sore from the brass nails in Neil Paraday's social harness' " (XV "DofL" 140). Many a Jamesian image comparing a person to a horse degrades not only the human but the beast. Thus, Tom Tristram, annoyed with his wife in *The American*, thinks that " 'she wants to be a bit touched up' " with " 'a flick of the whip' " (II *Ame* 509); another woman's mind is said to be " 'like a flogged horse—it won't give another kick' " (VIII *TM* II 241); and still another young lady objects to being stared at "as if she were a kicking horse" (V *PC* I 332). A more vicious, and more subtle, little pattern of metaphors pictures Charlotte in *The Golden Bowl* as being controlled by "a long silken halter." Adam Verver conceals one end of the line in his pocket, while the other is looped about his wife's "beautiful neck." When he smiles to his daughter Maggie, "the smile was the soft shake of the twisted silken rope." And he appears to be saying, " 'I lead her to her doom' " (XXIV *GB* II 287). We are later invited to wonder about "this gathered lasso . . . with what magic it was twisted, to what tension subjected" (331). Until the end, it is Adam's habit to "weave his spell and play out his long fine cord" (358). Once again, we have a high-spirited woman checked by a smiling but perhaps harsh master. James's sympathies go out to the woman. F. O. Matthiessen writes of the whole sequence that "this image is repeated on three occasions, and what James seems to want to keep uppermost through it is the unobtrusive smoothness of his 'dear man's' dealings. But James's neglect of the cruelty in such a cord, silken though it be, is nothing short of obscene."[8]

Images having to do with runaways and falls from horses make up a final group in this category; they generate enough feeling to make one suspect that they are based in part upon personal experience or at least observation. Thus, Felix likens Gertrude Wentworth's nature to "'a runaway horse. Now I like [he continues] the feeling of a runaway horse; and if I am thrown out of the vehicle it is no great matter'" (iii *Eurs* 169). The narrator of *The Sacred Fount* fears May Server's possible breakdown, he says, as he "might have dreaded some physical accident or danger, her fall from an unmanageable horse or the crack beneath her of thin ice" (xxix *SF* 117). And Strether's success in getting Madame de Vionnet to have breakfast with him resembles "the smash in which a regular runaway properly ends" (XXII *Amb* II 14-15); later, Sarah Pocock's situation, like that of "a person seated in a runaway vehicle and turning over the question of a possible jump," leads poor doomed Strether to conclude that "if she *should* gather in her skirts, close her eyes and quit the carriage while in motion . . . it would be appointed to him, unquestionably, to receive her entire weight" (162).[9] Persons caught up in circumstances of a powerful and an emotional nature are thus often described by runaway-horse imagery.

The fifty or more sheep images are often no more interesting than the far more numerous horse figures. Indeed, the qualities of lambs and sheep—and even of shepherds, as such—rarely yield much for use in modern imaginative prose. But James introduces these animals where he can, usually stressing their innocence, gentleness, passivity, and stupidity; persons

8. *Henry James: The Major Phase* (New York: Oxford University Press, 1944), p. 100. The animal held by the lasso is only impliedly a horse.

9. See also "CCon" 582, XIII *Re* 55, xxviii "Pap" 175.

or things endangered or squandered are often pictured as sacrificial lambs or sheep; and evil agents are likened to wolves assaulting the huddled fold.

Innocence is rarely isolated, in life or in Jamesian imagery: innocent young girls, when praised as lambs by James, are usually lambs amid vicious animals. Thus, the narrator of "The Married Son" recalls that his wife when they first met was "a little bleating stray lamb" in a "New York bear garden" ("MS" 538). In a more sinister passage, Longdon is shown regarding both Aggie and Nanda as lambs—of different sorts, to be sure—approaching the common doom of the slaughter house. "Both the girls struck him as lambs with the great shambles of life in their future; but while one [Aggie], with its neck in a pink ribbon, had no consciousness but that of being fed from the hand with the small sweet biscuit of unobjectionable knowledge, the other [Nanda] struggled with instincts and forebodings, with the suspicion of its doom and the farborne scent, in the flowery fields, of blood" (IX *AA* 239).

Stupid or vapid creatures often suggest lambs to James. Thus, at one point Francie Dosson of *The Reverberator* "bleated . . . like a bewildered interrogative lamb" (XIII *Re* 146); Francie does her bleating before Mme. de Brécourt, who is called "the sheepdog" (146). In an inept trope, Crawford's faithless fiancée appears "to have no more intelligence than a snowy-fleeced lamb" ("CCon" 572). The Prince Casamassima appears to be "as ignorant as one of the dingy London sheep browsing before" him in the park (V *PC* I 304). Occasionally, the whole lackluster public mind is comprehensively ridiculed by a sheep image of this same general sort. For example, in one story we read of "the public mind! —as if the public *had* a mind, or any principle of perception more discoverable than the stare of huddled sheep!" (xxvi

"SirD" 385); in another we read that "The London mind [is] so happy a mixture of those of the parrot and the sheep" (XVIII "BH" 400). Similarly, merely vapid creatures are sheepish: Miss Flora Saunt's target, Lord Iffield, "hadn't the spirit of a sheep" (xxvii "Gl" 208). And of the three silly daughters of stern Mrs. Goldie, in "The Solution," we read that "all they could do was to follow her like frightened sheep" (xxvi "So" 312). Pitiful Isabel Archer, seeking to avoid being sheeplike, is nonetheless led to the slaughter too; therefore, a statement she makes early in the novel is all the more pathetic in the light of her ultimate doom. She once says bravely, " 'I don't wish to be a mere sheep in the flock; I wish to choose my fate' " (III *PofL* I 228-29).

A stronger personality amid lesser or worse ones is frequently imaged as a shepherd. Miriam drives her fellow-actors "in front of her like sheep" (VIII *TM* II 243); the countess in "The Middle Years" calls to her initially too-docile companions, " 'Come, my little lambs; you should follow your old *bergère!*' " (XVI "MY" 85); and Stransom counts the candles before his "altar of the dead"—as we read—"head by head, till he felt like the shepherd of a huddled flock, with all a shepherd's vision of differences imperceptible" (XVII "AofD" 18).[10]

Blatantly victimized people—usually women—are often made out to be lambs or sheep shorn of their fleece, surrendered, led to the shambles, butchered, or sacrificed to strange or unnamed gods. The following are all compared to such sheep: Mrs. Hudson of *Roderick Hudson* ("a shorn sheep" [I *RH* 433]), Claire de Cintré ("the lamb" before "the butcher" [II *Ame* 448]), Caroline Spencer of "Four Meetings" ("a small pink shorn lamb [fleeced by her cousin!]" [XVI "FM" 292]), Catherine Sloper of *Washington Square* ("fattened . . .

10. See also "CE" 291, XXV *IT* 60.

sheep" [v *WS* 159]), Hyacinth Robinson ("'the lamb of sacrifice'" [V *PC* I 362]), Owen Wingrave ("a young lamb . . . marked for sacrifice" [XVII "OW" 303]), Effie Bream of *The Other House* ("'a poor little lamb of sacrifice'"[11] [*OH* 103]), and finally Mortimer Marshal of "The Papers" (a "lamb . . . [led] to the shambles" [xxviii "Pap" 152]).

In addition to making use of undifferentiated watchdogs, hounds, and puppies, James calls from his imagistic kennel a goodly pack of specific terriers, poodles, spaniels, greyhounds, and a pointer, in his nearly fifty dog images. The fact that terriers and poodles lead the statistical list perhaps attests to their creator's inveterate domesticity.

Only the greyhound shows any noble vitality. Thus, when Felix at one point waxes eloquent, "Mr. Wentworth and Charlotte both looked at him as if they were watching a greyhound doubling" (iii *Eurs* 193), while, to contrast practical Lillian and her more adventuresome sister Isabel Archer, James has the older woman "watching her as a motherly spaniel might watch a free greyhound" (III *PofL* I 39).

Comparing persons to little dogs is hardly complimentary: Maggie Verver, coming into contact for the first time with the cold, dark medium of double-dealing, is oddly pictured "as a silken-coated spaniel who has scrambled out of a pond and who rattles the water from his ears" (XXIV *GB* II 6-7). It is notable that as her social evolution progresses, James drops

11. Effie is the focal point for several similar images of sacrifice and contention, the first of which makes of her "a large white sacrifice, a muslin-muffled offering which seemed to lead up to a ceremony" (*OH* 68). Later, when Jean Martle humorously tells Tony that Effie "'doesn't trust our kitchen,'" he replies with a joke about poison and then adds, "'Leave the poor child, then, like the little princess you all make of her, to her cook and her "taster," to the full rigour of her royalty . . .'" (116). Finally, perched on Rose's lap, Effie is likened to "Helen on the walls of Troy" (158). A few pages later, Rose drowns the little child, in an insane and futile attempt to nullify Tony's vow so that she may wed him.

the dog figure and likens Princess Maggie to a tigress (10, 12) and later to an actress with a difficult part (33, 208, 222, 231). Little Bilham, socially a somewhat immature creature, is appropriately enough pictured as responding to Strether's suggestion that he marry Mamie Pocock by shaking "his good-natured ears an instant, in the manner of a terrier who has got wet" (XXII *Amb* II 173). If such a comparison is not actually degrading, others like it are. Thus, Blanche Wright of *Confidence* describes an ardent but frustrated follower as " 'like my dear little blue terrier. . . . If I hold out a stick he will jump over it' " (iv *Con* 207); and Crapy Cornelia is impliedly compared to "some shaggy old domesticated terrier or poodle" (xxviii "CCor" 330). Dominated persons are also often like poodles: Eugene Pickering is "like a poodle-dog that is led about by a blue ribbon [blue for boys], and scoured and combed and fed on slops" (xxiv "EP" 253), and the Countess Gemini, who in the first volume of *The Portrait of a Lady* is directed conversationally by the more forceful Madame Merle, aptly enough occasions the following comparison: "Isabel heard the Countess . . . plunge into the latter's lucidity as a poodle splashes after a thrown stick. It was as if Madame Merle were seeing how far she would go" (III *PofL* I 370).[12]

Only rarely does James stress the lovable fidelity of dogs, and the few resulting images are unelaborated. Thus, Osborne "worked like a horse and loved like a dog" ("OR" 8); Oronte has "a dumb dog-like fidelity in his eyes" (XVIII "RT" 331); and Owen Gereth is likened simply to "a big dog" (X *SpofP* 30). More often James's dogs are weak, in pain, or dangerous. For a few examples, Colonel Voyt of "The Story in It" remarks that British and American novels " 'show our sense of life as the sense of puppies and kittens' "

12. For somewhat similar images, see II *Ame* 323, VI *PC* II 328, xxvii "GiC" 316.

(XVIII "SinI" 419); the Northmore family, humbled in the eyes of Mrs. Hope, resembles "a dog with a dust-pan tied to its tail and ready for any dash to cover at the sound of the clatter of tin" (XVI "AofN" 219); and beautiful Flora of "Glasses" hopes soon to discard her unattractive spectacles— or, as a friend puts it, she thinks that "'if she leads a tremendously healthy life, she'll be able to take off her muzzle and become as dangerous again as ever'" (xxvii "Gl" 240).[13]

It would not do to move to James's thirty usually dull little cat images without first pausing to admire a final odd dog figure, this one from "Pandora": "when their daughter drew near them Mr. and Mrs. Day [lively Pandora's sluggish parents] closed their eyes after the fashion of a pair of household dogs who expect to be scratched" (XVIII "Pan" 115).

Many of James's cat images result from elaborated idioms such as "which way will the cat jump?", "bell the cat!", "at night all cats are gray," and "let the cat out of the bag."[14] Of the rest, an alarming proportion reveal frightened, blind, sick, and starved cats; only a few of the figurative felines are comfortable, still fewer attractive. When the promiscuous Selina of "A London Life" is recognized at one point, she "scrambled off like a frightened cat" (X "LL" 359). Mrs. Brookenham of *The Awkward Age* regards Cashmore's unbridled clique as "a litter of blind kittens" (IX *AA* 165).[15] At the end of his story, Newman knows that the Bellegarde mother and son are "as sick as a pair of poisoned cats" (II *Ame* 539). And poor Pinnie prefers "to die in a corner like a starved cat" (VI *PC* II 93) rather than recall Hyacinth from

13. A page later the narrator learns that Flora's rich fiancé, breaking his engagement with the now nearly blind girl, has "returned the animal as unsound" (241).

14. See, for examples, XIX *WofD* I 180, *Ou* 195-96, XXIII *GB* I 105, XV "CF" 318, XV "FinC" 265.

15. Later the Duchess says that Nanda is "'fairly sick—as sick as a little cat—with her passion'" (252).

his protracted visit with Princess Casamassima.[16] Only three women, compared to comfortable cats, can try to redress the almost universal misery of James's cats. When sleighing with an attentive friend, Lizzie Crowe looks, "curled up in the buffalo-robe beside him, like a kitten in a rug" ("SofY" 268). Wright mistakenly regards his flighty wife Blanche "chiefly as a pretty kitten" (iv *Con* 261). And the narrator remembers that he liked Greville Fane but that she wrote only potboilers: "To myself literature was an irritation, a torment; but Greville Fane slumbered in the intellectual part of it even as a cat on a hearth-rug" (XVI "GF" 113). One may rightly conclude again that most of James's animal kingdom is tangled in a jungle of misery.

Contributing to almost forty images, lions and tigers and their like are used chiefly to suggest the latent supple viciousness in people, rarely any controlled power. Most of these figures picture women—poised for a spring, with claws dug into flesh, hungry, or wounded. The men are usually harmless or merely attractive. Thus, Gloriani is simply "the glossy male tiger, magnificently marked," in whose garden habitat there is something "covertly tigerish" which comes to Strether "as a waft from the jungle" (XXI *Amb* I 219).[17] But the women usually inspire a good deal of variety. To be sure, Maggie Verver, in "her little crouching posture," is likened somewhat insipidly to "a timid tigress" (XXIV *GB* II 10), and Fanny Cashmore looks like "some beautiful tame tigress" (IX *AA* 107). But more often, tigerish women are active, violent, predatory. For example, to captivated Valentin, Noémie Nioche is "'a pretty panther who has every one of her claws in your flesh and who's in the act of biting your heart out'"

16. Earlier poor Pinnie was seen as "no better than a starved cat" (V *PC* I 162).

17. For the presumable source of this image, see Oscar Cargill, *The Novels of Henry James* (New York: The Macmillan Company, 1961), p. 326. For a pair of insipid lion-like men, see XVII "PL" 231, *Ou* 104.

(II *Ame* 305). Mrs. Ambient turns into "'a wounded tigress'" (XVI "AofB" 72) when her sick son grows worse. Kate Croy knows that her socializing aunt, Maud Lowder, is a domineering creature, "and she [Kate] compared herself to a trembling kid, kept apart a day or two till her turn should come, but sooner or later to be introduced into the cage of the lioness" (XIX *WofD* I 30).[18] Densher is aware of Maud's powerful feline quality too, and in her presence, early in the novel, he is perturbed: "She was in fine quite the largest possible quantity to deal with; and he was in the cage of the lioness without his whip—the whip, in a word, of a supply of proper retorts" (77). Aware that Maud is conscious of her power, Densher later imagines her saying to him, "'I can bite your head off, any day I really open my mouth . . .'" (84).[19] And Charlotte Stant, "the splendid shining supple creature" possessed of an energy like "a breaking of bars" (XXIV *GB* II 239), is pictured in a dozen varied images toward the end of the novel as a beast (or possibly large bird) of prey, escaping, dangerously at large, menacing poor Maggie—who imagines herself at one point to be "thrown over on her back with her neck from the first half-broken and her helpless face staring up" (242)—and finally caged again.[20]

18. Kate may be a kid to Maud, but to Milly, who is an even tenderer person, she is "a creature who paced like a panther" (282). The first words used to describe her after she is likened to a panther include the statement that "Kate flickered highest" (282). R. W. Short strangely includes the figure among "certain images of height"; "Henry James's World of Images," *PMLA*, LXVIII (December, 1953), 959. Surely regarding it instead as a fire figure would be more in keeping with the often-emphasized notion that Kate is lustrous, hard, feline, and down to earth. Fires "flicker" more often in James than birds do.

19. Elsewhere, Maud is imaged as a vulture, an eagle with a gilded beak, and a beneficent dragon (XIX *WofD* I 73, XX *WofD* II 34).

20. XXIV *GB* II 241, 283, 329. For a fine early discussion of this sequence, see A. J. A. Waldock, *James, Joyce, and Others* (London: Williams and Norgate, Ltd., 1937), p. 27. See also Miriam Allott, "Symbol and Image in the Later Work of Henry James," *Essays in Criticism*, III (July, 1953), 333-34.

Jungle and stalking imagery forms patterns in at least two of James's finest short stories, both late ones. They are "The Beast in the Jungle" and "The Jolly Corner." The first animal image concerning John Marcher supports the title, sets the tone for the remaining similar images, strikes an early ironic note, and foreshadows the fatal final revelation.

Something or other lay in wait for him, amid the twists and turns of the months and years, like a crouching beast in the jungle. It signified little whether the crouching beast were destined to slay him or to be slain. The definite point was the inevitable spring of the creature; and the definite lesson from that was that a man of feeling didn't cause himself to be accompanied by a lady on a tiger-hunt (XVII "BinJ" 79).

Marcher waits "for the beast to jump out" (85); his imagination glares out "quite as with the very eyes of the very Beast" (87); he once "threshed to vacancy" the jungle and concludes that "the Beast had stolen away" (116). At last, he pathetically learns that "the Beast, at its hour, had sprung" (126).

Spencer Brydon of "The Jolly Corner," knowing that "his *alter ego* 'walked'" (XVII "JC" 456), determines to spend his nights in his old house and stalk this "creature more subtle, yet at bay perhaps more formidable, than any beast of the forest" (457). And so

He found himself at moments—once he had placed his single light on some mantel-shelf or in some recess—stepping back into shelter or shade, effacing himself behind a door or in an embrasure, as he had sought of old the vantage of rock and tree; he found himself holding his breath and living in the joy of the instant, the supreme suspense created by big game alone (457).[21]

Further, Brydon feels at times "like some monstrous stealthy cat; he wondered if he would have glared at these moments

21. This rare hunting image does not ring true. For a more accurate indication of James's attitude toward hunters and hunting, see VIII *TM* II 372; XVII "SirE" 376; X *SpofP* 59, 61.

with large shining yellow eyes" (458). And the house "affected him as the very jungle of his prey" (459). Finally, confronted by the beastly *alter ego,* Brydon collapses "under the hot breath and the roused passion of a life larger than his own" (477).[22]

James pictures a crassly predatory public as lions and tigers to which prey are thrown like Christian martyrs. Daisy Miller is partly prophetic, though unconsciously so, when she sees herself and Giovanelli—who escapes—as " 'Christian martyrs,' " glared at by Winterbourne, whom she therefore likens to " 'one of the old lions or tigers' " (XVIII "DM" 85). Another victim of rigid social mores is poor little Lady Gwyther, whose outlandishly clad person a group of stiff guests are assembled to see " 'very much as the Roman mob at the circus used to be to see the next Christian maiden brought out to the tigers' " (XII "TF" 407).[23] Finally, at another social gathering, Maud, Kate, and Densher discuss the absent Milly too thoroughly to please Susan, who grows worried; we read that "Milly's anxious companion sat and looked—looked very much as some spectator in an old-time circus might have watched the oddity of a Christian maiden, in the arena, mildly, caressingly, martyred. It was the nosing and fumbling not of lions and tigers but of domestic animals let loose as for the joke" (XX *WofD* II 42).[24]

The remaining animals in James's well-stocked menagerie do not appear frequently enough to form patterns or to warrant much analysis. Usually their human equivalents behave

22. See also 461.
23. James did not like overdressed women. (Who does?) Lady Gwyther is later described as being " 'overloaded like a monkey in a show!' " (412), and Beale Farange's mistress in *What Maisie Knew* is likened to "a clever frizzled poodle in a frill or a dreadful human monkey in a spangled petticoat" (XI *WMK* 193).
24. F. O. Matthiessen mistakenly identifies the spectator in the circus as Densher; *Henry James,* p. 69.

as we might expect: thus, the rabbit is timid (a simple woman resembles "a pink-faced rabbit" [xxv "PofD" 138]), the donkey stupid (a foolish school might contain "five hundred grazing donkeys" [XI "Pu" 524]), the wolf rapacious (keeping tickets from a demanding theater-going public is like telling " 'the lamb to keep its tenderest mutton from the wolves!' " [VIII *TM* II 428]), the ox stolid (an unfortunate peasant is "yoked down like an ox, with . . . [his] forehead in the soil" ["GdeB" 238]), and so on.

Of the several isolated tropes displaying fine rhetoric, the following two reveal opposite qualities of tenderness and ferocity in their animals. Unlovely, massive Mrs. David E. Drack pays lovely Julia Bride the homage of noticing her spectacular beauty: "It had never been so paid, she [Julia] was presently certain, as by this great generous object . . . , who without optical aid, it well might have seemed, nevertheless entirely grasped her—might in fact, all benevolently, have been groping her over as by some huge mild proboscis" (XVII "JB" 517)! At the other extreme, Urbain de Bellegarde, Newman's insidious enemy, strikes the American early in their relationship as resembling a "queer, rare, possibly dangerous biped, perturbingly akin to humanity, in one of the cages of a 'show' " (II *Ame* 219); toward the end, he "evoked for our friend some vision of a hunched back, an erect tail and a pair of shining evil eyes" (489).[25]

25. Miriam Allott points out that this image was inserted during the revising of *The American*; she then adds that " 'Beast' images of this nature pervade the late stories but do not appear before 'The Marriages' of 1891, where, to the 'possibly poisoned and inflamed judgment' of Adela Chart, Mrs. Crutchley's [*sic*] 'high bony shoulders and the long crimson tail and the universal coruscating nod wriggle their horribly practical way through the rest of the night' " (XVIII "Ma" 260)— "Symbol and Image in the Later Work of Henry James," pp. 323-24. Incidentally, I regard the passage which Miss Allott quotes as not containing any explicit metaphor, since everything in it may be accepted literally as a description of a high-shouldered, crimson-clad, sinuous woman.

ii. Birds

James's bird imagery displays much virtuosity when it has to do with women, as it usually does. The Countess Gemini, for example, has "features that suggested some tropical bird —a long beak-like nose, small, quickly-moving eyes and a mouth and chin that receded extremely." The description of her attire adds to the resemblance: "voluminous and delicate, bristling with elegance, [it] had the look of shimmering plumage." And the sketching in of her manner completes the picture: "her attitudes were as light and sudden as those of a creature who perched upon twigs" (III *PofL* I 365). Mrs. Gereth deprived at Ricks of her Poynton spoils suggests to Fleda Vetch "the vision of some tropical bird, the creature of hot dense forests, dropped on a frozen moor to pick up a living" (X *SpofP* 146). To Strether, Miss Barrace is quick, frivolous, sharp; we read that "She seemed, with little cries and protests and quick recognitions, movements like the darts of some fine high-feathered free-pecking bird, to stand before life as before some full shop-window" (XXI *Amb* I 204). And Charlotte Stant, now Mrs. Verver, who may in one imagistic pattern be a supple predatory creature, is in another and a partially overlapping sequence a repeatedly caged bird. In sympathy Maggie envisages her rival's situation as comprised "of gilt wires and bruised wings" and pictures "the spacious but suspended cage, the home of eternal unrest, of pacings, beatings, shakings all so vain" (XXIV *GB* II 229) of the bitter woman. Still, Maggie is frightened and therefore "drew back as instinctively as if the door of the cage had suddenly been opened from within" (230). At the end, she considers the relationship of her husband and Charlotte "a hard glass," behind which "Mrs. Verver might at this stage have been frantically tapping from within by way of supreme irrepressible entreaty" (329). Thus Charlotte's consciousness resolves itself into its own prison. Far more simply, the Princess Casamassima, able to dazzle society and yet at one time strangely humble in her little London house, is pictured as "a creature capable socially of immeasurable flights sit[ting] dove-like and with folded wings" (VI *PC* II 270).

The dove is the bird most frequently named imagistically, even apart from dove figures in *The Wings of the Dove*, which provides only a third of the total number. James's first dove image, which is also his first bird figure, is dull: Lieutenant Ford of "The Story of a Year" sends Lizzie letters which "came week by week, flying out of the South like white-winged carrier-doves" ("SofY" 266).

Not until the magnificently modulated pattern of dove figures which help to elucidate Milly Theale's plight are these comparisons any better. Then, as F. O. Matthiessen has ably demonstrated,[26] they are matchless. Well before the first dove figure, Maud Lowder has been seen as both lioness and gilt-clawed bird of prey (XIX *WofD* I 30, 73), and just before it Kate Croy is imaged as a pacing panther (282). The contrast, then, is all the more dramatic when we hear Kate call Milly " 'a dove.' . . . She was a dove. Oh *wasn't* she?" (283).[27] The image is next used when Milly, sick unto death in Venice but dressed now in white and loaded with dove-colored pearls, inspires Kate to say to Densher, " 'She's a dove . . . and one somehow doesn't think of doves as bejewelled. Yet they suit her down to the ground' " (XX *WofD* II 218). If Kate thinks of the dove's pearls, Densher thinks of its "wings and wondrous flights" and "tender tints and soft sounds"; he continues by trusting that Milly's wings "could in a given case . . .

---

26. *Henry James*, pp. 68-70. See also Ernest Sandeen, *"The Wings of the Dove* and *The Portrait of a Lady*: A Study of Henry James's Later Phase," *PMLA*, LXIX (December, 1954), 1071-75, for an admirable discussion of the dove imagery in *The Wings of the Dove.*

27. The comparison is insisted upon through to 284.

spread themselves for protection" (218).[28] Next, back in London Densher learns from Maud that "'Our dear dove then, as Kate calls her, has folded her wonderful wings'"; Densher echoes the words, whereupon Maud goes on with unconscious truth, "'Unless it's more true . . . that she has spread them the wider.'" Densher, who is warmed now by his own magnificent vision of the immolated girl, again agrees, James telling us that "He again but formally assented, though, strangely enough, the words fitted a figure deep in his own imagination" (356). Finally, Kate, talking to Densher, says, "'I used to call her, in my stupidity—for want of anything better—a dove. Well she stretched out her wings, and it was to *that* [enabling them to marry] they reached. They cover us'" (404). But Densher replies singly to Milly's gesture of protection.

The final notable dove image, doubtless inspired by Milly, comes from James's 1907 revision of *Roderick Hudson*. In the 1876 version, Christina Light describes Mary Garland with these simple words: "'She looks very handsome when she frowns.'"[29] The revised text reads more excitingly: "'She looks magnificent when she glares—like a Medusa crowned not with snakes but with a tremor of doves' wings'" (I *RH* 381).

Images of violence and misery are also present in the bird group. The rich old gentleman in the short story "A Light Man" is "fair game for the race of social sycophants and cormorants" (xxv "LiM" 228-29); Mrs. Gereth, stripped of her art treasures and away from Poynton, at one point "had, like

28. Jean Kimball has valuably located and analyzed a central imagistic paradox in *The Wings of the Dove*: "If the abyss and her [Milly Theale's] position at the edge of the abyss define her 'practical problem of life,' the dove, with its wonderful wings, is the symbol of her final solution"; "The Abyss and The Wings of the Dove: The Image as a Revelation," *Nineteenth-Century Fiction*, X (March, 1956), 283.

29. Henry James, Jr., *Roderick Hudson* (Boston: James R. Osgood and Company, 1876), p. 347.

some great moaning bird, made her way with wings of anguish back to the nest she knew she should find empty" (X *SpofP* 246); and Abel Gaw, another rich old man, now dying but still mentally alert, is once said to "perch there like a ruffled hawk, motionless but for his single tremor, with his beak, which had pecked so many hearts out, visibly sharper than ever, yet only his talons nervous" (XXV *IT* 6).[30]

Minor patterns of bird imagery play some little part in the development of three short stories, all written rather late in James's career. In "Mora Montravers," the Traffles regard young Mora as a "fledgling of their general nest" (xxviii "MM" 244); Mrs. Traffle later has occasion to wonder whether her husband "might be having the gumption . . . to glean a few straws for their nakeder nest" (286), after Mora has left them, soaring as she now is doing on "wider wings of free-dom" (293). In "Glasses" Flora's doomed eyes "brushed with a kind of winglike grace every object they encountered" (xxvii "Gl" 189). When the beautiful girl is bespectacled later, "she seemed to speak . . . from behind a mask or a cage" (234). Next, when the narrator observes her, apparently recovered but in reality blind, "She . . . moved her eyes over the [opera] house, and I felt them brush me again like the wings of a dove" (246–47). The final image alters the pattern: now it is the girl's passion, freed and sustained by Dawling's love for her, which has wings: "If the music, in that dark-ness, happily soared and swelled for her, it beat its wings in unison with those of a gratified passion" (250). Finally, the first image in "Julia Bride" shows the heroine brightly smiling and "her radiance . . . travelling on the light wings of her brilliant prettiness. . . . Then with its extinction the sustaining wings drooped and hung" (XVII "JB" 490). The girl's testi-mony in the divorce court is likened to "the chatter of a

30. For other images comparing women to birds, see XI "InC" 420–21; XVI "Eur" 353; xxix *SF* 104, 106–7.

parrakeet, of precocious plumage and croak" (497). Later when she suicidally praises the second of her mother's two divorced husbands, "She measured every beat of her wing, she knew how high she was going and paused only when it was quite vertiginous. Here she hung a moment in the glare of the upper blue" (519).[31]

Motifs concerning the screaming eagle, bird's nests, perches held out, and wings brushing by combine to provide an accent assuredly Jamesian but not distinctive enough to warrant detailed consideration here.[32]

iii. Miscellaneous

Nor are the more than fifty fish comparisons worth pausing on for long, since they regularly show little development. For example, Mrs. Brissenden tells the narrator of *The Sacred Fount* that she considers May Server to be using poor Briss as a dodge, " 'Trailing him across the scent as she does all of you, one after the other. Excuse my comparing you to so many red herrings' " (xxix *SF* 69). The oddest fish figure in all of James is a metaphor more than impliedly sexual, which reveals the shining but lifeless Lady Beldonald; the painter-narrator says, " 'A box of sardines is "old" only after it has been opened. Lady Beldonald never has yet been—but I'm going to do it' " (XVIII "BH" 384).[33]

Of the sixty or more insect figures, none falls into patterns; instead, isolated examples are again usually the only ones of importance, as for example another disturbing image fixing the distressed Lady Beldonald firmly in her place: " 'that's the way, with a long pin straight through your body, I've got you' " (XVIII "BH" 388), the narrator tells her. This uncon-

31. See also 504, 517, 521.
32. II *Ame* 46, 112; *Ou* 219. "Pr" 702; xxvi "SirD" 435; XI "Pu" 518, 569; XVII "JB" 498. XIX *WofD* I 15, 85, 104-5, 189; XX *WofD* II 159, 229, 301. XII "TofS" 211, xxviii "Pap" 182, XXV *IT* 130.
33. For a discussion of a few other fish images, see pp. 32-33 above.

scious sexual figure—the narrator has only a professional interest in the cold lady—recalls an earlier, simpler one from *Confidence,* in which Angela Vivian tells Bernard Longueville of her annoyance at " 'knowing that I had been handed over to you [by Gordon Wright] to be put under the microscope —like an insect with a pin stuck through it!' " (iv *Con* 195).

Harmless, busy little people—or those thought so—are sometimes likened to insects. In *The Princess Casamassima* alone, for example, we read that Hyacinth is a flea (V *PC* I 18), Pinnie a caterpillar (25), and Rosy Muniment "a bedridden grasshopper" (VI *PC* II 75). Ralph Pendrel says that Aurora Coyne regards him as "a beautiful worm," "a delicate classified insect," and "a slow-crawling library beetle, slightly iridescent, warranted compressible" (XXVI *SeofP* 12). Bright, lithe women are sometimes just as oddly described: Gussy Bradham, for example, resembles "some shining humming insect, a thing of the long-constricted waist, the minimised yet caparisoned head, the fixed disproportionate eye and tough transparent wing, gossamer guaranteed" (XXV *IT* 50).[34]

Finally, of the few snake, serpent, and dragon figures, only the ones springing from the notion that a snake can hypnotize its victim have much excitement in them. Ray Limbert and Mortimer Marshal are thus imaged as immobilized by fear or fascination and are soon therefore "engulfed in the long, pink

34. Notice that James uses a diminishing image—that of an insect— to suggest the lack of importance of the thin-waisted Gussy. When he wants to convey a notion of the litheness, glitter, and sensuality of the equally thin-waisted Charlotte Stant, he uses a far different and more suggestive image: "He [the Prince] knew above all the extraordinary fineness of her flexible waist, the stem of an expanded flower, which gave her the likeness also to some long loose silk purse, well filled with gold-pieces, but having been passed empty through a finger-ring that held it together" (XXIII *GB* I 47). For a discussion of this image, see p. 172 below. Perhaps James is thinking of Isabella Stewart Gardner—"Mrs. Jack"—when he writes of thin-waisted, energetic little ladies; see Leon Edel, *Henry James: The Middle Years: 1882-1895* (Philadelphia and New York: J. B. Lippincott Company, 1962), p. 325.

throat" (XV "NT" 177) by the "serpent of shining scales" (xxviii "Pap" 155).[35]

Conclusion

And so our tour of James's menagerie is complete. The establishment is replete with noble and sturdy horses, innocent sheep in stupid herds, playful dogs, sick and scared cats, supple lions and lionesses, birds of various feathers, nondescript fish, and busy little insects. Rarely are men and women complimented in James by having their nobility, strength, and litheness likened to corresponding aspects of animals; far more often his characters are degraded when they are compared to beasts, birds, and bugs. It is clear that to James the natural world, when unimproved by art or religion, is fraught less with sweet pleasure than with sudden violence.

In fact, the main tendency of the imagery examined thus far—water, flower, and animal—has been to institute comparisons downward, which is flattering enough to the conquering wave, the passing bloom, and the fanged animal, perhaps, but not to mankind. As Robert Frost rightly says in "The White-Tailed Hornet,"

> Our worship, humor, conscientiousness
> Went long since to the dogs under the table.
> And served us right for having instituted
> Downward comparisons. As long on earth
> As our comparisons were stoutly upward
> With gods and angels, we were men at least,
> But little lower than the gods and angels.
> But once comparisons were yielded downward,
> Once we began to see our images
> Reflected in the mud and even dust,
> 'Twas disillusion upon disillusion.

35. For some representative dragon figures, see also VIII *TM* II 215-16, X "Ch" 498, xxv "NEW" 69, xxv "PR" 431; for other snake figures, see I *RH* 397, XXIII *GB* I 153.

To be sure, when we turn to the first of our next three categories of imagery, which are war, art, and religion, we should not expect man to emerge much higher than the beasts in the steamy, swarming jungle we are now leaving, since man as a warrior is more tigerish than the tiger. Gradually, however, we will rise along the great chain of being; and soon enough we will see James comparing man to the gods because of artistic endeavor and other efforts equally spiritual. In fact, Tennyson seems to provide the outline for the next three chapters:

> . . . Arise and fly
> The reeling Faun, the sensual feast;
> Move upward, working out the beast,
> And let the ape and tiger die.

V · A BRISTLING QUIVER

These words, he was well aware, left his wife—
given her painful narrowness—a bristling quiver
of retorts to draw from; yet it was not without
a silent surprise that he saw her, with her irri-
tated eyes on him, extract the bolt of finest point
(xxviii "MM" 265).

Introduction

Like many Americans even in our perilous century, James
was fortunately destined to view war only through the eyes
of others. His "horrid even if . . . obscure hurt"[1] was responsible for his being only an anguished civilian throughout the
Civil War, in which, however, his brother Robertson suffered

1. Henry James, "Notes of a Son and Brother," in *Autobiography*, ed.
Frederick W. Dupee (New York: Criterion Books, 1956), p. 415.

a severe sunstroke and his brother Garth Wilkinson was grievously wounded at Fort Wagner. Writing in his autobiography, James calls the memory of the stretcher-borne Wilky, more than half a century after he was wounded, "clear as some object presented in high relief against the evening sky of the west."[2] The image which closes "Owen Wingrave," James's fictional piece dealing most directly with militarism, must have been linked in James's mind with faded nightmares revolving about Wilky: "He was all the young soldier on the gained field" (XVII "OW" 319).

But since James was not to see war at first hand, perhaps it seemed right to him that it should not appear directly in many of his novels or tales.[3] Only a few involve the military at all intimately—"The Story of a Year," "Poor Richard," "A Most Extraordinary Case," "Owen Wingrave," "Georgina's Reasons," and "The Chaperon." Some few others, to be sure, have to do with retired or inactive officers—*The American*, "The Diary of a Man of Fifty," *The Bostonians*, and *The Golden Bowl*.

The more than seven hundred war and weapons images, relatively most numerous in the fiction of the 1860's, do not fall into easily distinguishable patterns. Their function is to point up the hazards and conflicts of life, to reveal the dominance of commanding personalities and show casualties among the meek, and to indicate how the peace-loving are frequently challenged to combat in situations which bewilder, frighten, or horrify them. The range of this imagery is from ancient to modern times, with the modern figures quantitatively the most numerous but with some of the Renaissance and most of the French Revolutionary ones the most startling. However,

2. *Ibid.*, p. 383.
3. For a brief discussion of James and the "big public noises—war, revolution, electoral struggles, reform movements, nationalism" and the like, see Elizabeth Stevenson, *The Crooked Corridor: A Study of Henry James* (New York: The Macmillan Company, 1949), pp. 26-29.

the vehicles of most of the war images cannot be dated: they have to do with the timeless weapons of our world and with the endless strife of human beings. Obviously James, who had no first-hand knowledge of modern arms, was inspired to create war figures by his reading and, to a less extent—it is to be assumed—from conversations with soldiers.[4]

i. Classical

Classical figures are few and routine in the war category. Thus, in the social pageant with which "Lady Barbarina" begins, the women on horseback with "Their well-secured helmets . . . [and] their firm tailor-made armour . . . look singularly like amazons about to ride a charge" (XIV "LaB" 10). Aware that M. Nioche has threatened to kill his wayward daughter Noémie, Valentin jokingly asks Newman, "'You didn't see the weapon of Virginius sticking out of his pocket?'" (II *Ame* 237).[5] Several figures are even more facetious, or are at least too heavy for their contexts. Thus, Daisy Miller's little brother Randolph is called an "'infant Hannibal'" (XVIII "DM" 49); Bob Assingham, a retired colonel, is said to have cheekbones and a bristling moustache "worthy of Attila the Hun" (XXIII *GB* I 66); and there are in addition hyperbolic Rubicons, St. Georges, and Valhallas.[6] The classical military formation of the phalanx appears imagistically many times in James, but not often so notably as when Lord Beaupré's stratagem foils the fortune-hunting females and we

4. Before he started writing fiction, James visited wounded Civil War troops—James, "Notes of a Son and Brother," in *Autobiography*, pp. 424-26—and he gallantly devoted much of the energy of his old age to boosting the morale of soldiers in England in 1914 and 1915—F. W. Dupee, *Henry James*, American Men of Letters ([New York]: William Sloane Associates, 1951), pp. 50, 286-88; *The Legend of the Master*, compiled by Simon Nowell-Smith (New York: Charles Scribner's Sons, 1948), p. 166.

5. See also 210.

6. See XVIII "Fl" 454, XV "LofM" 27, XVIII "Pan" 153, XV "DofL" 142.

read that "the phalanx of the pressingly nubile was held in check" (xxvii "LoB" 56). Often, when elements of anonymous but irresistible society invade the individual, they are imaged as doing so in a solid phalanx. Mrs. Headway's fight in "The Siege of London" is pitifully one-sided: "She was alone against many, and her opponents were a serried phalanx; those who were there [at Longlands] represented a thousand others" (XIV "SofL" 220-21); to Julia Bride the family of Frenches are "a serried phalanx" (XVII "JB" 500) against her; and so on.

ii. Medieval and Renaissance

Jumping forward to medieval and Renaissance times, we find that when James states plainly that a person is like a knight, the figure often is deliberately ludicrous. For example, Roderick Hudson returns from gambling foolishly and unsuccessfully at Baden-Baden looking "like the battered knight who yet sports a taller plume" (I *RH* 138); when Catherine Sloper moons over Morris Townsend, she "think[s] of a young knight in a poem" (v *WS* 36); a few persons inaccurately see Henry Wilmerding of "The Solution" as a "knight of romance" (xxv "So" 314, 343); and Lord Theign is ironically pictured as follows: "He was flushed, but he bore it as the ensign of his house; he was so admirably, vividly dressed, for the morning hour and for his journey, that he shone as with the armour of a knight" (*Ou* 148).[7]

But when James wishes to portray a man who is genuinely strong, self-denying, or chivalric, the fact may be suggested by serious and detailed knight imagery. For a late example, we find Ralph Pendrel sensing that in a compressed span of time he has gone far toward achieving a sense of the

7. See also the pseudo-chivalric pictures of poor Richard (xxv "PR" 443), Bantling (IV *PofL* II 394), and even little Miles (XII "TofS" 269).

past: "The impression was strong with him of having traversed a crisis—served, and all in half an hour, one of those concentrated terms of pious self-dedication or whatever by which the aspirants of the ages of faith used to earn their knighthood. . . . He had at all events grasped his candle as if it had been sword or cross . . ." (XXVI *SeofP* 84). Even more obviously different is the small set of armor images by which the tough, rigid character of Caspar Goodwood is revealed. Goodwood reminds Isabel of "the different fitted parts of armoured warriors—in plates of steel handsomely inlaid with gold" (III *PofL* I 165); further, his eyes once "seemed to shine through the vizard of a helmet" (218) and he "was naturally plated and steeled, armed essentially for aggression" (220).[8] Madame Merle is almost a match for him in hardness, however, for we read that "That personage was armed at all points; it was a pleasure to see a character so completely equipped for the social battle. She carried her flag discreetly, but her weapons were polished steel, and she used them with a skill which struck Isabel as more and more that of a veteran" (IV *PofL* II 154).[9]

Many items from James's war imagery can be assembled to provide a veritable medieval or Renaissance arsenal. Thus, Newman feels "cased in ancestral steel" (II *Ame* 510); "The fine web of authority, . . . woven about her [Verena Tarrant], was now as dense as a suit of golden mail" (viii *Bo* I 201); and the beard of Maisie's father is "burnished like a gold breastplate" (XI *WMK* 8).

It is already apparent that James often compares lithe

8. F. O. Matthiessen points out that this "recurrent image of armor" is a part of the rather extensive revisions of *The Portrait of a Lady* and not of the original text; *Henry James: The Major Phase* (New York: Oxford University Press, 1944), pp. 177-78.

9. See also 155, where Isabel is described as seeing the advantage of resembling such a woman, "of having made one's self a firm surface, a sort of corselet of silver."

young maidens to warriors armed cap-a-pie. He does so partly, I should say, in order to show how ill-suited many of them are for combat in ruthless modern society. The least well-equipped such fighter is pathetic Milly Theale, who nonetheless is pictured as positively marching out of the office of her doctor, Sir Luke Strett, armed with his advice: "It was as if she had had to pluck off her breast, to throw away, some friendly ornament, a familiar flower, a little old jewel, that was part of her daily dress; and to take up and shoulder as a substitute some queer defensive weapon, a musket, a spear, a battle-axe—conducive possibly in a higher degree to a striking appearance, but demanding all the effort of a military posture" (XIX *WofD* I 248).[10] In the second volume, confronting Susan Stringham, who has probably just been discussing the girl's case with Sir Luke,

. . . Milly, face to face with that companion, had . . . one of those moments in which the warned, the anxious fighter of the battle of life, as if once again feeling for the sword at his side, carried his hand straight to the quarter of his courage. She laid hers firmly on her heart, and the two women stood there showing each other a strange front (XX *WofD* II 99).

Thus Milly, so little a soldier, in rising to meet life and her troubles feels for her only weapon, which is her generous heart.

Verena Tarrant of *The Bostonians* also tries hard to be an effective warrior, in her crusade for women's rights; but in reality she is hardly more able than Milly. Thrice Verena is compared to Joan of Arc,[11] but before the climax of the novel has been reached, it is obvious that she is destined neither to

10. Alexander Holder-Barell analyzes this passage extremely well; *The Development of Imagery and Its Functional Significance in Henry James's Novels,* The Cooper Monographs (Bern: Francke Verlag, 1959), p. 74. See also XIX *WofD* I 249.

11. See viii *Bo* I 101, 145, 173.

lead a successful crusade nor to be a maiden martyr in a vast reform government.[12]

Except for a single image, James ignores the medieval maidens left behind by their warriors. Five years after Mrs. Temperley has taken her three daughters from America to Paris, the lover of one of them follows and finds the girl pensive and mute but still loyal to her mother: "his own version of her peculiarities was that she was like a figure on the *predella* of an early Italian painting or a medieval maiden wandering about a lonely castle, with her love gone to the Crusades" (xxvi "MrsT" 269).

Castles, citadels, and other outmoded fortresses loom large in James's imagery. In *The Wings of the Dove,* for example, Kate must choose between dealing with discoveries about her aunt and remaining in her upstairs refuge, where all worries "were at such a height only like the rumble of a far-off siege heard in the provisioned citadel" (XIX *WofD* I 29). Milly too is charmed by a refuge, her Venetian *palazzo.* "The romance for her . . . would be to sit there for ever . . . as in a fortress; and the idea became an image of never going down, of remaining aloft in the divine dustless air, where she would hear but the plash of the water against stone" (XX *WofD* II 147).[13] James almost totally varies the image, even though while doing so he reinforces the pattern of medieval warfare, when he has Susan Stringham contemplate the quiet but powerfully militant Maud Lowder with a sense of charm

12. One other woman is likened to Joan of Arc; she is Paule de Brindes in "Collaboration," but the comparison is not sustained. Félix Vendemer simply tells the narrator that "He considered that his intended bore a striking resemblance to Jeanne d'Arc, and he marched after her on this occasion like a square-shouldered armour-bearer" (xxvii "Col" 166). But all of this proves only that Vendemer does not call the tune.

13. See also XIX *WofD* I 31, 56-57. One is inevitably reminded of Hilda and her tower in Hawthorne's *The Marble Faun.* See Marius Bewley, *The Complex Fate: Hawthorne, Henry James and Some Other American Writers* (London: Chatto and Windus, 1952), p. 45.

—"a charm as of sitting in springtime, during a long peace, on the daisied bank of some great slumbering fortress" (XIX *WofD* I 169).

The loved one is often pictured as a fortress to be taken by storm, and love is often shown as activity within such a structure. For example, Mortimer Marshal of "The Papers" is attracted by Maud Blandy, but his mild nature can effect no conquest, as is suggested by the following unfortunately phrased image: "He wouldn't rage—he *couldn't,* for the citadel might, in that case, have been carried by his assault; he would only spend his life in walking round and round it, asking every one he met how in the name of goodness one did get in" (xxviii "Pap" 151). Nora in *Watch and Ward* feels that she loves Hubert but does not reveal the fact, all of which puzzles poor Lawrence, for "Search as he could, . . . he was unable to find her lover. It was no one there present; they were all alike wasting their shot; the enemy had stolen a march and was hidden in the very heart of the citadel" (xxiv *WandW* 148).[14] In the course of a particularly boring session with the Bellegardes early in his courtship of Claire, Newman watches while "the Marquis [Urbain] walked up and down in silence, like a sentinel at the door of some menaced citadel of the proprieties" (II *Ame* 260).[15] By contrast, Robert Acton in *The Europeans,* who toys with the idea of falling in love with Eugenia Münster, is oddly pictured as the building to be entered: in part we read that "he had flattered himself that his single condition was something of a cita-

14. The last two images are without doubt unconsciously sexual. See pp. 223-24 below.

15. Urbain later unbends long enough to give an entertainment in Newman's honor; however, at the opera, Newman sees that "he [Urbain] was as remotely bland as usual, but the great demonstration in which he had lately played his part appeared to have been a drawbridge lowered and lifted again. Newman was once more outside the castle and its master perched on the battlements" (339). These images well suggest the allurement of the female and the defensiveness of the *pater familias.*

del. . . . The draw-bridge had swayed slightly under Madame Münster's step; why should he not cause it to be raised again, so that she might be kept prisoner?" (iii *Eurs* 137).[16]

Those who have wealth are also besieged. Thus, the narrator of "A Light Man" lays siege to the dying financier's affections, and records, "I have made . . . a 'conquest' of his venerable heart. Poor, battered, bamboozled old organ! he would have one believe that it has a most tragical record of capture and recapture. At all events, it appears that I am master of the citadel. For the present I have no wish to evacuate. I feel, nevertheless, . . . that I ought to shoulder my victorious banner and advance to more fruitful triumphs" (xxv "LiM" 223).[17]

iii. French Revolutionary

Most intriguing is the imagery deriving from the French Revolution, the only identified war out of which a figurative phalanx of any size marches. James's sympathy with the political conservatives, unconsciously shown in several analogies, is fully as revealing, I think, as his consciously professed respect for the liberals in such works as *The Bostonians* and *The Princess Casamassima*. James, a doomed aristocrat from an increasingly capitalistic and industrial country, clearly sympathizes with the doomed aristocrats of an earlier era; however, nowhere does he contend that *ces aristocrates* were politically wise or even expedient. Isabel Archer may be voicing James's own position when she says, " 'In a revolution—after it was well begun—I think I should be a high, proud loyalist. One sympathizes more with them, and they've a chance to behave so exquisitely. I mean so picturesquely' " (III *PofL* I 100); to all of which her uncle replies, " 'I'm

16. This image, of 120 words—thus one of the longest James wrote in the 1870's—is inconsistent; Acton does not want to imprison Eugenia in his single condition but rather in his arms or his home.

17. See also XXV *IT* 216.

afraid . . . you won't have the pleasure of going gracefully to the guillotine here just now'" (101).[18] Thus the mention of revolutions in general brings quickly to James's mind specific thoughts of the execution of French nobles, even when the fictional context is British. Note further that Mrs. Gereth, whose plight when she is stripped of her Poynton art treasures James poignantly treats, is compared to "Marie Antoinette in the Conciergerie" (X *SpofP* 146). Hudson, on learning of Christina Light's marriage, is likened dramatically to "some noble young *émigré* of the French Terror, seized before reaching the frontier [does James regard love consummated as an escape?] and showing, while brought back, a white face, indescribable, that anticipated the guillotine" (I *RH* 463-64). The titular heroine of "Mrs. Medwin" is even more grotesquely pictured, for at one point "her white face—it was too white —with the fixed eyes, the somewhat touzled hair and the Louis Seize hat, might at the end of the very long neck have suggested the head of a princess carried on a pike in a revolution" (XVIII "MrsM" 481). These persons—a proud collector of art trophies, a stunned sculptor, and a would-be socialite —are sympathetically portrayed but are not entirely commendable.

It is a strange coincidence that each of James's three major novels of the early 1900's should also contain imagery drawn from the French Revolution. In a ghoulish, surrealistic figure, Milly Theale, amid luxury which she is fated soon to leave, is pictured as seeing her own doom bobbing at her from the vulgar streets below: "pity held up its telltale face like a head on a pike, in a French revolution, bobbing before a window" (XIX *WofD* I 240). Later, the condemned girl is clearly noble: "Milly had held with passion to her dream of a future, and she was separated from it, not

18. This is the literal end for the sympathetically presented Gabrielle de Bergerac and Pierre Coquelin in James's short story "Gabrielle de Bergerac."

shrieking indeed, but grimly, awfully silent, as one might imagine some noble young victim of the scaffold, in the French Revolution, separated at the prison-door from some object clutched for resistance" (XX *WofD* II 341-42). Next, through Madame de Vionnet's Parisian windows Strether credibly enough detects "the smell of revolution, the smell of the public temper—or perhaps simply the smell of blood"[19] (XXII *Amb* II 274); then he observes the dress of his polished French hostess and thinks that "Madame Roland must on the scaffold have worn something like it," all of which enables Strether to fill in "the mystic, the noble analogy" (275). Finally, Maggie Verver shares her subdued Italian husband's sense of imprisonment, before her father and his wife arrive to say farewell: "It was . . . as if she were waiting with him in his prison—waiting with some gleam of remembrance of how noble captives in the French Revolution, in the darkness of the Terror, used to make a feast or a high discourse of their last poor resources" (XXIV *GB* II 341). But there is a refreshing difference, since "For the people of the French Revolution assuredly there wasn't suspense; the scaffold, for those she was thinking of, was certain—whereas what Charlotte's telegram announced was . . . clear liberation" (341-42). In all of these images,[20] James definitely reveals a latent sympathy for noble victims of the Terror.

iv. Weapons

The more modern rooms of James's arsenal contain muskets, pistols, revolvers, big guns, artillery pieces of various

---

19. Back in 1872, James had written from Paris to his brother William that "Beneath all this neatness and coquetry, you seem to smell the Commune suppressed, but seething"; quoted in F. O. Matthiessen, *The James Family: Including Selections from the Writings of Henry James, Senior, William, Henry, & Alice James* (New York: Alfred A. Knopf, 1947), p. 256 n. 1.

20. See also ix *Bo* II 274-75, VI *PC* II 244, VII *TM* I 119, XXIV *GB* II 330.

sizes, and an odd tomahawk and bayonet or two. Sometimes the image is not functional but merely clever, as when opera glasses leveled at the ladies are called "an instrument often only less injurious in effect than a double-barrelled pistol" (XIV "SofL" 145). Occasionally a pistol is involved in a description of surprising, flaring energy: for example, Lady Agnes may look cold, but her son Nick Dormer of *The Tragic Muse* knows that "from time to time she would fire off a pistol" (VIII *TM* II 67), while Lord Theign's sudden laying down of the law in *The Outcry* "had a report as sharp and almost as multiplied as the successive cracks of a discharged revolver" (*Ou* 213-14).[21] Bullet imagery when suddenly released makes the reader jerk alert, as do the characters involved in the description in which such imagery is found: "Mrs. Wix gave the jerk of a sleeper awakened or the start even of one who hears a bullet whiz at the flag of truce" (XI *WMK* 271).[22]

A dreadful number of big guns imagistically crash through most of the fiction[23]—at least until World War I forced James to abandon *The Ivory Tower* and retreat to *The Sense of the Past,* which aptly enough contains no imagery deriving from modern war and only a few concerning romantic combat and somewhat archaic weapons.[24] When Isabel learns of old Mr.

21. See also XIV "PofV" 591, XXIII *GB* I 64, IX *AA* 87.

22. Dupee cites this image in support of his correct observation that James in the 1890's developed the "habit of turning abruptly and alarmingly concrete"; *Henry James*, p. 193. As for tomahawk, see II *Ame* 237; sabre, xxvi "MEC" 159; bayonet, XXII *Amb* II 222.

23. Such seemingly incongruous images, along with similar ones from other categories, help James to "show what an 'exciting' inward life may do for the person leading it even while it remains perfectly normal" (III, xx). John Paterson writes that "In spite of his professional mistrust of the primitive novel of adventure, . . . Henry James was as haunted as any Tom Sawyer by its crude and violent imagery"; "The Language of 'Adventure' in Henry James," *American Literature*, XXXII (November, 1960), 292.

24. See XXVI *SeofP* 10, 14, 119, 233. In the light of James's biography, the following image from the same late novel is most revealing:

Touchett's bequest to her, she is shocked, for as her aunt explains, "'It has been as if a big gun were suddenly fired off behind her; she's feeling herself to see if she be hurt'" (III *PofL* I 299). Isabel is entitled to her fear, because earlier it was explained that she "knew little of the sorts of artillery to which young women are exposed" (69). Elsewhere James says that ideas of a certain "calibre" "rumbled and flashed" (xxviii "Pap" 93) and further that "women of a larger experience" may be said to be "of a heavier calibre, as it were" ("SofM" 5). Ransom calls Miss Chancellor "'a battery of many guns'" (ix *Bo* II 57) when she defends Verena, who later plans "to take to the field in the manner of Mrs. Farrinder, for a winter campaign, carrying with her a tremendous big gun" (207-8). By contrast, Parson Hubert is "one of the light-armed troops of the army of the Lord. He fought the Devil as an irresponsible skirmisher, not as a sturdy gunman planted beside a booming sixty-pounder" (xxiv *WandW* 77). For this reason, perhaps, he fears Mrs. Keith, who, we read, "dragged a heavy gun to the front . . . [and] determined to fire her shot" (140).

For various reasons, many characters either go at the task of shooting without much vigor or else avoid it entirely. Aunt Maud considers Densher most unchallenging: "She fought him at any rate with one hand, with a few loose grains of stray powder" (XIX *WofD* I 79). Catherine Sloper is so passive that she fails to direct even mute reproaches at her father, who "was surprised at not finding himself exposed to these silent batteries" (v *WS* 95). And Ralph Touchett tells Lord Warburton, "'Osmond may after all not think me worth his gun-powder'" (IV *PofL* II 151).

It is interesting that these persons who are here described

"Recovering the lost was at all events on this scale much like entering the enemy's lines to get back one's dead for burial" (49).

as fearing or at least expecting direct attacks from those inimical to them are in fact not directly but instead only indirectly fought. Fear of forthright assault and then surprise at the nature of wily subterfuge contribute greatly to the dramatic and ironic clashes in James's fiction.

v. Miscellaneous

Many of the other war images fall into miscellaneous categories. German militarism, for example, with its determination and thoroughness, suggests a few figures. Thus, of one handsome but vacillating man it is said that he "would look like a Prussian lieutenant if Prussian lieutenants ever hesitated" (xxiv "IofC" 398); of another man, this one a captain, we read that "he had a first-rate power of work and an ambition as minutely 'down on paper' as a German plan of invasion" (X "Ch" 457).

James has a strangely small number of images deriving from sea-fighting, and most of those few are palpably romantic. Thus, a sunset is seen once as "a splendid confusion of purple and green and gold—the clouds flying and floating in the wind like the folds of a mighty banner borne by some triumphal fleet which had rounded the curve of the globe" (xxv "LaP" 372). But when James describes hidden lust for wealth, the result is more exciting: "the business of mere money-getting showed only, in its ugliness, as vast and vague and dark, a pirate-ship with lights turned inward" (II *Ame* 102).

Images in which military rank is specified permit the inference that James, unlike Herman Melville and Stephen Crane, preferred the upper orders.[25] There is but one

25. Among his dramatis personae, the same tendency is discernible; against lowly Lieutenant Ford and Captain Jay we may set among others Major Monarch, Colonels Mason and Assingham, the deceased Commodore Steuben, General Fancourt, and the general who wrote "The Diary of a Man of Fifty."

lowly corporal—the parlor maid in *The Other House,* who is "plainly the corporal of her squad" (*OH* 81) —while the rest rise from lieutenant (in "Osborne's Revenge" we find a woman "pressed into . . . service as a lieutenant" ["OR" 16]) through captain (Vanderbank in *The Awkward Age,* confronting his week-end, "sat down in front of [it] as a captain before a city" [IX *AA* 333]) and commodore ("Paste" offers us "a strange charming little red-haired black-dressed woman, a person with the face of a baby and the authority of a commodore" [XVI "Pas" 323]) to nothing less than commander-in-chief (Paul Muniment of *The Princess Casamassima* has "the complexion of a ploughboy and the glance of a commander-in-chief" [V *PC* I 114]).

It is noteworthy that far more persons seen imagistically as having specific military rank are women rather than men. Against Paul Muniment, a properly masculine commander-in-chief, we may place the redoubtable Mrs. Farrinder of *The Bostonians,* under whose banner Miss Chancellor hopes to see Verena enlist: "It had been Olive's original desire to obtain Mrs. Farrinder's stamp for her protégée; she wished her to hold a commission from the commander-in-chief" (viii *Bo* I 195). Further, Maggie, whose strategy of splitting the Prince and Charlotte apart Fanny can professionally appreciate, is seen by that meddling friend as follows: "She stood there, in her full uniform, like some small erect commander of a siege, an anxious captain who has suddenly got news . . . of agitation, of division within the place" (XXIV *GB* II 214). Also, of the seven grenadier figures in James, five are applied to women and one to a woman's principles, while only one concerns a man.[26] Once again, it seems that James's trope-making imagination was more engaged when challenged to picture women than it was when men were the subject.

26. See VII *TM* I 187; XVII "OW" 280, 284; xxvii "Gl" 188; *OH* 81; xxiv "EP" 273; and II *Ame* 3.

vi. War Patterns

Finally, only one short story and one novel have patterns of war imagery significant enough to warrant separate discussion. By all odds, "Owen Wingrave" has the largest proportion of such figures; nearly a third of its similes and metaphors concern the profession on which its young hero sees fit to turn his back. Spencer Coyle, the military tutor, whose initial argument with Owen was "an encounter in which each drew blood" (XVII "OW" 270), soon perceives that the young man's family are assembled to fight the youth. As Coyle explains it to his wife, " 'They've cut off his supplies—they're trying to starve him out . . . Owen feels the pressure, but he won't yield' " (292). The young man's aunt, Miss Wingrave, impresses Coyle as quite military herself—"not that she had the step of a grenadier or the vocabulary of a camp-follower" (280), it is added. When she tells Coyle early in the story that she has a weapon to use in the argument, "he didn't know in the least what this engine might be, but he begged her to drag it without delay into the field" (283). We learn that Owen has "a military steadiness under fire" (296) and can therefore bravely confront his family's wrath; so Coyle comes to admire "the sight of his pupil marching up to the battery in spite of his terror" (285). And even old Sir Philip, "higher in command" (284) than Miss Wingrave, whom Coyle finally concedes to be " 'a grenadier at bottom' " (284), cannot change the decision of Owen, who at his melodramatic death is imaged as "all the young soldier on the gained field" (319).

And a tenth of the images in *Washington Square* have to do with war and weapons, although few are worth mentioning in detail. We do find some figurative use of weapons, wounds, and neutral ground. Thus, when Dr. Sloper guesses —what is true—that Morris Townsend has decamped, Mrs. Penniman can only deny it, since "indignant negation was the only weapon in her hands" (v WS 197). Earlier, Morris has deeply hurt his sister Mrs. Montgomery, and we find Dr. Sloper busily trying to detect the fact: "she had contrived to plaster up her wounds. They were aching there . . . and if he could only touch the tender spot, she would make a movement that would betray her" (91). Mrs. Penniman seeks a tryst with Morris, and we read that "This interview could take place only on neutral ground" (99). The other war figures in *Washington Square* are of little import and do not materially alter the little battle plan sketched here. Dr. Sloper would like to be the commander and plan all the strategy; Mrs. Penniman romantically hopes to see Catherine and her lover outmaneuver the relentless man, but the daughter is too unconventional a fighter and the young man too pusillanimous.[27] *Washington Square* came too early in James's career for it to have a fine texture of imagery; and in addition, Miss Sloper could never be credibly pictured as is Miriam Rooth, for one example among many, pausing "in silent excitement, like a young warrior arrested by a glimpse of the battle-field" (VII TM I 353).[28]

Conclusion

It occasionally used to be thought that nothing much happens in a James novel or short story. But an honest recollection of the sweep of James's violent war imagery—with its serried phalanxes, embattled castles, heads on pikes, and big guns—should contribute toward quick surrender of such an untenable position.

James peppers his fiction with many routine bookish war images, concerning spears and battlements, helmets and flags of truce, knights and shining armor, and the like. More in-

27. See v WS 36, 43, 123, 143, 165, 193, 210, 218.
28. Holder-Barell finds a small pattern of war images in *The Spoils of Poynton* and analyzes it admirably; *Imagery in James's Novels*, pp. 72-73.

terestingly, he poignantly shows ill-equipped women, often courageous but essentially frail, struggling to do battle against awesome odds. He unconsciously places himself on the side of those French *émigrés* who when captured met their swift doom with aristocratic hauteur; more subtly, one might suggest that such images show James's disapproval of conspicuous social and political irresponsibility but also his concomitant ambivalent sympathy with those brutally destroyed for it. Further, the imagery displays his anti-Prussianism and his inclination toward the higher social orders, if the high figurative ranks he confers are any guide.

The same conclusion emerges from a consideration of these war tropes as does from a study of the water, flower, and animal figures: too often the sensitive are engulfed and the defenseless seized and rent. James's view of combative mankind is like that of Henry Adams, who, wondering what the year of his centenary might be like to his own returning shade and those of a few gentle friends, concludes his *Education of Henry Adams* as follows: "perhaps then, for the first time since man began his education among the carnivores, they would find a world that sensitive and timid natures could regard without a shudder."

VI · THE AESTHETIC LYRE

They twanged with a vengeance the aesthetic lyre—they drew from it wonderful airs (XXI *Amb* I 128).

Introduction

We have his entire life as proof that James was passionately interested in most of the arts. Books, paintings, and the theater—aside from his marvelous family—were literally the loves of his life. Among his earliest published pieces were book reviews. His travels took him to the great European art galleries. Theater-going began before he had entered his teens and became a lifelong habit. He wrote art and theater notes before he had become a really established fiction-writer and long before he had tried his hand at writing plays.

It is not surprising, therefore, that the largest single category of similes and metaphors in the fiction of James should be that of art. Nearly two thousand separate figures—more than a tenth of the total—concern art in one or more of its forms. Non-dramatic literature accounts for more than six hundred images, painting well over four hundred, the drama slightly more than four hundred, music over three hundred, sculpture less than two hundred, and the dance and architecture together only a scant fifty. The relative frequency of the art figures increases from the 1860's to the 1870's and then drops steadily but only slightly.

i. Literature

One of the most interesting groups of literary tropes is made up of sixty-odd direct imagistic references to twenty-six novelists or their works. Thackeray figures in nine, Balzac in six, Dickens and Cervantes in five each, and Goethe and Hawthorne in three each. The following novelists appear in two images each: Mrs. Radcliffe, George Sand, Sir Walter Scott, E. T. A. Hoffmann, and Oliver Goldsmith. And the following appear in one each: Bulwer, Feuillet, Mrs. Gore, Smollett, Jane Austen, Trollope, Kingsley, Poe, Mary Shelley, and Stendhal; also an unspecified Brontë sister, and even the James of "Daisy Miller" (really only a short story).[1] Judging from the imagery, I should say that Thackeray and Balzac were the two novelists most frequently on James's mind. James couples their names occasionally in letters, as for example in the one to William Dean Howells dated January 31, 1880, and dealing with American fiction: "I shall feel refuted only when we have produced (setting the present high company—yourself and me—for obvious reasons apart) a gentleman who strikes me as a novelist—as belonging to the com-

---

1. Goethe as author of *Faust* also inspires imagery, as do Washington Irving, Maupassant, and Chamisso.

pany of Balzac and Thackeray."[2] Half of the fiction-writers alluded to in imagery are English, with French and then American authors following. While this sort of evidence may be interesting, it is dangerously incomplete, because the omissions of George Eliot, Gustave Flaubert, and Ivan Turgenev, for example, were due in part to chance and in part to the fact that James mainly addressed Anglo-American audiences. Still, it would surely have been predictable that James's imagery should contain many references to Balzac and that Hawthorne should be the only American figuring in detailed imagistic sections. Nevertheless, it is a little puzzling that in imagery Thackeray should appear almost twice as often as Dickens, when the two names are frequently linked in critical passages by James.[3]

A social situation or a person is often imaged as coming from a novel: thus, the elements which make up the depressing life of Kate Croy's sister "work[ed] themselves into the light literary legend—a mixed wandering echo of Trollope, of Thackeray, perhaps mostly of Dickens" (XIX *WofD* I 192). The mother of Christina Light is likened by Madame Grandoni to " 'some extravagant old woman in a novel—in something of Hofmann or Balzac, something even of . . . Thackeray' " (I *RH* 164).[4] Impassioned or at least alert women often

2. *The Letters of Henry James,* ed. Percy Lubbock, 2 vols. (New York: Charles Scribner's Sons, 1920), I, 72.

3. F. O. Matthiessen, *The James Family: Including Selections from the Writings of Henry James, Senior, William, Henry, & Alice James* (New York: Alfred A. Knopf, 1947), p. 254; Henry James, "The Art of Fiction," in *The Future of the Novel: Essays on the Art of Fiction,* ed. Leon Edel (New York: Vintage Books, 1956), p. 3; Henry James, *Notes on Novelists with Some Other Notes* (New York: Charles Scribner's Sons, 1914), p. 113; Henry James, "The Middle Years," in *Autobiography,* ed. Frederick W. Dupee (New York: Criterion Books, 1956), p. 549.

4. Madame Grandoni's auditor is Rowland Mallet, who a few pages earlier is described as listening to Roderick's comments on a shadowy, predatory woman of the Kursaal and being "reminded of Madame de Cruchecassée in Thackeray's novel[s: *The Newcomes, Vanity Fair,* and

make James think of their counterparts in Thackeray. Thus, Nora Lambert when annoyed reminds Roger "of Lady Castlewood in Henry Esmond, who looked 'devilish handsome in a passion'" (xxiv *WandW* 70). The narrator of "The Liar" remarks of Everina, "'She used to remind me of Thackeray's Ethel Newcome'" (XII "Li" 324). And Strether tells Maria Gostrey that "she reminded him . . . of Major Pendennis breakfasting at his club" (XXI *Amb* I 35).[5]

Most of the Balzac references are imbedded appropriately in French scenes, usually of larger social groups.[6] For example, in a Parisian restaurant Hyacinth Robinson delightedly "had a vague sense of fraternising with Balzac and Alfred de Musset: there were echoes and reminiscences of their work in the air, all confounded with the indefinable exhalations, the strange composite odour, half agreeable, half impure, of the Boulevard" (VI *PC* II 120-21). Further, according to Louis Leverett, the various persons living at the Maisonrouge Pension in "A Bundle of Letters" "have a great deal of the Balzac tone" (XIV "BofL" 499). Valentin tells Newman that the Bellegardes are only "'fit for a museum or a Balzac novel'" (II *Ame* 162). Finally, James's high opinion of Balzac is implied when in *The Tragic Muse* he has Peter Sherringham call Madame Carré "'the Balzac, as one may say, of actresses'" (VII *TM* I 68).[7]

Pendennis]" (I *RH* 139). Joseph Warren Beach quotes both of these Thackeray images in his discussion of Thackerayan dialogue in James; *The Method of Henry James* (Philadelphia: Albert Saifer: Publisher, 1954), p. 75.

5. See also XXI *Amb* I 38, XIII "PP" 398, XIX *WofD* I 173.

6. James revered Balzac, of whom he once said, "I seem to see him . . . moving about as Gulliver among the pigmies"; *Notes on Novelists*, p. 111. Elsewhere James confessed that he had "learned from him [Balzac] more of the engaging mystery of fiction than from any one else"; *The Question of Our Speech* [and] *The Lesson of Balzac: Two Lectures* (Boston and New York: Houghton Mifflin Company, 1905), p. 70.

7. In "The Madonna of the Future" Mrs. Coventry acutely remarks

James uses only a few of the countless memorable scenes from Dickens which delighted him in his youth. It may be that, as was not the case with Thackeray, Dickensian situations and characters were usually below the social level of James's typical personae; further, James disapproved of some of Dickens's methods of characterization.[8] At any rate, often the tone of a passage in which James uses Dickens in imagery is blatant or satirical. For example, when Roderick Hudson explains that the measure of genius one person has is different from that of another, he goes on to add that " 'when you have consumed your portion it's as *naïf* to ask for more as it was for Oliver Twist to ask for more porridge' " (I *RH* 230). Julia Bride and Murray Brush meeting in Central Park are grotesquely likened to "Nancy and the Artful Dodger, or some nefarious pair of that sort, talking things over in the manner of 'Oliver Twist' " (XVII "JB" 529). Sir Claude asks the former Miss Overmore what Maisie's beloved Mrs. Wix has just said; the answer cheapens the speaker but does not elucidate the probable genuineness of Mrs. Wix's nature: " 'Why that, like Mrs. Micawber—whom she must, I think, rather resemble —she will never, never, never desert Miss [Maisie] Farange' " (XI *WMK* 126). Nor do I think that there is much Dickensian in the background of Felix Young, even though when she hears him spin it out in installments, the inexperienced Gertrude Wentworth thinks so: "While this periodical recital was going on, Gertrude lived in a fantastical world; she seemed to herself to be reading a romance that came out in

concerning inefficient Theobald's Madonna, " 'I shouldn't myself be surprised if, when one runs him to earth, one finds scarce more than in that terrible little tale of Balzac's—a mere mass of incoherent scratches and daubs, a jungle of dead paint!' " (XIII "MofF" 461). The fact that the entire story by James bears a resemblance to Balzac's "terrible little tale"—"Le chef-d'oeuvre inconnu," 1832—is more proof of James's respect for Balzac.

8. *Notes on Novelists*, p. 151; Henry James, *Views and Reviews* (Boston: The Ball Publishing Company, 1908), pp. 153-61.

daily numbers. She had known nothing so delightful since the perusal of Nicholas Nickleby" (iii *Eurs* 80).

The comparison seems somewhat forced at times when we read, as we very often do in James, that circumstances are "as queer as fiction, as farce" (XXII *Amb* II 257), that a situation is "'like something in a bad novel'" (I *RH* 511), or the like. But to James, who found life and letters equally vital,[9] the analogy must have seemed accurate and natural. So we find in "The Turn of the Screw" the narrator's story called "incomplete and like the mere opening of a serial" (XII "TofS" 151), and when Isabel Archer describes her romantic notion of happiness, the less imaginative Henrietta exclaims that the girl is "'like the heroine of an immoral novel'" (III *PofL* I 235). Further, Gabriel Nash tells Nick at one point, "'You talk like an American novel'" (VIII *TM* II 193). Perhaps the implied criticism here is not wholly Gabriel's: elsewhere—in "A Most Extraordinary Case"—an American doctor says that the heroine "'looks as if she had come out of an American novel. I don't know that that's great praise; but, at all events, I make her come out of it'" (xxvi "MEC" 124). On the other hand, there is obviously no disrespect in the Princess Casamassima's picture of odd Lady Aurora's selfless life—so "'quaint and touching'"—as "'like something in some English novel'" (VI *PC* II 198). The image is only one of many like it in the same novel: eight out of its fifty art images deal with fiction. Thus, Hyacinth is "'like a young man in an illustrated story-book'" (V *PC* I 235), and, "like some famous novel, he was thrilling" (VI *PC* II 56); further, to this thrilling young man, the Princess once

9. "It is art that *makes* life, makes interest, makes importance, and I know of no substitute whatever for the force and beauty of its process," James wrote to H. G. Wells in July of 1915; *Henry James and H. G. Wells: A Record of Their Friendship, Their Debate on the Art of Fiction, and Their Quarrel,* ed. Leon Edel and Gordon N. Ray (London: Rupert Hart-Davis, 1958), p. 267.

appears "as a sudden incarnation of the heroine of M. Feuillet's novel, in which he had instantly become immersed" (16). In addition, Captain Sholto's chambers remind poor Hyacinth "somehow of certain of Bulwer's novels" (V *PC* I 267), while the Princess's Madeira Crescent house "evoked the idea of the *vie de province* he had read about in French fiction" (VI *PC* II 269). Finally, the Princess tells Hyacinth that his pledge to the anarchist Hoffendahl is " 'like some silly humbug in a novel' " (274). The analogies are regularly careful, not casual: London lives are like lives in English novels; continental persons and places suggest French novels.

James regarded Hawthorne as the best of American novelists, as is attested sufficiently, to be sure, by his 1879 monograph *Hawthorne*; so it is not surprising that he used a few of that novelist's creations in short, simple comparisons. Thus, the woman narrator of "The Impressions of a Cousin" finds Adrian Frank "a charming creature—a kind of Yankee Donatello." And she adds, "If I could only be his Miriam, the situation would be almost complete, for Eunice is an excellent Hilda" (xxiv "IofC" 379). Ralph Pendrel feels that he must go to the Ambassador with his curious discovery concerning the portrait of the young man in his ancestral home.

He recalled the chapter in Hawthorne's fine novel in which the young woman from New England kneels, for the lightening of her woe, to the old priest at St. Peter's, and felt that he sounded as never before the depth of that passage. *His* case in truth was worse than Hilda's and his burden much greater, for she had been but a spectator of what weighed upon her, whereas he had been a close participant (XXVI *SeofP* 89).

The whole situation in *The Sense of the Past* here is so Hawthornean—with the central character mysteriously conscience-stricken, attempting to dig into the past, to come to terms with a secret, to assay the spirit of an ancient house, to study an eerie family portrait—that the image might well have been predictable; yet it is to be wondered at that James did not here—or ever—make use of elements from *The House of the Seven Gables* for imagistic purposes. In fact, the only other figurative employment of things Hawthornean comes when Nick, while he is painting Gabriel Nash's picture, diverts himself, we read, by

. . . imagining in the portrait he had begun an odd tendency to fade gradually from the canvas. He couldn't catch it in the act, but he could have ever a suspicion on glancing at it that the hand of time was rubbing it away little by little—for all the world as in some delicate Hawthorne tale [or one only planned in his notebook]—and making the surface indistinct and bare of all resemblance to the model. Of course the moral of the Hawthorne tale would be that his personage would come back in quaint confidence on the day his last projected shadow should have vanished (VIII *TM* II 412-13).[10]

James evokes the ghost of Don Quixote several times in imagery. Taken together the references form a rather detailed portrait of the grim, sad, idealistic knight. The ill-regulated ambition of Fenton in *Watch and Ward* inspires this extravagant bit of rhetoric: "The Knight of La Mancha, on the torrid flats of Spain, never urged his gaunt steed with a grimmer pressure of his knees than that with which Fenton held himself erect on the hungry hobby of success. Shrewd as he was, he had perhaps, as well, a ray of Don Quixote's divine obliquity of vision" (xxiv *WandW* 59). And the narrator of "Professor Fargo" suddenly hits upon the right comparison for the reluctant partner of the quack spiritualist: "The next moment I identified him—he was Don Quixote in the flesh; Don Quixote, with his sallow Spanish coloring, his high-browed, gentlemanly visage, his wrinkles, his moustache, and

10. Here James surely reveals his own—not Nick Dormer's—knowledge of Hawthorne's notebooks—not tales.

his sadness" ("PF" 237-38). Similarly, Searle of "A Passionate Pilgrim" stares after a ghost and strikes the narrator as
possessed: "His cadaverous emaciated face, his tragic wrinkles
intensified by the upward glow from the hearth, his distorted
moustache, his extraordinary gravity and a certain fantastical
air as the red light flickered over him, all re-enforced his fine
likeness to the vision-haunted knight of La Mancha when laid
up after some grand exploit" (XIII "PP" 412). A woman can
even remind James of Don Quixote. Thus, Mrs. Gereth impresses Fleda Vetch, early in *The Spoils of Poynton*, as like
the tragic knight: "Her handsome high-nosed excited face
might have been that of Don Quixote tilting at a windmill"
(X *SpofP* 31).[11] To complete the record, Gabrielle and her
friend Marie de Chalais remind the narrator of "Gabrielle de
Bergerac" of "the beautiful Duchess in Don Quixote, followed
by a little dark-visaged Spanish waiting-maid" ("GdeB" 233).

Goethe's *Wilhelm Meister* is the only German novel specified in James's imagery.[12] Mignon is the only character in it
which seems to have appealed to James, who in an early story
pictures a daughter sitting beside her father "with all the
childish grace and serenity of Mignon in 'Wilhelm Meister,' as
we see her grouped with the old harper" ("PF" 237); Mallet
writes to his cousin that the pleasures of wintering in Rome
are so intense that "'after-life, to spare your aesthetic nerves,
must play upon them with a touch as dainty as the tread of
Mignon when she danced her egg-dance'" (I *RH* 7); and
Sherringham of *The Tragic Muse* sets up a forced comparison: "the occasion reminded him of pages in 'Wilhelm
Meister.' He himself could pass for Wilhelm, and if Mrs.

11. This image does much, I think, to qualify the generally held
opinion that Mrs. Gereth is only a scheming and materialistic woman.

12. E. T. A. Hoffmann is mentioned twice in James's imagery (I *RH*
164, "GhR" 667), but no works are named. Adelbert von Chamisso's
Peter Schemihl, also mentioned ("Ad" 39), is unimportant.

Rooth had little resemblance to Mignon, Miriam was remarkably like Philina" (VIII *TM* II 130).[13]

Few American fiction-writers other than Hawthorne inspire the trope-making faculty of James. But before his marriage, the Prince in *The Golden Bowl* does tediously compare the obscure motives of Maggie and her friends to the concealing white mist figuring in Edgar Allan Poe's *Narrative of Arthur Gordon Pym*. (Even though Amerigo could not be expected to have read Melville's *Moby-Dick*, it is a pity that James could not somehow have adumbrated ambivalences by citing the whiteness of the whale instead.) And Longdon tells Nanda in *The Awkward Age* that he is as out of touch with the times as Rip Van Winkle was (IX *AA* 222).[14] Finally, the young German count Otto Vogelstein in the story "Pandora" is intrigued by the titular heroine but, having just read "the story . . . of a flighty forward little American girl who plants herself in front of a young man in the garden of an hotel" (XVIII "Pan" 105), is prepared to read into Pandora's family all sorts of unwarranted criticism, including the belief that the girl's "sister should be a Daisy Miller *en herbe*" (114). Thus does James pleasantly invade his own fiction once for an image. The particular usage here is not surprising, since "Pandora" was planned as a continuation of James's study of the American girl in society begun with the story of "Daisy Miller."[15]

Understandably, James refers in his figures to far fewer

---

13. See Henry James, *Literary Reviews and Essays*, ed. Albert Mordell (New York: Grove Press, Inc., 1957), pp. 267-72, for James's careful review of Thomas Carlyle's 1865 translation of *Wilhelm Meister*.

14. James was probably less familiar with the Rip of Irving's *Sketch Book* than with the stage adaptation by Dion Boucicault for the actor Joseph Jefferson, whose performance James admired; see Henry James, *The Scenic Art: Notes on Acting & the Drama: 1872-1901*, ed. Allan Wade (New Brunswick: Rutgers University Press, 1948), pp. 82, 182.

15. *The Notebooks of Henry James*, ed. F. O. Matthiessen and Kenneth B. Murdock (New York: Oxford University Press, 1947), p. 56.

poets than to fiction-writers. Leading the list of poets used imagistically are Keats with nine appearances, Tennyson with eight, and Goethe with seven;[16] then come Dante and Coleridge with two each, and finally—with one each—Burns, Cowper, Gray, Musset, Shelley, and Whittier.[17] In addition, James refers to ballads—usually in very vague terms—half a dozen times.

"On First Looking into Chapman's Homer" inspires a number of images. For example, a long, ornate sequence tells in part that Adam Verver of *The Golden Bowl* "had stared at *his* Pacific. . . . His 'peak in Darien' was the sudden hour . . . of his perceiving . . . that a world was left him to conquer" (XXIII *GB* I 141). A couple of pages later Adam concludes that it probably was all for the best that his first wife died, since she might have interfered with his conquest as a collector of art treasures: "Would she [he wonders] have prevented him from ever scaling his vertiginous Peak?—or would she otherwise have been able to accompany him to that eminence, where he might have pointed out to her, as Cortez to *his* companions, the revelation vouchsafed?" (143).[18] But the text would be turned against Mr. Verver if he should chance to ponder on the poem later, as he sets sail with Charlotte for American City, beyond the Mississippi. The charming expression "swims into his ken," from the same Keats sonnet, starts a few other figures, none very important. Thus, "the answer to their question must have swum into her ken" (XVII "BinJ" 99), and the like.[19] The one other Keats reference worth mentioning has more point than the woman who utters it is aware: Mrs. Tristram of *The American* compares Valentin to "'the hero of the ballad'" "La Belle Dame sans

16. I consider *Faust* a poem.
17. I omit here consideration of imagistic allusions to classical poetry.
18. See p. 25 n. 14 above.
19. See also XXIII *GB* I 265, XXIV *GB* II 324, xxviii "CCor" 339. Note that all of these uses are in works written after 1900.

Merci" (II *Ame* 325). If the young nobleman is the knight-at-arms—and later he does fight a duel—the merciless lady surely is Noémie Nioche.

James in 1877 met Tennyson and wrote that he had "a face of genius,"[20] but there is nothing in James's fiction or other writings to indicate any high regard for the laureate's poetry.[21] With the imagery, it is simply a matter of James's recalling lines or situations, with greater or lesser consciousness, from the better-known poems. For a hackneyed example among several, we read the following of foolish Sanguinette, who is fascinated into stillness before "Rose-Agathe": "like the warrior's widow in Tennyson's song, he neither spake nor moved" (xxv "RA" 395). Also, the Prince speaks to Charlotte of cracks in situations and bowls: " '. . . as to cracks, . . . what did you tell me the other day you prettily call them in English? "rifts within the lute"? . . .' " (XXIII *GB* I 360). Imbedded in what is perhaps the wildest and most abandoned Jamesian image, one from "Crapy Cornelia"—it is more than three hundred words in length—is a Tennysonian quotation: "Thus, as I say, for our friend [White-Mason], the place itself, while his vivid impression lasted, portentously opened and spread, and what was before him took, to his vision, though indeed at so other a crisis, the form of the 'glimmering square' of the poet" (xxviii "CCor" 333). Finally, it should perhaps be mentioned that James makes undistinguished use of lotus-eating and "a cycle of Cathay."[22]

20. *The Letters of Henry James,* I, 53. For a discussion of James and Tennyson, see Leon Edel, *Henry James: The Conquest of London: 1870-1881* (Philadelphia and New York: J. B. Lippincott Company, 1962), pp. 372-74.

21. James preferred Browning's recitation of his works to Tennyson's reading; see James, "The Middle Years," in *Autobiography,* pp. 585-94. James lectured on *The Ring and the Book*; see *Notes on Novelists,* pp. 385-411. Yet Browning does not inspire any Jamesian imagery. However, see Sidney E. Lind, "James's 'Private Life' and Browning," *American Literature,* XXIII (November, 1951), 315-22.

22. See I *RH* 7, 465; XIX *WofD* I 119; XXVI *SeofP* 4.

Typical of the few images stemming from Goethe's *Faust* is the description of the Princess Casamassima's Captain Sholto "hover[ing] there like a Mephistopheles converted to inscrutable good" (V *PC* I 203). Such an apparently simple figure, like many in James, repays scrutiny: Sholto is trying to entice Hyacinth to go to the Princess, who, as the former Christina Light, becomes Lucifer, while Hyacinth is the endangered Faust. Later, it may be noted, Prince Casamassima remarks of his wife that "'she's the Devil in person'" (VI *PC* II 310).[23] Also the good Brother explains the sort of perfection which the place in "The Great Good Place" has: "'the thing's so perfect that it's open to as many interpretations as any other great work—a poem by Goethe, a dialogue of Plato, a symphony of Beethoven'" (XVI "GGP" 257). Such an image gives precisely the universality and generality James wishes to suggest; and, in the presence of no other Plato allusion and only a few other Beethoven usages, it may also suggest the unworkable idealism of the utopian place. The other Goethe images are routine and merely picturesque.[24]

Additional specific references to poetry in the imagery are few in number and elementary in character; thus, an inn sign resembles "the Dantean injunction to renounce all hope" (iv *Con* 1); if one of a long-married couple dies, "It will be quite 'John Anderson my Jo'" (xxviii "MEv" 39); a rich but comparatively rustic young woman sees herself as "at the very most a sort of millionaire Maud Müller" (xxv "PR" 435).[25]

James must have been somewhat interested in ballads, to which there are a few general allusions in his imagery. For

23. Back in *Roderick Hudson*, when the young sculptor compares Miss Light's poodle to "'the black dog in *Faust*,'" Rowland replies, "'I hope at least that the young lady has nothing in common with Mephistopheles. She looked dangerous'" (I *RH* 95-96). Later, Gloriani pulls his moustache "like a genial Mephistopheles" (123).

24. VIII *TM* II 192, xxvii "Col" 176.

25. This Whittier usage is the only image in all of James's fiction springing from American poetry, and an inept one it is, too.

example, we read of Maisie, caught between her bellicose parents, that "only a drummer-boy in the ballad or a story could have been so in the thick of the fight" (XI *WMK* 9). May Server walking through a grove toward the narrator of *The Sacred Fount* is "like the reminiscence of a picture or the refrain of a ballad" (xxix *SF* 103). From "Adina" we may glean another image, which though no more specific, is much more vivid. Scrope whistles delightfully at having tricked Angelo out of his precious stone, but the passive narrator feels guilty: "When I heard him I had a sudden vision of our friend Angelo staring blankly after us, as we rode away like a pair of ravishers in a German ballad" ("Ad" 38). This image has possibilities: Angelo, ravished of his gem, obtains a Gothic revenge by stealing the love of Adina, the whilom fiancée of Scrope.

Only about a hundred figures in all of James's fiction[26] refer to classical literature. One frequently employed image derives from the ancient belief that gods and goddesses—James clearly preferred the latter—could wrap themselves in clouds and walk unseen among men, scattering good or evil. Thus, Hubert hopes that Nora will not analyze the mystery out of him: " 'Let me walk like an Homeric god in a cloud; without my cloud, I should be sadly ungodlike' " (xxiv *WandW* 122). The once bookish Isabel Archer—herself initially a kind of archer goddess Diana—finds that "Her reputation of reading a great deal hung about her like the cloudy envelope of a goddess in an epic" (III *PofL* I 45). And

26. Adeline R. Tintner remarks that James "gave himself the background training of a painter, and instead of classical literature (Brownell takes him to task for the lack) it was classical art which gave him those 'impressions' his father had taught were 'the dearest things in the world' "; "The Spoils of Henry James," *PMLA*, LXI (March, 1946), 241. Ford Madox Hueffer and Rebecca West similarly "take him to task"; but see the spirited refutation of all those who regarded James as unversed in classicism by Daniel Lerner and Oscar Cargill, in their "Henry James at the Grecian Urn," *PMLA*, LXVI (June, 1951), 316-17.

Hyacinth thinks that the Princess will "engage to save him—to fling a cloud about him as the goddess-mother of the Trojan hero used in Virgil's poem to *escamoter* Aeneas" (VI *PC* II 127).[27] Typically, the later the treatment of this common image, the more elaborate it is.

Although James did not use his acquaintance with the more familiar classical myths to create many patterns, they were there for him to draw upon for the enrichment of many separate sections of his fiction. He occasionally called his characters godlike, as we have seen, and also often compared them to those gods' mortal friends and enemies, and children. Thus, Isabel regards the mysterious Madame Merle's hair arrangement as classical and "as if she were a Bust, . . . a Juno or a Niobe" (III *PofL* I 249). This image is superb, because later Madame Merle has occasion to wail for her child Pansy, surely lost to her.[28] The bewildered narrator of "The Solution" regards the redoubtable Mrs. Goldie as possessed of "a monstrous Gorgon face" which stares "with a stony refusal to comprehend" (xxvi "So" 349). This story, laid in and around Rome, appropriately has a few other classical Italian images: Wilmerding reminds the narrator of "the busts of some of the old dry-faced powerful Roman lawgivers and administrators" (313), but the narrator is tempted to call him " 'another Antinous' " (345) upon another occasion; further, Wilmerding's superior waits once in a carriage "like a sitting Cicero" (362). Next, in *The Other House* the sight of Mrs. Beever's face immobilizes gentle Jean Martle; but Tony notes "how far the gaze of the Gorgon was from petrifying Rose

27. See also XX *WofD* II 335, in which Densher thinks of Kate as such a goddess. James used foreign words and phrases in nearly 150 images. The following contains the longest quotation from classical literature: "The few scattered surviving representatives of a society once 'good'—*rari nantes in gurgite vasto*—were liable . . . to meet" (xxviii "CCor" 339).

28. See also I *RH* 460, in which Mrs. Hudson is prophetically likened, before her son's death, to Niobe.

Armiger" (*OH* 67). Later, it is Rose who seems to wear "the mask of Medusa" (182).[29] Several other women wear the Medusa mask in James, none more notably than Georgina, the child-abandoning bigamist of "Georgina's Reasons": "This woman's blooming hardness, after they got to Rome, acted upon her [Mrs. Portico, a friend] like a kind of Medusa-mask" (xxv "GeR" 287). As is natural, dominating females suggest Medusa to James, who prefers his heroines to be dove-like. It will be recalled that Christina Light—neither Medusa nor dove, but rather an Aphrodite—pictured Mary Garland as "'a Medusa crowned not with snakes but with a tremor of doves' wings'" (I *RH* 381).[30]

Hercules is the male among the ancients who inspired James most often; but, since fewer of his heroes are herculean than his women are gorgonian, references to the mighty warrior are usually either simple or somewhat satirical. Thus, Angelo Beati of the story "Adina" "had the frame of a young Hercules" ("Ad" 35), while Roderick Hudson's Roman studio has an archway which "might have served as the portal of the Augean stables" (I *RH* 97). The petulant Marco Valerio, of "The Last of the Valerii," is likened to "the infant Hercules" (xxvi "LofV" 10), and—oddly—the April day which Charlotte shares with her Italian lover at Matcham is said to

29. There are other classical references in the imagery of this novel, the plot of which has been compared to that of the *Medea* of Euripides (Lerner and Cargill, "Henry James at the Grecian Urn," p. 327 and *passim*). Thus, cool Mrs. Beever, comparing herself to the really phlegmatic Paul, "thanked God, through life, that she was cold-blooded, but now it seemed to face her as a Nemesis that she was a volcano compared to her son" (95). Tony finally sees Jean as "a tall, slim nymph on a cloud" (118). And, significantly, he remarks of Jean and his own daughter Effie, "'She looks . . . like the goddess Diana playing with a baby-nymph'" (131). Tony perhaps unconsciously sees Jean, a chaste nymph herself—as proved by the earlier image, in conjunction with the Diana reference—as psychically ideal as the foster-mother of his child.

30. See p. 77 above.

be "all panting and heaving with impatience or even at moments kicking and crying like some infant Hercules who wouldn't be dressed" (XXIII *GB* I 332). These herculean images involve Italians and things Italian, as is often the case with the classical figures by which James describes women.

A welter of other references, all loosely classical, extends from Atlas, Avernus, Acheron, and Orpheus, forward to Sardanapalus, Aristides, and Hypatia. James often uses these half-lost names brilliantly, to enrich the texture of his fiction. For example, Mallet perversely thinks that if Roderick is going to fizzle out, "one might help him on the way—one might smooth the *descensus Averni*" (I *RH* 314). But the Neapolitan Prince, Gennaro Casamassima, who naturally lives near Lago Averno, is the one who unwittingly smooths Roderick's path to the infernal regions, by marrying Christina. Even more apt is this passage concerning Miss Bordereau of "The Aspern Papers," which is cast in Venice: "The worst of it was that she looked terribly like an old woman who at a pinch would, even like Sardanapalus, burn her treasure" (XII "AP" 69). Sardanapalus, though not a woman, is said to have been effeminate; the Tigris is sufficiently Venetian; and the palace in which the king destroyed his treasures and himself by fire may be likened to Miss Bordereau's rickety *palazzo,* which contained the priceless Aspern letters—finally burned.

The numerous references in the imagery to fairy tales and children's stories should convince everyone that James remained young at heart and very gentle.[31] Fairy tales are used in figures whose purposes are to dismiss inexplicable relationships as magical, to describe ineffably blissful situations, and to show what the world looks like to a child—for example, Maisie Farange, in whose story several such images play an

31. See *The Legend of the Master,* compiled by Simon Nowell-Smith (New York: Charles Scribner's Sons, 1948), pp. 90-95, for a delightful selection of anecdotes concerning James and children.

important part: "he was her good fairy" (XI *WMK* 160), "the Arabian Nights had quite closed round her" (175), and the like.[32] And in *Watch and Ward*, Nora remarks typically: " 'I feel to-night like a princess in a fairy-tale' " (xxiv *WandW* 44).[33] Through his imagery, James unwittingly reveals that his favorite reading in this genre was *The Arabian Nights*, "Sleeping Beauty," and "Bluebeard"; mentioned also are "The Babes in the Woods," "Beauty and the Beast," "Cinderella," "Hop-o'-my-Thumb," and "Nick of the Woods."[34] The early fictional works contain most of the figures of this sort, with *Watch and Ward* showing the most elaborate development:

There came to him [Roger Lawrence] . . . a vague, delightful echo of the "Arabian Nights." The room was gilded . . . into the semblance of an enamelled harem court; he himself seemed a languid Persian, lounging on musky cushions; the fair woman at the window a Scheherazade, a Badoura. . . . She smiled and smiled, and, after a little . . . she blushed, not like Badoura or Scheherazade, but like Nora (xxiv *WandW* 143).

The Sleeping Beauty comparisons are ordinary enough, involving such Rossetti-like, aroused creatures as Miss Searle of "A Passionate Pilgrim" and old Miss Wenham of "Flickerbridge."[35] The Bluebeard usages seem uniformly weak, especially such a one as the following from the early story "A Day of Days," the heroine of which feels her brother Herbert's house to be sadly prosaic: "She felt a delectable long-

32. One of the spectacular successes of this novel is the imagery, much of which is exactly the sort which a clever little girl would think of or respond to; see, for example, 61, 68-69, 197, and see pp. 181-82 below.

33. See also 31.

34. James's comments concerning the two general types of fairy-tales—"the short and sharp and single," and "the long and loose"—are to be found in his preface to the volume containing "The Turn of the Screw" (XII xvi) and reveal his full and accurate memory of childhood reading.

35. XIII "PP" 374, 381; XVIII "Fl" 456-57, 462.

ing . . . to discover some Bluebeard's closet. But poor Herbert was no Bluebeard" (xxv "DofD" 182).[36] The relative superiority of the Sleeping Beauty figures over the Bluebeard figures helps to support the conclusion that James was stimulated imaginatively far more by the dullest sleeping beauty than by the most licentious Bluebeard.

Brief mention should now be made of the nearly two hundred images having to do with books and reading of a very general nature. Most of these figures are not very challenging: "'The book of life's padded, ah but padded—a deplorable want of editing!'" (VIII *TM* II 26); "The women one meets—what are they but books one has already read? You're a whole library of the unknown, the uncut'" (XX *WofD* II 62); and the like. Still, a philobiblon's anthology can be put together out of various such images, and taken as a unit they show James's fertility. "He had looked . . . like a page—fine as to print and margin—without punctuation" (XIII "Li" 317). "She had long cheeks, like the wide blank margins of old folios" (X "LL" 273-74). "She was like an odd volume, 'sensibly' bound, of some old magazine" (*OH* 10). "'You know what I'm driving at: some chapter in the book difficult to read aloud—some unlucky page she'd like to tear out. God forgive me, some slip'" (xxvii "GrC" 271). "'It's like the new edition of an old book that one has been fond of—revised and amended, brought up to date, but not quite the thing one knew and loved'" (XXI *Amb* I 177). "The intention remained, like some famous poetic line in a dead language, subject to varieties of interpretation" (XXIV *GB* II 345). ". . . Morgan had been as puzzling as a page in an unknown language. . . . Indeed the whole mystic volume in which the boy had been amateurishly bound demanded some practice in translation" (XI "Pu" 518). "To see a place for the

36. The others are little better: see xxvi "MEu" 52, II *Ame* 111, XXVI *SeofP* 208.

first time at night is like reading a foreign author in a translation" (ix *Bo* II 166).[37] "It sounded like a sentence from an English-French or other phrase-book" (XV "CF" 303). And finally, "it might perhaps be an inspiration to . . . begin again on a clean page" (X *SpofP* 48).

ii. Painting

James loved the art which was within a picture-frame almost as dearly as that embraced by the covers of a book. Definite references are made in the vehicles of seventy or so images to thirty-four painters, from Cimabue to Sargent. Interestingly, the works James did not revise—including the post-1907 fiction—although it amounts to about half of his total production, has less than a fourth of the painting imagery now under consideration.[38] Quantitatively, the Italian painters win easily over the next two nationalities combined. English and French groups tie for next place, with Flemish following, then German and Spanish, and finally a solitary Dutch and a lone American trailing at the end. In order of frequency the painters mentioned in imagery are as follows: Titian and Holbein, nine times each; Veronese, seven; Gainsborough and Van Dyke, four each; Michelangelo, Raphael, and Velasquez, three each; Lambinet, Lawrence, Reynolds,

37. James deplored the need for translations; see his letter to Auguste Monod of September 7, 1913, in *The Selected Letters of Henry James,* ed. Leon Edel (New York: Farrar, Straus and Cudahy, 1955), p. 107.

38. In the light of this fact, not much significance should be assigned to the fact that in 1892 from Siena James wrote to Charles Eliot Norton, apropos of painting, "it is true I have ceased to feel it very much"; *The Letters of Henry James,* I, 197. James sufficiently approved of the painting analogies in the works selected for revision and inclusion in the New York Edition to let them remain; in revision he added others; further, *The Outcry,* his only completed post-1907 novel, concerns collectors of paintings. But it is also true, as John L. Sweeney has pointed out, that James "wrote . . . little about the pictorial arts after 1882"; "Introduction," Henry James, *The Painter's Eye: Notes and Essays on the Pictorial Arts* (London: Rupert Hart-Davis, 1956), p. 31.

Rossetti, and Watteau, twice each; and finally, Andrea del Sarto, Boucher, Bronzino, Cimabue, Carpaccio, Corot, Doré, Dürer, Ghirlandaio, Goya, Greuze, Hogarth, Longhi, Memling, Pinturicchio, Rembrandt, Romney, Rubens, Sassoferrato, Sargent, and Tintoretto, once each. James should not be held to account for omissions from a list already impressive in length, but it does seem surprising that he was not inspired to imagery by Copley, Delacroix, or Daumier, for example, of whose works he wrote reviews, or by any of the Impressionists, about whom he later changed his early adverse opinion.[39]

If the imagery is any guide—and here it indubitably is—Titian was James's favorite painter. Indeed, James wrote to his brother William as early as 1869, "I admire Raphael; I enjoy Rubens; but I passionately love Titian."[40] An image from *The Portrait of a Lady* shows clearly the great respect James had for Titian's mastery. Ralph muses as follows on the subject of the spontaneously charming Isabel: " 'A character like that,' he said to himself—'a real little passionate force to see at play is the finest thing in nature. It's finer than the finest work of art—than a Greek bas-relief, than a great Titian, than a Gothic cathedral' " (III *PofL* I 86).[41] We find Densher referring aptly enough to the Venetian master when he explains to Milly his joy at remaining a while in Venice. "He [Densher] brought out the beauty of the chance for him—there before him like a temptress painted by Titian—to do a

39. Miss Tintner is obviously too harsh on James when she says that painting is "a field he never really understood other than as metaphor for writing"; "The Spoils of Henry James," p. 246; she is distressed that James rated Gavarni over Daumier. For a more sympathetic and more comprehensive view of James as an informal art critic, see Sweeney, "Introduction" to James, *The Painter's Eye*, pp. 9-31.

40. Quoted in Matthiessen, *The James Family*, p. 255.

41. Contrast this image with the one from "The Great Good Place" (XVI "GGP" 257) quoted above, p. 113. The one from *The Portrait of a Lady* is obviously more laudatory and more representative of the mind of James.

little quiet writing" (XX *WofD* II 243). Peter Sherringham's complexion, moustache, and beard remind Biddy Dormer of Charles I; but "At the same time—she rather jumbled her comparisons—she thought he recalled a Titian" (VII *TM* I 49). And beautiful, insincere Amy Evans of "The Velvet Glove" is aptly said to have the "rich and regular young beauty . . . of some divine Greek mask overpainted say by Titian" (xxviii "VG" 215).

When a search for an image ends with Titian, Veronese is often there too in James's mind. For example, the narrator of "Travelling Companions," which takes place in several of the art centers of Italy, tells Miss Evans his impressions of Italians seen on his little tour: " 'They only need velvet and satin and plumes . . . to be subjects for Titian and Paul Veronese' " ("TC" 612). Mrs. Coyne in *The Sense of the Past* is said to have a "resemblance to some great portrait of the Renaissance"; and Ralph continues by thinking that "That was the analogy he had . . . fondly and consistently found for her: she was an Italian princess of the *cinquecento*, and Titian or the grand Veronese might, as the phrase is, have signed her image" (XXVI *SeofP* 7). Much later, Ralph is beautifully described as wondering about the resemblance as follows: ". . . didn't it place round the handsome uplifted head, as by the patina of the years, the soft rub of the finger of time, that ring of mystic light? In the Titian, the Tintoret or the Veronese such a melting of the tone, such a magic as grew and grew for Ralph as soon as he once had caught the fancy of it, would have expressed the supernatural even as the circling nimbus expresses" (79-80). The other Veronese references are to be found in *The Wings of the Dove*. Lord Mark may know his Bronzinos and his Veroneses, but he certainly cannot fathom poor Milly. When she wails in her Venetian *palazzo* that she wishes she might never have to go down, he replies ineptly, "'But why shouldn't you . . . with that tremendous old staircase in your court? There ought of course always to be people at top and bottom, in Veronese costumes, to watch you do it'" (XX *WofD* II 147). Later Susan Stringham blocks out a Veronese canvas to show Densher the sort of life Milly is meant to lead—still in Venice.

"It's a Veronese picture, as near as can be—with me as the inevitable dwarf, the small blackamoor, put into a corner of the foreground for effect. If I only had a hawk or a hound or something of that sort I should do the scene more honour. The old housekeeper, the woman in charge here, has a big red cockatoo that I might borrow and perch on my thumb for the evening." These explanations and sundry others Mrs. Stringham gave, though not all with the result of making him feel that the picture closed him in (206).[42]

The smooth glow of Titian contrasts dramatically with the crabbed carefulness of Holbein, not least in James's "The Beldonald Holbein." When the hard beauty, Lady Beldonald, speaking of plain Louisa Brash, asks the narrator, "'You call her a Holbein?,'" the reply is quick: "'She brings the old boy to life! It's just as I should call you a Titian. You bring *him* to life'" (XVIII "BH" 388). And at the end, poor Mrs. Brash's successor, hired to bring out the picturesqueness of the Lady and not to compete with it, is said to be "as little a Holbein, or a specimen of any other school, as she was, like Lady Beldonald herself, a Titian" (404). Holbein is mentioned in imagery seven other times in the tale.[43] And related to the specific references to painters in it are several general art images. For example, Outreau the French painter

---

42. The enormous "Marriage of Cana" by Veronese, mentioned in a literal passage of *The American* (II *Ame* 16) and alluded to in James's *Autobiography* (p. 199), is the sort of canvas James means in this image, which is twice repeated later in *The Wings of the Dove* (XX *WofD* II 207, 213).

43. See 384, 386, 391, 395, 400, 403, 405.

describes Mrs. Brash's appearance to his practiced eye: "'. . . the wonderful sharp old face—so extraordinarily, consummately drawn—in the frame of black velvet'" (386). When jealous Lady Beldonald discharges the old woman, the act produces "a consternation . . . as great as if the Venus of Milo had suddenly vanished from the Louvre" (403). Finally, deprived of applause, poor Mrs. Brash resists her fate for a time but then dies: "what had occurred was that the poor old picture, banished from its museum and refreshed by the rise of no new movement to hang it, was capable of the miracle of a silent revolution, of its turning, in its dire dishonour, its face to the wall" (405).[44]

As for the other painters, James's Gainsboroughs are usually of English ladies, of whom Mrs. Ambient, the novelist's wife in "The Author of Beltraffio," is typical: "she was clothed in gentleness as in one of those vaporous redundant scarves that muffle the heroines of Gainsborough and Romney" (XVI "AofB" 11).[45] Oddly, "The Author of Beltraffio" has far more painting than fiction images: thus, the house of the Ambients seems "copied from a masterpiece of one of the pre-Raphaelites" (8); "the light hand of Sir Joshua might have painted Mark's wife and son" (56); the sister "suggested a symbolic picture, something akin even to Dürer's Melancholia" (26); and we read that the odd woman's "chin rested on a cinquecento ruff" (37). The Van Dykes in the imagery concern clever but unpleasant persons: in *The American*, "Madame de Bellegarde, in purple and pearls and fine laces, resembled some historic figure painted by Vandyke" (II *Ame* 313); and in "The Figure in the Carpet" the arrogant Corvick dies before he can write his book on Vereker, the full-length study

44. Aged Julia Ward Howe was the model James used for his picturesquely ugly Mrs. Brash; see his *Notebooks*, pp. 290-91. Further, I wonder whether Mrs. Howe's sister Louisa Ward Crawford Terry, whom James knew, provided Louisa Brash's first name.

45. See also XIII "PP" 364, XIV "BofL" 502, IX *AA* 145.

of whom "was to have been a supreme literary portrait, a kind of critical Vandyke or Velasquez" (XV "FinC" 266). Other Velasquezes charmingly picture sad little Pansy Osmond, who, "in her stiff little dress, only looked like an Infanta of Velasquez" (IV *PofL* II 108), and the depleted Guy Brissenden, who reminds the narrator of *The Sacred Fount* "of some fine old Velasquez or other portrait—a presentation of ugliness and melancholy that might have been royal" (xxix *SF* 125).

The gallery is nearly complete. When James chooses to particularize, he often makes use of lesser-known masters, usually Italian. Thus, Mrs. Touchett compares Isabel to a Cimabue Madonna, while Gilbert Osmond says that Mrs. Touchett's likeness may be found in a Ghirlandaio fresco (III *PofL* I 300, 372); further, we read that Osmond's ragged footboy might "have issued from some stray sketch of old-time manners, been 'put in' by the brush of a Longhi or a Goya" (387).[46] The valley and far horizon of "The Great Good Place" are likened to similar elements in "some old Italian picture, some Carpaccio or some early Tuscan" (XVI "GGP" 252). May Server, another of the exhausted characters in *The Sacred Fount*, "might have been herself—all Greuze tints, all pale pinks and blues and pearly whites and candid eyes—an old dead pastel under glass" (xxix *SF* 41-42). Milly Theale regards Matcham as "the centre of an almost extravagantly grand Watteau composition" (XIX *WofD* I 208).[47] Finally, of a florid American woman in a super-heated New York hotel James wrote in 1910, after his last American visit,

46. This last image James brushed in during the revision of *The Portrait of a Lady;* see F. O. Matthiessen, *Henry James: The Major Phase* (New York: Oxford University Press, 1944), p. 166.

47. John Cowper Powys presumably had this sort of image in mind when he wrote as follows of James's scenes: "among the terraces in a soft artificial fairy moonlight dimmed and tinted with the shadows of passions and misty with the rain of tender regrets"; *Suspended Judgments: Essays on Books and Sensations* (New York: G. Arnold Smith, 1916), p. 398.

that "she would have tumbled on a cloud, very passably, in a fleshy Boucher manner, hadn't she herself been over-dressed for such an exercise" (xxviii "RofV" 371). Many other examples might be added, to prove even more thoroughly James's familiarity with European masters, particularly Italian.

With very few exceptions—and the exceptions notably include Madame de Bellegarde and Mrs. Touchett—persons likened to subjects of celebrated painters are passive and in addition are usually victimized by others too dynamic to be immobilized, even by Titian or Veronese.

Often art imagery, while not so specific as to name an individual artist, is precise enough to evoke a detailed picture. Thus, Miss Congreve in "Osborne's Revenge" "looked as if she had stepped out of the frame of one of those charming full-length pastel portraits of fine ladies in Louis XV's time, which they show you in the French palaces" ("OR" 13). Adina "wore her auburn hair twisted into a thousand fantastic braids, like a coiffure in a Renaissance drawing" ("Ad" 39). Prince Casamassima resembles "some old portrait of a personage of distinction under the Spanish dominion at Naples" (V *PC* I 269). Gilbert Osmond "was not handsome, but he was fine, as fine as one of the drawings in the long gallery above the bridge of the Uffizi" (III *PofL* I 356). And, for a final instance, the prevaricating Colonel Capadose "was a fine specimen of the period of colour: he might have passed for a Venetian of the sixteenth century" (XII "Li" 335). When James wishes to particularize, to evoke a special mental picture, he habitually avoids the literal and often recalls—as though by instinct—his beloved Renaissance Italian art.

All the mechanical phases of painting—from preparing canvas, through chalking in outlines and mixing pigments, to applying paint, retouching, varnishing, and hanging work in the crowd-filled gallery—are used in numerous images. Thus—

"How the art of portraiture would rejoice in this figure" (XV "CF" 283); "she called for a canvas of a finer grain" (XVII "PL" 228); "She sketched with a light hand a picture of their preconcerted happiness" (xxvii "WofT" 110); "They gave Ralph [Limbert] time to block in another picture" (XV "NT" 178); "Modern she was indeed, and made Paul Overt, who loved old colour, the golden glaze of time, think with some alarm of the muddled palette of the future" (XV "LofM" 55); "He lays on colour" (XII "Li" 350); "one has to take a big brush to copy a big model" (XIV "PofV" 503); "She was nothing but a tinted and stippled surface" (X "Ch" 442); "He suggested a stippled drawing by an inferior master" (IX *AA* 66); "Her lovely grimace . . . was as blurred as a bit of brush-work in water-colour spoiled by the upsetting of the artist's glass" (xxix *SF* 104); "It [the attention paid to Felix Young] was like a large sheet of clean, fine-grained drawing-paper, all ready to be washed over with effective splashes of water-colour" (iii *Eurs* 61);[48] "The great smudge of mortality across the picture" (XX *WofD* II 298-99); "All nature seems glazed with light and varnished with freshness" (xxiv "IofC" 419); and finally "It was vital she should hang as straight as a picture on the wall" (XVII "JB" 497). Of considerable interest are the two following images: "Was experience to be muffled and mutilated like an indecent picture?" (XIII "MdeM" 299); and "She had had her picture of the future, painted in rather rosy hues, hung up before her now for a good many years; but it struck her that Mrs. Bowerbank's heavy hand had suddenly punched a hole in the canvas" (V *PC* I 22). Literal mutilation of paintings figures in "The Story of a Masterpiece" (1868) and "The Liar" (1888); and most curiously,

48. Edwin T. Bowden isolates and effectively analyzes a little pattern of four painting images in *The Europeans*, and notes that "Felix as an artist quite properly should use such images drawn from the arts"; *The Themes of Henry James: A System of Observation Through the Visual Arts* (New Haven: Yale University Press, 1956), pp. 51-52.

John Singer Sargent's admirable portrait of James was knifed in 1914 at the Royal Academy.[49]

iii. Drama

It is surprising that James's imagery drawing upon the theater should be somewhat disappointing and often rather casual. Since James must have spent more time attending plays, most often at the Théâtre Français, than writing them —though he did complete twelve—it is perhaps to be expected that the important images concerned with the drama are usually from the point of view of watcher and not that of creator or actor. There are very few direct references in the imagery to playwrights or their specific works: Shakespeare is used in imagery twenty-three times, with *Hamlet* the play named or alluded to most often (five times), *Romeo and Juliet* next (four times), then *The Tempest* and *King Lear* (twice each) and finally *Antony and Cleopatra, As You Like It, King Henry IV—Part 2, Much Ado About Nothing, Othello, Twelfth Night,* and *The Winter's Tale* (once each). In addition, Orestes, Electra, and Antigone, from the Greek theater, are named a time or two, and—once each—Aristophanes, Juvenal, *A School for Scandal*, Ibsen, and Maeterlinck. Finally, passing mention is made of the French stage. And that is all.

Shakespeare does almost nothing for James's imagery. Roderick Hudson sprawling beside Miss Light is said, in a figure with absolutely no overtones, to resemble "Hamlet at

49. C. Hartley Grattan, *The Three Jameses: A Family of Minds: Henry James, Sr., William James, Henry James* (New York: Longmans, Green and Co., 1932), p. 352; F. W. Dupee, *Henry James,* American Men of Letters ([New York]: William Sloane Associates, 1951), p. 283. The one feeble Sargent image in James appears in "The Beldonald Holbein": the London set is described as " 'bounded on the north by Ibsen and on the south by Sargent!' " (XVIII "BH" 400). James wrote a fine essay on Sargent, however; see Henry James, "John S. Sargent," in *Picture and Text* (New York: Harper and Brothers, 1893), pp. 92-115.

Ophelia's feet" (I *RH* 199). For no simple or subtle reason, the abandoned Saltram "wandering roofless . . . about the smoky Midlands" reminds the narrator of "The Coxon Fund" of "the injured Lear . . . on the storm-lashed heath" (XV "CF" 320). And Searle in "A Passionate Pilgrim" has "a romantic vision free as the flight of Ariel" (XIII "PP" 392). It is somewhat more suggestive to read that Madame de Vionnet "was, like Cleopatra in the play, indeed various and multifold" (XXI *Amb* I 271).[50] Perhaps a representative enough example of the regularly unchallenging Shakespeare usages may be this one from "The Aspern Papers," during the early part of which the narrator returns one evening to the Venetian garden of his *padrone*, old Miss Bordereau:

. . . it was such a night as one would gladly have spent in the open air . . . now the only thought that occupied me was that it would be good to recline at one's length in the fragrant darkness on a garden-bench. . . . It was delicious—just such an air as must have trembled with Romeo's vows when he stood among the thick flowers and raised his arms to his mistress's balcony. I looked at the windows of the palace to see if by chance the example of Verona—Verona being not far

50. The charming Frenchwoman is indeed various: James has just described her as resembling a Renaissance coin, a goddess in a cloud, and a sea-nymph waist-deep in the water (270). A few pages earlier, anticipating the Cleopatra reference, Miss Barrace says of her, " 'She's various. She's fifty women' " (265); and much later Strether says of her, " 'She has such variety and yet such harmony' " (XXII *Amb* II 300). William M. Gibson acutely calls this Cleopatra image one of "A series of historical comparisons . . . [which] contributes to the continual redefinition of the essential conflict" in *The Ambassadors;* "Metaphor in the Plot of *The Ambassadors,*" *New England Quarterly,* XXIV (September, 1951), 292, 293. Only two other profoundly attractive women in James's fiction—Kate Croy and Charlotte Stant—are noted for having similar mysterious variety, but neither is likened to Cleopatra. For the contention that James's allusion to Cleopatra here suggests affinities between *The Ambassadors* and *Antony and Cleopatra* (with Woollett resembling Rome and Paris resembling Egypt), see Herbert R. Coursen, Jr., "The Mirror of Allusion: *The Ambassadors,*" *New England Quarterly,* XXXIV (September, 1961), 382-84.

off—had been followed; but everything was still. Juliana might on the summer nights of her youth have murmured down from open windows at Jeffrey Aspern, but Miss Tina was not a poet's mistress any more than I was a poet (XII "AP" 52-53).

Now, I submit that possibly Lorenzo's famous "in such a night as this" speech from *The Merchant of Venice* may have been in his mind when James began to write the strange passage quoted above, and that if so, he would have done better to follow with a suggestion that old Miss Bordereau might be likened to an embattled Shylock. The conclusion is clear: James, with the possible exception of the Cleopatra reference already quoted, used Shakespearean allusions to suggest that some of his personae, like most of T. S. Eliot's, are no Prince Hamlets, nor were meant to be.

No appreciable use is made of British dramatists aside from Shakespeare. There is one negligible paraphrase of a now hackneyed line from Sheridan: "The Ingrams . . . , quitting New York, quite left, like the gentleman in 'The School for Scandal,' their reputations behind them" ("CCon" 577). One reason for this dearth may be provided by Madame Carré, the proud old actress in *The Tragic Muse:* when Miriam makes it known that she wants to play Shakespeare, the distinguished Frenchwoman replies, "'That's fortunate, as in English you haven't any one else to play'" (VII *TM* I 135).

Of the very few references to classical drama, two usages of the Electra-Orestes theme are apt. The close relationship between Nick Dormer and his sister Biddy is suggested as we read that "She was a devoted Electra, laying a cool healing hand on a distracted perspiring Orestes" (VIII *TM* II 279). It is true that the two are nearly killing their mother Lady Agnes, because Nick has quit politics and Biddy cannot seem to attract Sherringham. But a closer parallel to the Greek source is found in a brilliant little image from *The American* by which Valentin describes his close relationship to his sister

Claire: "'Well we're very good friends; such a brother and sister as haven't been known since Orestes and Electra'" (II *Ame* 149). The mother in this novel, it will be recalled, murdered her husband—if we can believe Mrs. Bread.[51]

One might expect images in James drawn from the French stage to be numerous—they are not—and occasionally captivating, for example in *The Tragic Muse*, which concerns the training by Madame Carré of Miriam Rooth, a talented Jewish girl, for the stage. Only two such references materialize in that novel. First, Miriam is compared without elaboration to Rachel, the French actress Élisabeth Félix, whom James evidently never saw.[52] And also, when Madame Carré begins to speak at one point, we find Gabriel Nash gallantly crying out, "'Ah la voix de Célimène!'" (VII *TM* I 117), a reference doubtless to the venerable actress's success long ago in Molière's *Le Misanthrope*. Further, in only one other James work do we find imagistic use of material from the French theater. In "The Siege of London" the *donnée* is provided by two French plays, *Le Demi-Monde* by Alexandre Dumas, *fils*, and Émile Augier's *L'Aventurière*, both of which Littlemore and Waterville have seen at the Comédie Française. Later these plays provide the basis for a simple image. Waterville tells his friend, "'You're in the position of Olivier de Jalin in "Le Demi-Monde."'" He goes on, "'Or like Don Fabrice in "L'Aventurière."'" When Littlemore tells Waterville to warn Mrs. Headway's present lover about her adventurous past, the reply is "'Play the part of Olivier de Jalin? Oh I can't. I'm not Olivier'" (XIV "SofL" 259).[53]

51. And John A. Clair cannot; see his intriguing but finally not convincing "*The American*—A Reinterpretation," *PMLA*, LXXIV (December, 1959), 613-18.

52. Leon Edel, "Henry James: The Dramatic Years," in *The Complete Plays of Henry James*, ed. Leon Edel (Philadelphia and New York: J. B. Lippincott Company, 1949), p. 26.

53. Augier's *L'Aventurière* may have been the first play James saw

The images deriving from technical terms of the stage (*mise-en-scène,* properties, entr'acte, *coup de théâtre,* and the like) are less numerous and certainly less appealing than those concerning actors and actresses, particularly their voices. "There was that about Gaston de Treuil that reminded you of an actor by daylight. His little row of foot-lights had burned itself out" ("GdeB" 64)—thus is a decadent *vicomte* neatly pictured. Rose Tramore of "The Chaperon" has a father who is indifferent to his children's development; he is said to be "like a clever actor who often didn't come to rehearsal" (X "Ch" 444). And we read that Rose Armiger, villainess of *The Other House,* stops once "before her mirror, still dealing, like an actress in the wing, with her appearance, her make-up" (*OH* 58). At Matcham Milly Theale pathetically has "a sense of pleasant voices, pleasanter than those of actors" (XIX *WofD* I 218), while the equally impressionable Strether hears from the Paris streets "a voice calling, replying, somewhere and as full of tone as an actor's in a play" (XXII *Amb* II 24). *The Ambassadors,* however, is sparer in imagery of this theatrical sort—as in other sorts—than either *The Wings of the Dove* or *The Golden Bowl.* For we read that "Densher saw himself . . . as in his purchased stall at the play; the watchful manager was in the depths of a box and the poor actress [Kate Croy] in the glare of the footlights" (XX *WofD* II 34-35). And Maggie Verver is tempted to regard herself "as some panting dancer of a difficult step who had capered, before the footlights of an empty theatre, to a spectator [the Prince] lounging in a box" (XXIV *GB* II 222). Earlier, the sorely challenged Maggie is said to resemble "an actress who

at the Comédie Française, about 1870. He saw *Le Demi-Monde* by Alexandre Dumas, *fils,* in 1877, to his agitation; see Edel, ed., *The Complete Plays of Henry James,* pp. 37, 38, 826, and Edel, *Henry James: The Conquest of London,* p. 294. "The Siege of London" was first published in 1883.

had been studying a part and rehearsing it, but who suddenly, on the stage, before the footlights, had begun to improvise, to speak lines not in the text" (33). And she is also described as feeling at one point like "some young woman of the theatre who, engaged for a minor part in the play . . . , should find herself suddenly promoted to leading lady and expected to appear in every act of the five" (208). So the women caper and cavort before somewhat bored men. Naturally *The Ambassadors* lacks such imagery, since it lacks such young men. Chad, to be sure, however, comes close, and Strether has an early moment of fearing what sort of drama may be going forward on "Chad's private stage" (XXI *Amb* I 88).

An amusing little set of images concerning theater tickets smacks of the personal, or perhaps they came from James's amused or exasperated observation. Waterville is delighted to accept an invitation to a celebrated British estate: "It seemed to him that through a sudden stroke of good fortune he had received a *billet d'auteur*" (XIV "SofL" 216). Necessary lies are brilliantly contrasted with gratuitous specimens: "For the falsehood uttered under stress a convenient place can usually be found, as for a person who presents himself with an author's order at the first night of a play. But the mere luxurious lie is the gentleman without a voucher or a ticket who accommodates himself with a stool in the passage" (XII "Li" 350). The following peculiar image suggests to me that its vehicle was evolved through observation, before its tenor was evolved through thought: "the way in which she could show prompt lips while her observation searchingly ranged might have reminded him of the object placed by a spectator at the theatre in the seat he desires to keep during the entr'acte" (XVI "FC" 395).[54]

54. I similarly judge the evolution of the following figure: "Maurice, in a word, was not 'approached' [with a job] from any quarter, and meanwhile he was as irritating as the intended traveller who allows you the pleasure of looking out his railway-connections" (xxvii "WofT" 101).

Amusingly, James's theater images cover nearly every act of the play. Thus, " 'It was a first act for a melodrama' " (II *Ame* 152); "it seemed to her that she had come in at the second act of the play" ("SofY" 268); "He felt as if he had been called away from the [figurative] theatre during the progress of a remarkably interesting drama. The curtain was up all this time, and he was losing the fourth act" (iii *Eurs* 138); and "he occupied the interval in refurnishing his house, and clearing the stage for the last act of the girl's childhood" (xxiv *WandW* 40).

As almost every reader of James must have noticed, the word "mask" is used very frequently. Often it is used literally, but in addition it figures nearly a hundred times in imagery, usually without significantly enriching the fiction. Masks may be observed to be moulded, varnished, glazed, elastic, comic, or tragic; also they may be ill-fitting, falling, and thrown off. Taken together, these images show once again James's perception of the complexity of life and human motives, and also his awareness of the distinction between appearance and reality. Here are two simple examples: the exemplary servant Brooksmith "wore in an exceptionally marked degree the glazed and expressionless mask of the British domestic *de race*" (XVIII "Br" 370); and the narrator of "The Altar of the Dead" recalls Creston's "blurred ravaged mask bent over the open grave" (XVII "AofD" 8). But the most challenging mask image is to be found in "The Beast in the Jungle," the inactive hero of which is curiously provided "a mask painted with the social simper, out of the eyeholes of which there looked eyes of an expression not in the least matching the other features. . . . May Bartram . . . achieved . . . the feat of at once—or perhaps it was only alternately—meeting the eyes from in front and mingling her own vision, as from over his shoulder, with their peep through the apertures" (XVII "BinJ" 82). In this single, sustained, brilliant image, James suggests at least this, that Marcher believes himself to have a ready personality suppressed by his public role and that Miss Bartram both sees through the false face—if not through him—and sees reality with him.[55]

Several stories and novels have sizeable patterns of drama images. The leading works in this respect are "The Madonna of the Future," *Roderick Hudson, The American, The Portrait of a Lady,* "The Aspern Papers," and "The Private Life." *The Ivory Tower,* with but one drama image, and *The Sense of the Past,* with only five, are thin in this category and perhaps attest to the distance time, by 1910 or so, had taken James from his *années dramatiques.* By contrast, "The Private Life," written in 1892, has a fascinating sequence of drama figures, nearly all of which help to place in the spotlight the histrionic Lord Mellifont, who in private is literally nothing. Thus, we read that the good lord "was always as unperturbed as an actor with the right cue" (XVII "PL" 226). He wants Adney to play his violin before Vawdrey recites—" 'You must [he intones] give us the overture before the curtain rises. That's a peculiarly delightful moment' " (230). Mellifont smooths things over when Vawdrey forgets his lines; the lord's bridging over the pause has a way "like the actors of the Comédie Française" (231). The narrator has his suspicions concerning the man: "I had secretly pitied him [we read] for the perfection of his performance, had wondered what blank face such a mask had to cover" (247). Mellifont must of course be utterly inactive at times: "how intense an *entr'acte* to make possible more such performances!" (248). Blanche Adney, an actress, eerily pic-

55. Apropos of this dual vision, L. C. Knights aptly observes of "The Beast in the Jungle" that "the two points of view—the subjective and the objectively critical—not only alternate swiftly and with almost unnoticed transitions, they are often presented simultaneously"; "Henry James and the Trapped Spectator," *Southern Review,* IV (Winter, 1939), 613.

tures the empty scene after he has withdrawn: "'At any rate the stage was as bare as your hand'" (255). But when she looks for him, he is there; and she seems to be saying to the narrator, "'He fills the stage in a way that beats us'"; and the narrator as silently adds, "We could no more have left him than we could have quitted the theatre till the play was over" (257). When Mellifont goes to his room, the narrator describes his exit in this manner: "'The *entr'acte* has begun'" (258).

The following modern image, by which James describes the Gothic weather closing in upon the scene of "The Turn of the Screw," appropriately draws the curtain on this section of drama figures: "The summer had turned, the summer had gone; the autumn had dropped upon Bly and had blown out half our lights. The place, with its grey sky and withered garlands, its bared spaces and scattered dead leaves, was like a theatre after the performance—all strewn with crumpled playbills" (XII "TofS" 243).[56]

iv. Miscellaneous

There are several significant groups of music, sculpture, gem, coin, pottery, dance, and architecture images in James's fiction.

The three hundred and fifty or so images drawn from the realm of music are never technical and usually are not elaborate or even very interesting. Rarely are they precise enough to name composers.[57] These facts mark such images off com-

56. But this image is more James's than that of the governess, who when describing Quint earlier as looking like an actor revealingly added, "'I've never seen one, but so I suppose them'" (191). Consequently, this image too may be used in partial refutation of those who feel that the best way to study imagery is to consider speaker and context.

57. Further, music of specified composers figures only infrequently in literal passages as well. At Gardencourt, Isabel hears Madame Merle competently playing "something of Schubert's" (III *PofL* I 245). But in the original version of this novel, it was "something of Beethoven's"—

pletely from those deriving from fiction, painting, and the drama.[58] Significantly, almost all of the images which name composers have to do with the opera, as do a number of more general figures. James clearly preferred the drama of operatic score and setting to purer forms of music.

The following composers, musicians, or their works appear in uniformly ordinary music figures: Wagner, four times; Mozart, three times; Beethoven, twice; and Paganini, once. The Wagner usages all happen to be in works published after 1900.[59] The narrator of *The Sacred Fount* calls his private enjoyment of the situation "a revel—that of the exclusive king with his Wagner opera" (xxix *SF* 230). When Mrs. Stringham is launched on her trip to Europe with Milly, petty considerations "sounded with as little effect as a trio of penny whistles might sound in a Wagner overture" (XIX *WofD* I 114). Maggie, once she is realistically married to her Prince, "ceased to see . . . the pair of operatic, of high Wagnerian lovers . . . interlocked in their wood of enchantment" (XXIV *GB* II 280). And loud, large Rosanna Gaw of *The Ivory Tower* "ring[s]

---

an indication that James did not use music for its overtones; see Matthiessen, *Henry James*, p. 168. And at Mrs. Burrage's tea there was for Olive Chancellor "the perfume of Schubert and Mendelssohn" (viii *Bo* I 184).

58. Matthiessen is right, as usual, when he remarks that James "was unlike the symbolist poets in that the suggestiveness of music was not his chief concern. His own analogies for his work were always with painting or with the stage"; *Henry James*, p. 71. A contrary opinion, surely twice erroneous, is that of C. Hartley Grattan: "music meant nothing to him [James] though for a man so indifferent he made liberal use of music metaphors to convey the 'shades' of emphasis in the condensation of his characters. The drama, a life-long devotion, was to be of small final use to him except as an adjunct to the development of a fictional method"; *The Three Jameses*, p. 229. Such a statement represents the sort of conclusion concerning James's imagery which too many critics have made, without first having read all of James and studied all of his figures.

59. For a note on James and Wagner, see Oscar Cargill, *The Novels of Henry James* (New York: The Macmillan Company, 1961), p. 375 n. 3.

out like Brünnhilde at the opera" (XXV *IT* 40).[60] Regularly, then, Wagner is called upon when James wishes to suggest the unrealistic, the romantic, or the grotesque. The Mozart allusions all appear in *The American,* in close proximity; during a performance of *Don Giovanni,* Newman and Urbain's wife indulge in some harmless comparisons—they agree that Donna Elvira is like Claire, and Zerlina like Urbain's wife— until the Marquis Urbain sours the pleasantries with this remark: " 'I'll go to the *foyer* for a few moments . . . and give you a chance to say that I'm like the Commander—the man of stone.' " His wife caps the line in his absence: " 'Not a man of stone, a man of wood' " (II *Ame* 340). The titular hero of "Eugene Pickering," who is ridiculously naïve, is so foolish as to say that listening to the preposterous Madame Blumenthal's conversation is " 'like hearing the opening tumult of one of Beethoven's symphonies, as it loses itself in a triumphant harmony of beauty and faith!' " (xxiv "EP" 281). For a change, the music figure which concerns Paganini is almost entirely sincere: Miriam Rooth is described as interrupted while she is rehearsing by the entrance of Peter, who loves her; "the cold passion of art had perched on her banner and she listened to herself with an ear as vigilant as if she had been a Paganini drawing a fiddle-bow" (VII *TM* I 335). It is true that the other Beethoven image, previously quoted,[61] is also sincere. But for the most part, James pays composers no such respect as he accords Thackeray and Balzac, Titian and Veronese, or Shakespeare.

Most of the many general references to unspecified opera in the imagery also indicate scant respect for that medium.

60. This is only one of several images by which James suggests Rosanna's bigness: elsewhere she is compared to a large ship and to a great Buddhist idol, and she is of such Wagnerian proportions that her parasol is once likened to the roof of a Burmese palanquin (1, 15, 68-69).

61. See p. 113 above.

The rather theatrical Verena Tarrant makes of her father's residence "such a scene as a prima donna makes of daubed canvas and dusty boards" (ix *Bo* II 5). And the frustrated Peter Sherringham momentarily contends that "art" resembles " 'some irritating chorus of conspirators in a bad opera' " (VIII *TM* II 355)—surely Basil Dashwood and Miriam, actor and actress, are soon to unite, through marriage, in what Peter may well regard as a conspiracy against him. In an image somewhat more complimentary to opera, the narrator's nephew in the short story "Louisa Pallant"—he is naïve, to be sure—finds an Italian lake scene to be "as pretty as the opera" (XIII "LoP" 523). But elsewhere we read of "the flimsy and tarnished properties of a superannuated comic opera" ("GdeB" 63). Such seems to have been James's impression of opera as an art form.

Technical terms stemming from music are rare and rather elementary: minor or lower key, transposing, crescendo, and the leitmotif fairly represent their extent and kind.[62] And James used the words "pitch" and "note" in non-figurative passages so often as to constitute a little mannerism.

The imagery mentions pianos more frequently than other instruments, with violins and harps following, and organs, lyres, and flutes lagging far behind. Occasionally James dramatizes a tension within one character by putting him through a figurative performance on a piano. The two incomplete novels contain an unusually similar pair of such images:

. . . what he [Graham Fielder] inwardly and fantastically compared it [his joy] to was some presented quarto page, vast and fair, ever so distinctly printed and ever so unexpectedly vignetted, of a volume of which the leaves would be turned for him one by one and with no more trouble on his

62. See, for example, iv *Con* 121, XVIII "Pan" 137, "SofB" 770, xxvii "WofT" 131, xxvi "RofC" 105, III *PofL* I 122, xxviii "RofV" 374.

own part than when a friendly service beside him at the piano, where he so often sat, relieved him, from sheet to sheet, of touching his score (XXV *IT* 86).

And

He [Ralph Pendrel] was in actual free use of the whole succession of events, and only wanted these pages, page after page, turned for him: much as if he had been seated at the harpsicord and following out a score while the girl beside him stirred the air to his very cheek as she guided him leaf by leaf (XXVI *SeofP* 125-26).

The sensibilities of fine persons are likened to the delicate balance of musical instruments; thus, of Isabel Archer we read that "vibration was easy to her, was in fact too constant with her, and she found herself now humming like a smitten harp" (III *PofL* I 232). Gentle expression of affection is sometimes likened to music; thus, "this uttered sweetness . . . was like some quaint little old air . . . played upon a faded spinnet with two girlish fingers" (XIV "LaB" 112). Voices, which were almost as provocative as the human eye to the trope-making faculty of James, are often compared to the tones made by various musical instruments. For example, Fenton's monotonous voice "was an instrument of one string" (xxiv *WandW* 56); further, when Stransom visits his altar mate at her home, "her late aunt's conversation lingered like the tone of a cracked piano" (XVII "AofD" 45); and the voice of odd Miss Wenham of "Flickerbridge" has "the possible tone of the old gilded silver-stringed harp in one of the corners of the drawing-room" (XVIII "Fl" 458); and finally, Milly Theale delightedly meets a real-life bishop, who has "a voice like an old-fashioned wind instrument" (XIX *WofD* I 147).[63]

The insensitive are indifferent to life's subtle melodies, but the highly conscious listen—and remember. Thus, to crass,

63. See also VII *TM* I 118, "CE" 255.

gross M. de Mauves "the life of the spirit was as closed . . . as the world of great music to a man without an ear" (XIII "MdeM" 255),[64] and dense though harmless Owen Gereth "had no more sense for a motive than a deaf man for a tune" (X *SpofP* 20). On the other hand, when perceptive Longmore sees Madame de Mauves a second time, "her charm came out like that of fine music on a second hearing" (XIII "MdeM" 219); and when the highly intelligent narrator of "The Next Time" reads Limbert's new two-volume novel, his hope that he will find it a possible best-seller rather than simply another in a series of uncommercial masterpieces is doomed, because "the wretched volumes . . . were like a beautiful woman more denuded or a great symphony on a new hearing" (XV "NT" 196). But note that in none of these little music figures does James specify a composer.

Most of the infrequent images coming from sculpture describe the physical appearance of people, usually women— often hard, cold women. Thus, Madame Merle "had thick, fair hair, arranged somehow 'classically' and as if she were a Bust, . . . a Juno or a Niobe" (III *PofL* I 249).[65] The eyes of another hard woman, the titular heroine of "Lady Barbarina," are said to be "as beautiful as if they had been blank, like those of antique busts" (XIV "LaB" 128).[66] After Kate Croy has received Densher's kiss, "she kept the position in which, all passive and as a statue, she had taken his demon-

---

64. Perhaps it would be more accurate to say that M. de Mauves only seems crass and gross in the opinion of Longmore, the aptly named central consciousness through whose frustrations the story "Madame de Mauves" is refracted; see Charles Kaplan, "James' MADAME DE MAUVES," *The Explicator*, XIX (February, 1961), Item 32. On the whole matter of "unreliable narrators" in James, see Wayne C. Booth, *The Rhetoric of Fiction* ([Chicago]: The University of Chicago Press, 1961), pp. 339-74, 425, 427.

65. See also XVI "FM" 268. For my comment on the aptness of the Niobe image, see p. 115 above.

66. See also xxv "LaP" 343, 345; "CCon" 570; VII *TM* I 335.

stration" (XX *WofD* II 379). One pure and lovely woman is somewhat similarly described: of aloof Madame de Mauves we read that "her delicate beauty acquired to his [Longmore's] eye the serious cast of certain blank-browed Greek statues" (XIII "MdeM" 246); and although this woman is unsatisfactory for the arms of a would-be lover, it is probably not because she is cold, for toward the end it is explained that Longmore "couldn't clasp her to his arms now, any more than some antique worshipper could have clasped the marble statue in his temple. But Longmore's statue spoke at last with a full human voice and even with a shade of human hesitation" (310). As for yet another proscribed object of yet another lover's adoration, the Prince notes that Charlotte Stant's arms have "the completely rounded, the polished slimness that Florentine sculptors in the great time had loved and of which the apparent firmness is expressed in their old silver and old bronze" (XXIII *GB* I 46-47).[67] This image, along with several others similar to it, suggests that Charlotte is, like fine metal, smooth, hard, glittering, and costly. By contrast Maggie to her devoted but possessive father, who has what Adeline R. Tintner has neatly called "the Cortez-complex," suggests

. . . the appearance of some slight slim draped "antique" of Vatican or Capitoline halls, late and refined, rare as a note and immortal as a link, set in motion by the miraculous infusion of a modern impulse and yet, for all the sudden freedom of folds and footsteps forsaken after centuries by their pedestal, keeping still the quality, the perfect felicity, of the statue . . . (XXIII *GB* I 187).[68]

James's men are seldom flatteringly likened to sculptured objects. Thus, Crawford's "face had been cast first in a rather

67. See also V *PC* I 207.
68. Miss Tintner valuably notes that to Adam Verver "the Prince becomes a crystal; Charlotte, oriental tiles; and even his daughter, some 'draped antique of Vatican or Capitoline halls' "; "The Spoils of Henry James," p. 250.

rugged and irregular mold, and the image had then been lightly retouched, here and there, by some gentler, more feminine hand" ("CCon" 570). Captain Diamond has an equally ugly face: "The lines in his face were as rigid as if they had been hacked out of a block by a clumsy wood-carver" ("GhR" 668); and later the same man is said to resemble "some ruggedly carven figure on the lid of a Gothic tomb" (676).[69] Humorously, a minor literary critic is sardonically said to look "like a dim phrenological bust" (XV "FinC" 274); moreover, when he blushes, "the numbers on his bumps . . . come out" (275). But, as if partially to redress the insult to the less molded sex, James describes Valerio as having "a head . . . like some of the busts in the Vatican . . . a head as massively round as that of the familiar bust of the Emperor Caracalla, and covered with the same dense sculptural crop of curls" (xxvi "LofV" 4).[70]

Attractive if somewhat dangerous or enigmatic European women suggest gem or fine coin figures. Thus, Scholastica in the short story "Benvolio" resembles "a certain exquisite little head on a Greek silver coin" (xxiv "Be" 322); Christina Light predictably is compared to "a nymph on a Greek gem" (I *RH* 297); and Noémie Nioche is said to be " 'as hard and clear-cut as some little figure of a sea-nymph on an antique intaglio' " (II *Ame* 299). Further, Madame de Brindes in "Collaboration" has a "delicate cameo-face" (xxvii "Col" 165), while Madame de Vionnet has a "head . . . like a happy fancy, a notion of the antique, on an old precious medal, some silver coin of the Renaissance" (XXI *Amb* I 270). On the other hand, men are rarely so imaged. To Isabel, the flawed Gilbert Osmond at first "suggested, fine gold coin as he was, no stamp nor emblem of the common mintage that provides for general circulation; he was the elegant complicated medal

69. See also XVI "TofK" 180, XVIII "Pan" 132.
70. See also xxviii "MM" 253.

struck off for a special occasion" (III *PofL* I 329). Much more simply, Basil Ransom is said to have "a head to be seen above the level of a crowd, on some judicial bench or political platform, or even on a bronze medal" (viii *Bo* I 4).

Porcelain, china, and pottery figures may be important to Ned Rosier, the bibelot-collector in *The Portrait of a Lady*, but James treats them with scant consideration. The following are typical enough to stand for the rest. Mademoiselle Voisin, the French actress, is said to have "'a hard polish, an inimitable surface, like some wonderful porcelain that costs more than you'd think'" (VII *TM* I 370). Thus James suggests repellent surface hardness.[71] And of Delia Dosson's face, looming in *The Reverberator*, we read the following: "It was a plain clean round pattern face, marked for recognition among so many only perhaps by a small figure, a sprig on a china plate, that might have denoted deep obstinacy; and yet, with its settled smoothness, it was neither stupid nor hard" (XIII *Re* 11).[72]

The very infrequent dance images rarely involve choreographic artistry but usually come from the world of simple entertainment. Thus, one of Mrs. Gereth's impassioned speeches directed to Fleda Vetch "affected our young lady as if it had been the shake of a tambourine borne toward her from a gipsy dance" (X *SpofP* 220). And the curiously ambivalent Christina Light is aptly described as looking "'half like a Madonna and half like a *ballerina*'" (I *RH* 195): she inspires rapturous adoration at the same time that she is making a decorative public spectacle of herself. A more elaborate image

71. See also XIX *WofD* I 30, 256; XXVI *SeofP* 261. See Tintner, "The Spoils of Henry James," p. 243.

72. This image was added when James revised the novel for inclusion in the New York Edition. For a discussion of this image and others added, see Sister Mary Brian Durkin, "Henry James's Revisions of the Style of THE REVERBERATOR," *American Literature*, XXXIII (November, 1961), 339-45, especially 341.

suggests Miss Dormer's passivity: "Biddy had a momentary sense of being a figure in a ballet, a dramatic ballet—a subordinate motionless figure, to be dashed at to music or strangely capered up to" (VII *TM* I 26). An equally exposed and endangered girl, but one finally more active and determined, is described in an only slightly different image: Maggie Verver during her engagement strikes her supercilious Prince as resembling "a little dancing-girl at rest, ever so light of movement but most often panting gently, even a shade compunctiously, on a bench" (XXIII *GB* I 322).[73] References in the imagery to types of dances—*pas seul*, minuet, and quadrille[74]—complete this grouping.

And finally, images drawn from architecture, like those from dancing, are ornamental rather than vital to the fiction. There is, for example, nothing functional about the following contrived picture of elderly Miss Wenham in "Flickerbridge": "She wore on the top of her head an upright circular cap that made her resemble a caryatid disburdened" (XVIII "Fl" 450). Similarly, the Princess Casamassima, being a pillar neither of society nor of the revolutionary movement, is inappropriately described by the burdened Hyacinth as "raising and upholding the weight that rested on him very much after the form of some high bland caryatid crowned with a crushing cornice" (VI *PC* II 399). And the following typical figures are also only decorative: Mrs. Rooth's "upper lip . . . projected over the under as an ornamental cornice rests on its support" (VII *TM* I 116), and the dramatist Allan Wayworth "felt more and more that his heroine was the keystone of his arch" (xxvi "NV" 464). Exceptional for the architecture group of figures is the following baroque expression of Adam Verver's early quiet rejoicing that his daughter's Prince is round instead of square: " 'Say you had been formed all over in a lot of little

73. See also XXIV *GB* II 222.
74. XIII "PP" 375-76, X *SpofP* 73, IX *AA* 255.

pyramidal lozenges like that wonderful side of the Ducal Palace in Venice—so lovely in a building, but so damnable, for rubbing against, in a man, and especially in a new relation'" (XXIII *GB* I 138). But it is to be assumed that, with or without his "Cortez-complex," Verver would not have attempted to buy the Ducal Palace of Venice! Nonetheless, by this curious image James has him unconsciously adumbrate Amerigo's Italianate versatility, approachability, and almost complete impenetrability.[75]

Conclusion

Now that we have followed James through the separate but interconnected rooms of his imagistic museum, we are surely prepared to agree that he used his knowledge of many of the arts, especially literature, painting, and the drama, in elaborating a large proportion of his metaphors and similes.

With these images to guide us, we may conclude that Thackeray, Balzac, and Hawthorne were among the most consistently inspiring of the writers whom this novelist's novelist revered; however, the imagery also demonstrates what Professor William T. Stafford has concluded from a study of literary allusions in the critical prefaces—that James "knew well much of the . . . literature of Europe."[76] To be sure, there are relatively few references in the imagery to poetry, which indicates both James's at most only moderate interest in poets other than Keats, Tennyson, and Goethe and also his sense of belonging to the Anglo-French stream of fiction.

If England and France provide the bulk of literary analogies for James, Italy clearly takes the lead in inspiring pictorial ones. Gainsborough and Reynolds—certainly Watteau

75. Later Maggie images the unapproachability of the Prince as a porcelain-plated pagoda (XXIV *GB* II 3); see p. 6 above.
76. William T. Stafford, "Literary Allusions in James's Prefaces," *American Literature*, XXXV (March, 1963), 70.

and Corot—do little for his imagery compared to the distinctive and varied inspiration of Titian, Veronese, Raphael, and many another Italian *pittore* whose masterpieces grace museum walls in his beloved Venice, Florence, and Rome. Again, James is to be complimented, since, writing as he was for an English-speaking, cosmopolitan, fiction-reading and traveling public, he tactfully employed art tropes most frequently concerned with fiction in English and with paintings whose messages are in the universal language of the Italian Renaissance.

Less can be said in defense of James's somewhat misplaced enthusiasm for French drama. And a word of explanation should perhaps be added for his apparent lack of appreciation for music, the dance, and architecture. Here, in part at least, the imagery seems to be an unreliable guide. But it is simply that, being in essence a pictorial dramatist, James could not make use in imagery of all of the art forms which his ranging and imaginative intellect found curious and challenging in a life dedicated to art. For example, he was always an able if amateur student of architecture, making many highly perceptive comments in criticism of the American skyscraper;[77] and in addition he often likened himself in his critical prefaces to an architect.[78] Yet, as we have seen, the imagery fails to reflect this critical and imaginative interest. It must be concluded that not even in approximately two thousand similes and metaphors concerning literature, painting, drama, music, sculpture, the dance, and architecture could James fully express his devotion to the artistic way of life and to the manifold objects of that pilgrimage.

77. See pp. 200-1 below.
78. See III xii, xvi, xix; IX xvi; X viii-ix; XIX xii-xiii, xxi; and see Robert L. Gale, "Henry James's Imagistic Portrait of Henry James," *Forum* (University of Houston), III (Summer, 1961), 33.

VII · BLEST IMAGES AND SANCTIFIED RELICS

He was, to an extent he never fully revealed, a collector of impressions as romantically concrete, even when profane, as the blest images and sanctified relics of one of the systematically devout, and he at bottom liked as little to hear anything he had picked up with the hands of the spirit pronounced unauthentic (II Ame 211).

Introduction

The ever-growing body of critical writing on the subject of religion in the James family is proof enough of its significance in the fictional works of Henry James. His father was a Swedenborgian and a spiritually luminous family-head, whose theology undoubtedly impressed the son's unconscious mind. Consciously, however, the novelist shied away from religious matters; more than that, he was a little critical of his father when in a letter to his brother William he wrote of *The Literary Remains of the Late Henry James,* "It comes over me . . . how intensely original and personal his whole system was, and how indispensable it is that those who go in for religion should take some heed of it. I can't enter into it (much) myself—I can't be so theological nor grant his extraordinary premises, nor throw myself into conceptions of heavens and hells . . ."[1] I agree with F. O. Matthiessen, who reports that "James's religion was phrased very accurately by Eliot as an 'indifference to religious dogma' along with an 'exceptional awareness of spiritual reality.' "[2] In addition, extrasensory phenomena obviously intrigued James, who wrote at least ten short stories having in them ghosts—real, imagined, or feigned.[3] Also, James was an admirer of his brother's *Varieties of Religious Experience,* which he said in 1902 he was "reading . . . with . . . rapturous deliberation."[4] And toward the end of his life he wrote a gentle little essay called "Is There a Life after Death?" as his part in an anthology called *In After Days: Thoughts on the Future Life.*[5]

So, if James did not formally "go in for religion," he still was well aware of the dramatic impact of religion through the ages and turned religious functions, functionaries, and trap-

1. *The Letters of Henry James,* ed. Percy Lubbock, 2 vols. (New York: Charles Scribner's Sons, 1920), I, 111-12. See also Leon Edel, *Henry James: The Middle Years: 1882-1895* (Philadelphia and New York: J. B. Lippincott Company, 1962), p. 63.

2. F. O. Matthiessen, *Henry James: The Major Phase* (New York: Oxford University Press, 1944), p. 145.

3. See Leon Edel, "Family Ghosts," pp. v-x, in *The Ghostly Tales of Henry James* (New Brunswick: Rutgers University Press, 1948), which contains eighteen stories, some not especially "ghostly."

4. Unpublished letter to William James and his wife, October 25, 1902, quoted in F. O. Matthiessen, *The James Family: Including Selections from the Writings of Henry James, Senior, William, Henry, & Alice James* (New York: Alfred A. Knopf, 1947), p. 338.

5. This essay is discussed in Matthiessen, *Henry James,* pp. 145-48, and is reprinted in Matthiessen, *The James Family,* pp. 602-14.

pings to excellent and frequent use in fashioning well over eight hundred figures of speech. They concern Greek and Roman deities and concepts, pagans alone or in conflict with Christians, Biblical references in abundance and variety, and many elements of Christianity. To be found in this group of images are hosts of oriental items, oracles, ghosts, priestesses, pilgrims, and angels, occasionally so clustered in individual works as to form iterative patterns. Most surprisingly, these figures decline steadily in relative frequency from their greatest density in the fiction of the 1860's to hardly one-third that proportion after 1900. However, as might be expected, some of the most elaborate religion tropes are to be found in the later works.

i. Greco-Roman

Of all non-Christian religions, James found the Greco-Roman the most rewarding for his imagery. For every rococo Hindu, Buddhist, Egyptian, or Mohammedan religion figure, there are at least ten somewhat more conventional—if less dramatic—ones concerning Greek or Roman gods and goddesses, sacrifices, and oracles. However, Maggie Verver's predicament, seen as "a Mahometan mosque"[6] which she cannot enter since she is a "base heretic" (XXIV *GB* II 4), Rosanna Gaw's parasol, likened to "the roof of some Burmese palanquin or perhaps even pagoda" (XXV *IT* 1), represent many such images which are arrestingly bizarre compared to the simpler though still radiant enough procession of figurative Junos and Dianas, and their divine companions. Thus, Miriam Quarterman, Mrs. Farrinder, Lady Bradeen, and Rosanna Gaw are compared to Juno; Caroline Hofmann, Jean Martle, and Amy Evans—as we shall see in detail in a moment—are likened to Diana in varying degrees of appropriateness; Verena Tarrant is a Minerva; Nora Lambert, a Pallas Athene; and so on. As

6. See p. 6 above, where the image is quoted in some detail.

for the men, Roger Lawrence is compared to Jove; Harold Staines, Roderick Hudson, and Vanderbank, to Apollo; and Lieutenant Ford and Davey Bradham, to Mercury.

But Kate Croy's massive and irresistible Aunt Maud, when she is pronounced by Densher to be " 'on the scale altogether of the Car of Juggernaut' " (XIX *WofD* I 90), Roderick Hudson, who is at one point "like a Buddhist in an intellectual swoon" (I *RH* 394), and Fanny Assingham, who is imaged as the "immemorially speechless Sphinx" because of her "free orientalism of type" (XXIII *GB* I 364), are, with several others, far more sharply etched in imagery from eastern religions than as a rule is even the divinely beautiful western goddess Amy Evans, heroine of "The Velvet Glove" and inspiration of a whole pattern of Greek god-goddess figures. Thus, the novelist John Berridge, entranced by the beauty of Amy, is still more delighted when she speaks sympathetically of his art. But all is spoiled when the young man learns that she is offering her graciousness only in the hope that he will write a preface for her latest worthless novel. An attractive young lord approaches Berridge, who, "under the blighting breath of the false gods, stupid conventions, traditions, examples" (xxviii "VG" 207), cannot recall where they once met but decides that "One placed young gods and goddesses only when one placed them on Olympus, and . . . they glimmered for one, at the best, through their silver cloud" (209). When Amy follows the lord to greet Berridge flatteringly, he remembers having seen them both on an Italian train. "If she was Olympian—as in her . . . beauty, that of some divine Greek mask . . . , she more and more appeared to him—this offered air was that of the gods themselves: she might have been . . . Artemis decorated, hung with pearls, for her worshippers . . ." (215-16). Having "snatched the cup of gold from Hebe" (216), the goddess descends upon Berridge, for, after all, "every goddess in the calendar had, when you came to look, sooner or later liked some prepossessing young shepherd" (218). Since she must "cure him, as goddesses *had* to cure shepherds, of his mere mortal shyness" (223), she is soon whisking him toward her home in her automobile, now "their chariot of fire" (229). Awaiting his answer to her request for the preface, "she hung there, she quite bent over him, as Diana over the sleeping Endymion" (234). But Berridge refuses, and tells the surprised and pearly-teared girl, who is finally a "miraculously humanised idol, all sacred, all jewelled, all votively hung about," " 'Princess, I adore you. But I'm ashamed for you' " (237). Is James, like Melville before him and Twain with him, enunciating the position that most human beings have more honor than divinities?

ii. Oracles and Priestesses

Images stemming from oracles, augurs, pagan idols, high-priests and even priestesses, and sacrificial altars and their victims are while very numerous rarely elaborated, as three representative examples will show. Nora Lambert "handled this letter somewhat as one may imagine a pious maiden of the antique world to have treated a messenger from the Delphic oracle" (xxiv *WandW* 141); Verena Tarrant's parents "had . . . often been in the position of the two augurs behind the altar" (viii *Bo* I 87); and for Milly Theale in Venice "Palazzo Leporelli held its history still in its great lap, even like a painted idol, a solemn puppet hung about with decorations" (XX *WofD* II 135). James's few high-priests are dull fellows: Theodore Lisle, in "A Light Man," is "destined to become a high priest among moralists" (xxv "LiM" 223); Eugene Pickering's father is merely "a sort of high-priest of the proprieties" (xxiv "EP" 248); and at one point Breckenridge Bender in *The Outcry* "remained . . . solemnly still, . . . like some high-priest circled with ceremonies" (*Ou* 242-43).

Far more interesting, and appearing in better stories and novels, are the high-priestesses—which fact is added proof that women stirred James's imagination more than men did. Such enigmatic, dedicated women as Rose Armiger and Miriam Rooth are likened to priestesses: the former once "stood there in her vivid meaning like the priestess of the threatened altar" (*OH* 102); the latter, about to recite for Madame Carré, is "the priestess on the tripod, awaiting the afflatus and thinking only of that" (VII *TM* I 126). Occasionally a passive but inspiring woman is called a priestess, as, for example, Milly is, whose "infinite number of yards of priceless lace . . . hung down to her feet like the stole of a priestess" (XX *WofD* II 96).[7] Finally, in a rare sequence involving a man at a gory altar, Strether, although he enjoys the worldliness of Paris, is pictured as feeling stained by it, " 'as if my hands [he says] were embrued with the blood of monstrous alien altars—of another faith altogether' " (XXII *Amb* II 167-68).

iii. Pagan *vs.* Christian

The clash of pagan and Christian provides a basis for many dramatic images. For example, Grace Whittaker of "Poor Richard" oddly wants one suitor to act as an ennobling influence upon another: "But women have been known to show their affection for a man by sending him as a missionary to the cannibals" (xxv "PR" 433). And a suitor in "The Chaperon" sympathizes with Rose Tramore at the death of her father; "he had spoken of her bereavement very much as an especially mild missionary might have spoken to a beautiful Polynesian" (X "Ch" 460). Confusion comes during a reading of the latter image when one tries to reconcile the figure to the suitor's dual mission—conversion from grief and persuasion toward marriage. Perhaps the missionary is subtly saying to the bereaved native

7. See also Catherine Sloper, as described v *WS* 14.

that she should now put her faith in the true Lord's emissary. Several figures liken innocent victims of crass social groups to Christian martyrs under the gaze of pagan Romans. Thus, barbaric society, because it loves a spectacle even if it is at the expense of an innocent victim, hopes that the hero of "The Path of Duty" will break his engagement: "As it would prolong the drama . . . , there was a considerable readiness to see the poor girl sacrificed. She was like a Christian maiden in the Roman arena" (xxv "PofD" 153-54). Similarly, a heartless group of house-party guests, hoping for a laugh at the guileless young wife in "The Two Faces," is described as "assembled . . . very much as the Roman mob at the circus used to be to see the next Christian maiden brought out to the tigers" (XII "TF" 407). And Mrs. Stringham, when she listens to the way the Londoners are conversationally handling her absent friend Milly Theale, "sat and looked—looked very much as some spectator in an old-time circus might have watched the oddity of a Christian maiden, in the arena, mildly, caressingly, martyred. It was the nosing and fumbling not of lions and tigers but of domestic animals let loose as for the joke" (XX *WofD* II 42).[8] The last image is superb. Lions and tigers, vicious though they may be, assure a better martyrdom than would domestic animals, in the center of which is poor Milly, the dove, the princess of peace, the crucified victim and victor. It is certainly no accident at all that Merton Densher makes a kind of Christmas resolution to honor Milly's faith.

iv. Bible

James's imagery makes specific mention of numerous Biblical persons. The favorites, appearing five times each, are Samson and the Queen of Sheba; then comes Solomon, mentioned three times; next, used twice each, are David, Joshua,

8. See also XVII "DM" 85, XVII "OW" 293, xxix *SF* 216.

Mary Magdalene, and Moses; finally, each of the following appears once: Daniel, Delilah, Ezekiel, Herod, Herodias, Jacob, Jeremiah, Joseph, Judas, Samuel, Salome, and Saul. There are several other Biblical, mostly Old Testament, usages which do not contain specific names. Taken as a whole, these images reveal only a normal awareness of the more dramatic scenes in the Bible. But we should bear in mind that modern fiction would seem didactic or at least affected if decorated with numerous Biblical allusions, and that James wrote to elucidate characters in an epoch of waning interest in the Bible.[9] It is curious that Adam and Eve—vitally important names for James's Swedenborgian father—are not named, although Eden and the Fall are used slightly.[10] Imagistic use of the New Testament is rather infrequent, as are elaborations of general Biblical situations and idioms—i.e., money-changers in the temple, oil from a golden cruse, and the like. Nearly all of the Bible usages are simple; most are undeveloped exaggerations; and many seem deliberately rather trivial—particularly those which appear in conversation. A few representative examples will suffice. When the ineffectual painter in "The Madonna of the Future" complains that America is barren of art, the narrator exclaims, " 'Be you our Moses . . . and lead us out of the house of bondage!' " (XIII "MofF" 442). The beauty of that evil angel Christina Light is compared by the observant Gloriani to that of " 'the young woman . . . who pranced up to the king her father with a great bloody head on a great gold tray' " (I RH 190). Although much relevant conversation follows Gloriani's introduction of this

9. Edwin T. Bowden rightly remarks that "Henry James . . . would have been embarrassed to use the religious terms of a Hawthorne or a Bradford"; *The Dungeon of the Heart: Human Isolation and the American Novel* (New York: The Macmillan Company, 1961), p. 89.

10. In general, I should say, James's imagery offers no support whatever to the main thesis of Quentin Anderson, *The American Henry James* (New Brunswick: Rutgers University Press, 1957).

comparison, it is really not a thorough-going figure. Nor is the next Bible image any more rewarding: all the mother of Eustace means is that she hopes her aging fiancé will solve her emotional and domestic problems, but what she says is this: "'*He* will drive the money-changers from the temple!'" (xxvi "MEu" 68). Worst of all is a Samson image from "Guest's Confession," in which story Guest believes that his relative Mrs. Beck may have surmised the fact that he is financially tottering: "He had slept in the arms of Delilah, and he had waked to find that Delilah had guessed, if not his secret, something uncomfortably like it" ("GuC" 579). The image simply does not work: to be sure, Mrs. Beck is slightly mysterious—in fact, she may not actually be a relative of the Guests—but there is not the slightest suggestion of any liaison between her and Guest.

It must be concluded, therefore, that the Bible did almost nothing for James's style but provide it with an occasional ornamental allusion.

v. Catholicism

"'Things that involve a risk are like the Christian faith; they must be seen from the inside.—Yours ever, E.S.'" (xxv "DofM" 41). Thus young Stanmer closes his letter to the diarist in the short story "The Diary of a Man of Fifty," revealing that in spite of the older man's advice he has married the ambiguous countess. One may use this thought to explain in part why James's images involving Catholicism, while almost uniformly respectful, remain usually only general and at most only colorfully dramatic. Impressed with Catholicism, James still saw it only from the outside.[11]

11. Mallet says to Christina Light at Saint Cecilia's in the Trastevere in Rome, "'I've never ceased for a moment to look at the Faith simply from the outside. I don't see an opening as big as your finger-nail where I could creep into it!'" (I *RH* 279). This remark is quoted in its unrevised form by Robert M. Slabey, in "Henry James and 'The

Only a few of the many tropes likening women to the Madonna are to be interpreted as Catholic. Often these largely pictorial figures are only decently pious. For example, Marco Valerio, who is a confessedly poor Catholic, is described as idolatrous of an exhumed statue of Juno: " 'But the Count treats her as if she were a sacrosanct image of the Madonna' " (xxvi "LofV" 21). Sometimes the comparison proves unfortunate, as when in "Rose-Agathe" a pretty face is thrice likened to that of a Madonna and then we learn that one of the enraptured men involved has been referring all along to a hair-dresser's dummy.[12] Usually a similarity to the Madonna is mentioned for its pictorial effects alone. Thus, the Italo-American Christina Light is appropriately said to look " 'half like a Madonna and half like a *ballerina*' " (I *RH* 195). One wonders whether the Cavaliere Giacosa's contribution to Miss Light's composition is responsible for her madonna-like qualities. Our friend the diarist in "The Diary of a Man of Fifty," fancying that he was once wronged by an Italian countess, warns the young man in the story against that woman's daughter: " 'My dear fellow, . . . they are mother and daughter —they are as like as two of Andrea's Madonnas' " (xxv "DofM" 24). Andrea del Sarto is undoubtedly meant, and therefore the figure is diabolically subtle, because most of the Madonnas of "the faultless painter" were modeled by his wife Lucrezia, a woman as scheming as James's diarist regards both of his suspicious acquaintances, and also, like them, a Florentine.

Almost always the saint images are inappropriate and

Most Impressive Convention in All History,' " *American Literature*, XXX (March, 1958), 99. Slabey demonstrates most ably that James shows in his writings from 1870 to 1875 an attraction toward and a deep interest in Catholicism; "Numerous characters in the stories express views regarding Catholicism: most of them consider themselves as outsiders, Protestants, 'passionless tourists,' 'heretics,' but, more significantly, many express dissatisfaction with viewing the Church only from the outside" (p. 101).

12. See xxv "RA" 393, 395, 397-98.

merely graphic, and sometimes also ironic. Selina Berrington of "A London Life" should hardly be called "a picture of Saint Cecilia" (X "LL" 320), since she is highly immoral. Nor is the amoral Christina Light a proper candidate; nonetheless, she is said, when she loosens her magnificent hair in Hudson's studio, to resemble "some immaculate saint of legend being led to martyrdom" (I *RH* 178).[13] However, two admirable non-materialists, Lady Aurora of *The Princess Casamassima* and Graham Fielder of *The Ivory Tower*, are aptly compared to Saint Francis of Assisi. Lady Aurora is said simply to be "as good in her way as Saint Francis of Assisi" (VI *PC* II 271). And following his receipt of the inheritance, Fielder asks Vinty, who is in reality corrupt, to "act" for him in the business world; Vinty replies: " 'Do you mean as your best man at your marriage to the bride who is so little like St. Francis? much as you yourself strike me . . . as resembling the man of Assisi' " (XXV *IT* 249). This sort of comparison, with others similar to it, James might well have formed into a pattern had he lived to complete *The Ivory Tower*, since the tragic opposition of art—which James often looked upon as a religion, in and out of imagery—and money was to have formed the core of the novel. There is only one other saintly man so designated in James: Theobald of "The Madonna of the Future" is called " 'one of the blessed saints' " (XIII "MofF" 479) by Serafina—hardly a reputable judge. Further, of the score or more women compared to saints, only half deserve the compliment. Certainly Christina Light, Mrs. Gereth, and Fanny Cashmore, for three examples, do not.[14] On the other

13. I suppose that we could agree that the European institution of arranged marriages is martyring Christina, but I prefer to see her as sold by her mother to the highest bidder: "Rowland had never been in the East [nor had James], but if he had attempted to make a sketch of an old slave-merchant calling attention to the 'points' of a Circassian beauty he would have depicted such a smile as Mrs. Light's [as she shows off her daughter's hair]" (I *RH* 179).

14. I *RH* 178, X *SpofP* 210, IX *AA* 110.

hand, Claire de Cintré, Pansy Osmond, Mildred Theory, and Miss Birdseye—among James's hagiography—merit the high praise they receive when called saintly.[15] Incidentally, by repetition of a simple saint image concerning little Miss Osmond, James subtly underlines her real parentage. In the first volume of *The Portrait of a Lady,* "'Ah,' cried Gilbert Osmond beautifully, 'she's a little saint of heaven!'" (III *PofL* I 383). A volume later, the girl's unacknowledged mother, Madame Merle, praises her in the same words—"'She's a little saint of heaven . . .'" (IV *PofL* IV 377). Further, Isabel is the auditor of both speeches, but between them she has been enlightened as to Pansy's real mother; undoubtedly the echo falls on attentive ears.

Jamesian people are likened to functionaries and communicants of the Catholic church, from priests and confessors, and nuns and monks, to devout pilgrims and persons cherishing rosary, medal, and cross. Often the person-to-person comparisons are brief and rather insignificant. Thus, Captain Diamond "made his obeisance like the priest before the altar" ("GhR" 675), while Longueville in *Confidence* admits to being "'as ignorant of women as a monk in his cloister'" (iv *Con* 58). However, three Catholic-order images, used principally for moderate dramatic value, permit an interesting, tentative conclusion. First, Hyacinth Robinson's subservience to the revolutionary plan involves him in "a vow of blind obedience, the vow as of the Jesuit fathers to the head of their order" (VI *PC* II 54). Next, the titular hero of "Poor Richard," hoping at one point to break his habit of drinking, "went to bed that night fasting as grimly as a Trappist monk" (xv "PR" 447). And last, the narrator of "The Next Time" says of Ralph Limbert's masterly but unpopular novels, "I used to

15. II *Ame* 283, III *PofL* I 377, xxv "GeR" 290, ix *Bo* II 216. *The Bostonians* appropriately has a number of images by which oppressed women are placed in a semi-religious "sisterhood."

talk about his work, but I seldom do now: the brotherhood of
the faith have become, like the Trappists, a silent order" (XV
"NT" 166). Now, it is notable that these three figures concerning orders all center upon activity characterized by failure: Hyacinth fails to shoot the duke, Richard fails to stop
drinking, and Limbert's writings fail to reach a wide audience.
In spite of conscious sympathy and partly unwilling self-identi-
fication with the monastic life,[16] James may be revealing here
his unconscious opposition to what he might term renunciation
of life. The literal goals of James's figurative pilgrims include
art in its many forms, the richness of Continental civilization,
and the beauty of women—an interesting series in the light
of James's own life. Thus, the splendid art treasures of Poynton attract Fleda Vetch: "She would go down to Poynton as a
pilgrim might go to a shrine" (X SpofP 259). Hyacinth will go
from London to the Continent as to a Mecca, leaving Millicent
Henning, a kind of girl friend, behind him: "Hyacinth thought
of her as some clever young barbarian who in ancient days
should have made a pilgrimage to Rome might have thought
of a Dacian or Iberian mistress awaiting his return to the
rough provincial shore" (VI PC II 131). And Rowland Mallet
writes of Christina Light in part as follows: "'About Miss
Light it's a long story. She's one of the great beauties of all
time and worth coming barefoot to Rome, like the pilgrims of
old, to see'" (I RH 296). Of the many images concerned with
rosaries, medals, and crosses, two from The Golden Bowl are
perhaps the finest, brilliantly contrasting as they do the two
central women in the novel. In the first volume, Charlotte's

16. Max Beerbohm said that when shaven James resembled a lay
cardinal; see "Note on the Cover to This Edition," The Notebooks of
Henry James, ed. F. O. Matthiessen and Kenneth B. Murdock, A Galaxy
Book (New York: Oxford University Press, 1961), opp. p. [i]. Further,
note that Overt angrily condemns St. George's implication that the truly
dedicated artist is "'a mere disfranchised monk and can produce his
effect only by giving up personal happiness'" (XV "LofM" 77).

awareness of the Prince's love is something "she might . . . have been carrying about with her like a precious medal— not exactly blessed by the Pope—suspended round her neck" (XXIII *GB* I 301). The second volume reports, in a neatly related image, that Maggie's courageous determination to win back her husband is always with her, "like that little silver cross . . . blest by the Holy Father" (XXV *GB* II 112). In a superficial way, the two women are the Prince's evil angel and his good angel, and "virtue" triumphs—and pays.

Only one image in all of James's fiction even slightly ridicules the Catholic faith, and that one appears in dialogue in "The Birthplace," a short story which satirizes the practice of making shrines and relics out of trivia. " 'Exactly so; the whole thing becomes a sort of stiff smug convention—like a dressed-up sacred doll in a Spanish church—which you're a monster if you touch' " (XVII "Bi" 174);[17] thus does a critical young American tourist picture "the birthplace," a meretricious literary shrine, to its increasingly unhappy curator. It is true that in a couple of instances James turns miraculous Catholic Church occurrences into imagery, but he does so without a trace of contempt. Thus is the uncomplaining nature of Catholic little Pansy pictured when we read that it may be occurring to her that her "magnificent father" and her "gentle stepmother" are in opposition to one another: "Her heart may have stood almost as still as it would have done had she seen two of the saints in the great picture in the convent-

17. James wrote lugubriously to his brother William in 1903 that "These visions I've had, one by one, all to give up—Spain, Greece, Sicily, any glimpse of the East, or in fact of anything . . ."; *The Letters of Henry James*, I, 417. However, as Leon Edel has shown, James did briefly set foot in Spain in 1876, and while there "he studied a life-sized Virgin in a church with a flamboyant façade"; in fact, James's description of the "gloomy, yet bedizened" statue, "emotional as a woman and mechanical as a doll"—quoted by Edel—is somewhat similar to the image above from "The Birthplace" (1903); *Henry James: The Conquest of London: 1870-1881* (Philadelphia and New York: J. B. Lippincott Company, 1962), p. 266.

chapel turn their painted heads and shake them at each other. But as in this latter case she would (for very solemnity's sake) never have mentioned the awful phenomenon, so she put away all knowledge of the secrets of larger lives than her own" (IV *PofL* II 383). A similar supernatural event forms the basis of an even more dramatic image when Ralph Pendrel finds himself waiting to see if the figure in the painting will turn: "He was like the worshipper in a Spanish church who watches for the tear on the cheek or the blood-drop from the wound of some wonder-working effigy of Mother or of Son. When he moved away a little it was to let these things start at their ease, and when he next turned upon them it was to assist at the prodigy before it should stop" (XXVI *SeofP* 78). Later, after pacing through the darkness of time and the London house, Ralph strikes a light and looks again: "It was like the miracle prayed for in the church—the figure in the picture had turned" (86-87). I ignore Strether's amused suggestion that from Waymarsh's point of view Maria Gostrey is "a Jesuit in petticoats" recruiting for society, for Europe, for what Waymarsh would call "The Catholic Church, . . . that was to say the enemy, the monster of bulging eyes and far-reaching quivering groping tentacles" (XXI *Amb* I 41). Strether is sympathetic to Madame de Vionnet's religion, and in most respects it is obviously he rather than Waymarsh who reflects many of James's opinions and attitudes. Finally, as a counteraction, consider Newman's admittedly prejudiced praise of Claire de Cintré: "If such flawless white flowers as that could bloom in Catholic soil they but attested its richness" (II *Ame* 422).

vi. Protestantism

Totally different from Catholic imagery are most of the Protestant figures of speech, which are infrequent as such and are rarely anything but frivolous. The following typical examples should lead one to deduce less a fundamental dislike of Protestantism in James than simply a love of indulgent jibing. " 'A man should only marry in self-defense, . . . as Luther became Protestant. He should wait till he is driven to the wall' " ("CCon" 571); " 'It's as negative . . . as a Protestant Sunday' " (XXI "AP" 10); "he despised her; she had no traditions and the moral horizon of a Unitarian minister" (IV *PofL* II 201); "she struck him as a sort of transfigured Quakeress—a mystic with a practical side" (iv *Con* 12); and " 'You look as if you were taking me to a prayermeeting or a funeral' " (XVIII "DM" 41). Admittedly, these comments are sometimes reflections or paraphrases of the thoughts of biased observers.

vii. Religion Patterns

Religion images form the principal figurative pattern in a few of James's works, but usually—as in the case of the ghost metaphors in "Travelling Companions"[18] and the angel and devil tropes in "The Impressions of a Cousin"[19]—in only a very plain fashion. More interesting are the motifs in "The Velvet Glove," already noted,[20] "The Altar of the Dead"—the title of which focuses numerous figures—and "The Birthplace," which has already been said to have satirical elements. The following tropes help to establish an almost allegorical tone and an occasional Biblical idiom in "The Altar of the Dead": "what came to pass was that an altar . . . reared itself in his spiritual spaces" (XVII "AofD" 5) which soon comprised the "chapel of his thoughts" (15); the candles, which are "as dazzling as the vision of heaven in the mind of a child" (52), have a message and "sing out like a choir of angels" (57).[21] But the

18. "TC" 600, 607, 611, 695.
19. See xxv "IofC" 401, 426, 427, 429, 434, 437.
20. See pp. 151-52 above.
21. More than 10% of the imagery in this story is of a religious nature while only 3% is animal by contrast; "The Beast in the Jungle" has

cleverest pattern of religion figures is to be found in "The Birthplace." Miss Putchin, "the priestess in black silk" (XVII "Bi" 144), shows Morris Gedge around the "shrine at which he was to preside . . . , the Mecca of the English-speaking race" (134). In the adjoining museum, "the vestibule of the temple" (186), "votive offerings glimmered" (192). Gedge, once he is "the priest of the idol" (162), soon finds himself "hurled by his fate against the bedizened walls of the temple, quite in the way of a priest possessed to excess of the god" (183); but he reforms, even though to do so he must destroy his fine critical sense "on the altar of sacrifice . . . for ever splattered" (189). At the end, he may be seen delivering his new and successful ritualistic speech "as solemnly and softly . . . as over a pulpit edge" (195).

Conclusion

A consideration of the vast mosaic of religion images in James's fiction leads to several conclusions. In the first place, James creates some of his most bizarre effects by means of Oriental references, while he uses more conventional religion tropes—those having to do, for example, with priestesses, sacrificial altars, and literary staples like Juno and Jove—as a kind of metaphoric reinforcement or ground base. Also, it may be safely inferred that James finds women suitable subjects (if often only ironically so) for similes and metaphors of this sort at least twice as often as he does men: that is to say, in his world there are, fortunately, more Dianas than Endymions. Further, it is strikingly apparent that the most provocative religion tropes appear in the later works of James, and in the works revised for inclusion in the New York Edition—for example, "The Altar of the Dead," "The Birthplace," and "The

nearly 10% animal figures but less than 3% religion. Thus the titles, in reality indicative of master metaphors to follow, control the figures beneath them.

Velvet Glove"—rather than in the earlier and unrevised ones. Next, it is notable that while James—like Hawthorne—respects those who profess to sense spiritual actualities, he deplores the excesses of zealots, exploiting as he does such wildness in many graphic, comic, and ironic figurative comparisons. And it should also be emphasized that James excellently uses the clash of opposing religions to image dramatic clashes of various secular sorts in his fictional world, that he likens professional dedication to monkish asceticism, and that to him a worldly pilgrim's worthy goal is the adoration of beauty. Finally, James reveals a sensitive awareness of spiritual matters but no belief in any specific creed.

Indeed, the only religion to James seems to have been the adoration of art. This supposition is supported by several intriguing images. For example, in "Collaboration," a story concerning two dedicated men of art, we read that "Art protects her children in the long run—she only asks them to trust her. She is like the Catholic Church—she guarantees paradise to the faithful" (xxvii "Col" 158). And in the short story "Mora Montravers," Traffle, an art lover, meets by chance the young heroine Mora while he is visiting what James calls a place "of pilgrimages" to see "the idol in the numbered shrine" —that is, a painting—in one of the Dutch rooms of London's National Gallery, which is "a temple" and "an unprofaned place" (xxviii "MM" 287). More illuminating still is James's use of the most inspiring symbol in all secular Christian literature, the holy grail. There are only two holy grail images in James's fiction, and they both concern art. In "The Author of Beltraffio," the narrator is enraptured by the eloquence of Mark Ambient, the author in question: "On that high head of the passion for form—the attempt at perfection, the quest for which was to his mind the real search for the holy grail—he said the most interesting and inspiring things" (XVI "AofB"

30). And Vendemer of "Collaboration," which concerns the friendship and co-operation of a German musician and a French poet, asks an assembled group to name the greatest crime against art; he elaborates the phrasing of his query thus: " 'Against the religion of art—against the love of beauty— against the search for the holy grail?' " (xxvii "Col" 177). The answer, patriotism, shows that Henry James saw such a power for international good in art that to him it was little short of a religion.

VIII · OTHER ALLUSIONS STILL

Their real meetings must have been constant, for half of it was appointments, and allusions, all swimming in a sea of other allusions still, tangled in a complexity of questions that gave a wondrous image of their life (XI "InC" 383).

Introduction

Fully one third of the imagery in the fiction of Henry James falls into the six major categories which have now been discussed. Of the remaining figures, which have escaped thus far, several thousand may be placed in what I regard as the nine largest minor groups. These are fire, metals, sensations, children, games, cups, jewelry, court life, and astronomical bodies. Some of these categories are of little interest, some are of considerable interest. All reveal James's mind and personality to a degree, while most characterize, point up tensions, and advance action.

i. Fire

Although some of James's several hundred fire images refuse to drop into distinct pigeon-holes, most—as is the case with Hawthorne's similar imagery—are found in descriptions of passion or of intellectual activity, while a few are only momentarily clever rhetorical flashes.

Fire figures having to do with unspecified passion are frequent. Thus, "Passion, in him [Christopher Newman], by habit, nevertheless, burned clear rather than thick" (II *Ame* 525); and Lord Warburton's eyes are "charged with the light of a passion . . . that burned as steadily as a lamp in a windless place" (III *PofL* I 148).[1] Often a particular emotion is seen to be fiery. For example, "Searle blazed up into enthusiasm" (XIII "PP" 391); "'His hatred of you burns with a lurid flame—the flame that never dies'" (v *WS* 178); "Mrs. Magaw quite flamed with excitement" (XVI "FC" 424); and "the flicker of his fear . . . sprang up, for its moment, only to die down and then go out for ever" (XXII *Amb* II 94).

Love is a flame. It is often a hidden one;[2] but oddly, as though James grew to recognize the platitudinous quality of the figure, we almost never find love so imaged in the works of the New York Edition. Usually the examples are simple: "he had fanned his flame at Homburg" (xxiv "EP" 298); "the timid little flame which was kindled at Nice was beginning to shoot up again" (xxiv "LoM" 235); and so on. Rarely does James elaborate on the fiery pit of love, but we do read once that "the thick, smoky flame of a sentiment that knew itself forbidden, and was angry at the knowledge, now danced upon

1. Eyes also suggest to the trope-making James candles, coals, embers, fire, flames, gas-light, lanterns, lights, motor-lamps, sparks, stars, and torches! See pp. 225-26 below.
2. See iii *Eurs* 167, iv *Con* 173, xxvi "WofT" 143.

the fuel of his good resolutions" (xxv "GeR" 311). Sometimes the fire dies out: "'Mrs. Donner is dust and ashes to me'" (IX *AA* 172).

Characters in James who seek knowledge are frequently imaged as seeking light, flame, fire. Undoubtedly the most dogged and ingenious such seeker in all literature is the unnamed narrator of *The Sacred Fount,* which is adazzle with torches, blazes, flickering flames, flaring fires, and simple struck sparks. But that narrator, whose pleasures evidently are all intellectual, does not trouble himself with any emotional heat. The painter Obert leads off by saying of the narrator's tentative theory that "'it sheds a great light'" and that "'it's . . . a torch in the dark'" and even "'dazzling'" (xxix *SF* 51). The narrator in turn admires "Obert's blaze of ingenuity" (51) but confesses that he is "'quite in the dark—or in a darkness lighted, at best [he adds], by what you have called the torch of my analogy'" (53). When later the same busy narrator spots Obert in the smoking-room, he explains that on seeing him again "'my prospects gave something of a flare'" (163). Finally, in the course of the ensuing conversation, "the torch of the analogy" is mentioned again fully five times, during the last of which Obert wildly develops the image: "'I've blown on my torch . . . till, flaring and smoking, it has guided me, through a magnificent chiaroscuro of colour and shadow, out into the light of day'" (173-74).

Torches can be raised to gentle memories, simple facts, and sources of possible information: "I hold up the torch to the dusky years" (XV "NT" 157); "Madame de Vionnet had by her visit held up the torch to these truths, and what now lingered in poor Maria's face was the somewhat smoky light of the scene between them" (XXII *Amb* II 297); and "this inquiring authoress was constantly flashing her lantern into the quiet darkness of his soul" (IV *PofL* II 243).

Memory itself is often compared to a fire, mild or blazing vigorously, or turning to mere ashes. Thus, "the flame of memory turned to an equalising glow, that of a lamp in some side-chapel in which incense was thick" (XXIV *GB* II 11); "for everything they spoke of he positively cultivated extravagance and excess, piling up the crackling twigs as on the very altar of memory. . . . It was the game of feeding the beautiful iridescent flame, ruddy and green and gold, blue and pink and amber and silver, with anything they could pick up, anything that would burn and flicker" (xxviii "CCor" 348); and we see in a dying old man's eyes "the faint ghost of an old story, the last strange flicker, as from cold ashes, of a flame that had become the memory of a memory" (VII *TM* I 301-2).

Flames blown out are frequent; they suggest naturally enough the end of something or the death of someone. Poor Claire de Cintré's youthful marriage, " 'like a lamp that goes out, turned all to smoke and bad smell' " (II *Ame* 151), says her brother Valentin aptly. A literary critic senses the rightness of a new theory only to lose it again—or, as James puts it, "he would clasp his hands over new lights and see them blown out by the wind of the turned page" (XV "FinC" 244). And rejected by Lady Beldonald, poor Mrs. Brash dies, "going out like a snuffed candle" (XVIII "BH" 405).

Appropriately enough, Maggie Verver of *The Golden Bowl,* who is imaged as an actress before footlights and as a tender creature menaced by escaped beasts or birds of prey, is also involved in a pair of brilliant figures concerning her fear of losing the protection of fire. "It would be all in vain to have crouched so long by the fire; the glass would have been smashed, the icy air would fill the place" (XXIV *GB* II 151). Later, her condition with Charlotte is likened to "the predicament of the night-watcher in a beast-haunted land who has no means for a fire" (299-300).

Finally, numerous clever fire images are concerned with the illuminating of faces: "his face was like a lighted lantern patched with paper and unsteadily held" (IV *PofL* II 59); "her huge eyes, her red lips, the intense marks in her face formed an *éclairage* as distinct and public as a lamp set in a window" (XI *WMK* 211);[3] and when John Marcher sees an intensely grief-stricken man's face, we read that it "flared for him as a smoky torch" (XVII "BinJ" 125).

ii. Metals

Of the many metal images in James's fiction, only a relatively small number are exclusively metallic, without also belonging to more prominent and significant categories. Thus, the armor images belong in James's imagistic arsenal, cage and trap figures in his menagerie, bronze statues in his museum, and so on. Still, a few fictional works take on a hard, high luster because of patterns of metal imagery. For example, in "The Lesson of the Master" Overt praises St. George's writings as "'a mine of gold'" (XV "LofM" 52). But later the master, discussing his production, insists, "'I've touched a thousand things, but which one of them have I turned into gold? The artist has to do only with that—he knows nothing of any baser metal'" (72). Finally, the now well-remarried older novelist tells the younger, celibate artist that he will read only him now; whereupon the young man wonders— "Did he mean this . . . as a covert intimation that the assistance he should derive from that young lady's fortune . . . would make the difference of putting it in his power to cease to work ungratefully an exhausted vein?" (94-95). So far, gold is a blessing.

The Golden Bowl has nearly thirty metal images, more than half of which concern gold. Thus, the erotic Prince

3. This image, concerning Maisie's mother, is very appropriate since the woman is most common and "public."

likens his Charlotte's lithe body to "some long loose silk purse, well filled with gold-pieces but having been passed empty through a finger-ring that held it together" (XXIII *GB* I 47). This magic-act image is arresting: how can the purse be filled if it is slipped while still empty through a ring? It must be visualized as not opening at the top but unfastening lengthwise. This makes the image more suggestive. When combined with other elements in the same context, the figure becomes rather sensual. And Adam Verver is pictured as carrying the little glass with which he tastes life "in an old morocco case stamped in uneffaceable gilt with the arms of a deposed dynasty" (196). I think that this image arises from an unconscious fear in James of the deposing of capitalism. When they are at a party Adam gives, Charlotte and the Prince sense "a mystic golden bridge between them, strongly swaying and sometimes almost vertiginous" (325). Later, when he overhears Charlotte say that she is staying on a while with him at Matcham, "Amerigo, with the chink of this gold in his ear, turned straight away, so as not to be instantly appealed to" (345). Maggie toys with the sight of the Prince and her friend Charlotte exchanging a glance, "as she might have played with a medallion containing on either side a cherished little portrait and suspended round her neck by a gold chain of a firm fineness that no effort would ever snap" (XXIV *GB* II 35-36). This interesting image shows that Maggie cherishes both the Prince and Charlotte, that they "depend" upon her, and—most neatly—that in this unchangeable conjunction of the two lovers in Maggie's mind they are faced away from each other. Maggie and her father continue to enjoy Fawns; she recalls how, earlier, "they had let their happy confidence lull them with its most golden tone" (85). When the Prince tardily confesses that he has been acting all in good faith, self-reliant Maggie casually watches the words "settle like some handful of gold-dust thrown into the air" (350). At the last, Maggie looks back with relief and satisfaction upon her final vision of the defeated Charlotte: "The shade of the official, in her [Charlotte's] beauty and security, never for a moment dropped; it was a cool high refuge, the deep arched recess of some coloured and gilded image, in which she sat and smiled and waited . . ." (357). But the reader is apt to look back further to the far more graphic image of Charlotte in a gilded cage, from which she escapes only temporarily but then terrifyingly.[4] Often, therefore, gold is a dubious blessing.

The Other House has a fine little motif of terse metal figures, which throw a revealing light on Dennis Vidal. He is strong and inflexible, like Caspar Goodwood, who is bodied forth in a few glittering armor images.[5] Rose Armiger, whose last name means "armor bearer to a knight," tells Dennis, her impatient suitor who is just back from China, " 'You look young just as a steel instrument of the best quality, no matter how much it's handled, often looks new' " (*OH* 27-28). Four years later, again home from the Far East, "he only sat rather stiffly back and let her see how fine and firm the added years had hammered him" (151). When after the murder Vidal is asked if he and Rose are engaged, he thinks fast and answers untruthfully that they are—to protect Rose—and we read that "He spoke with a clearness that proved the steel surface he had in a few minutes forged for his despair" (203). But his metal has its match; in Rose's "hard embrace" "he might . . . have been a creature trapped in steel" (200).

4. See pp. 71, 75-76 above; see also XXIV *GB* II 229-30, 239, 241, 283, 329. It should finally be noted incidentally that the title *The Golden Bowl* focuses a good deal of forceful symbolism but only three minor images: XXIII *GB* I 359; XXIV *GB* II 216-17, 236. J. A. Ward, in *The Imagination of Disaster: Evil in the Fiction of Henry James* (Lincoln: University of Nebraska Press, 1961), pp. 148-51, acutely analyzes the relationship of gold usages (some literal) and evil.

5. See p. 87 above.

"Why should Madame de Mauves have chosen a French-woman's lot—she whose nature had an atmospheric envelope absent even from the brightest metals?" (XIII "MdeM" 247). From this charming image we may conclude that it is not attractive, in James's estimation, for women to appear metallic. Far more often than otherwise, when metal is used in imagery portraying his heroines or subordinate women, there is an implication of stolidity, coldness, inflexibility. For example, Catherine Sloper is compared to " 'a copper kettle that receives a dent; you may polish up the kettle, but you can't efface the mark' " (v WS 136). Henrietta reminds Osmond " 'Of a new steel pen—the most odious thing in nature' " (IV PofL II 287). Hard, clever Linda Pallant, who resembles Hawthorne's Lady Eleanore to a degree, is said to be " 'cased in steel; she has a heart of marble' " (XIII "LoP" 532). Unfeminine Julia Dallow occasions this epitome: " 'the surface so delicate, the action so easy, yet the frame of steel' " (VII TM I 257). And Greville Fane's cold, over-protected daughter Ethel impresses the frank narrator as being "surrounded with a spiked iron railing. . . . Who would be inspired to clamber over that bristling barrier? What flower of tenderness or of intimacy would such an adventurer conceive as his reward?" (XVI "GF" 118). Rarest of all, perhaps, is Maud Lowder: she is Britannia with "a helmet, a shield, a trident and a ledger" (XIX WofD I 30-31). She has "gilded claws" (73). She is like a projectile "loaded and ready for use" (169). And she is, although "ugly in form," nevertheless of "precious metals" in contrast to Densher's "comparative brummagem" (XX WofD II 33). She even manages once to throw "a fine floating gold-dust" (XIX WofD I 168).[6]

6. Austin Warren says that for Maud "the master metaphor is metallic"; "Myth and Dialectic in the Later Novels," *Kenyon Review*, V (Autumn, 1943), 560.

iii. Sensations

James compares things to sensations of various sorts, usually gustatory, with olfactory following, and tactual and auditory coming last.[7] The word "taste" is much overworked in James, and instances are very numerous in which it is difficult to decide whether the usage is figurative or literal. However, more than a hundred times the word "taste" appears in clearly if sometimes hackneyed imagistic contexts. The fancied sensation may be pleasant, merely present, or revolting. Thus, one young lady "tasted very soberly of the sweets of defiance" (iv *Con* 52); another "kindled a perception of raciness in a mind to which the usual fare of life seemed unsalted" (III *PofL* I 312); and a sad man hears something which "embittered again the taste of his tragedy" (*OH* 228).

In two late, tragic works we can trace the progress of figurative tastes from sweet to bitter. Early in "The Beast in the Jungle" May Bartram's revelation that John Marcher told her long ago of his obsession gradually begins "to taste sweet to him" (XVII "BinJ" 69). Later Marcher paces May's little drawing-room, "in which he had, as he might have said, tasted their intimate communion with every sauce" (86). At the end, the searing truth may be hideous, but "he kept it there before him so that he might feel the pain. That at least, belated and bitter, had something of the taste of life. But the bitterness suddenly sickened him . . ." (126).

7. Abstractions compared to things visible can hardly be sensibly considered here, since almost every figurative image in James is also visual. In addition, I ignore such excessive refinements as organic, kinesthetic, and motor sensation imagery, with which—added to the five main types of sensation figures—Richard Harter Fogle complicates something essentially simple enough except for its vocabulary, in his *Imagery of Keats and Shelley* (Chapel Hill: The University of North Carolina Press, 1949), pp. 26-29. But see I. A. Richards, *Principles of Literary Criticism* (New York: Harcourt, Brace and Company, 1924), p. 119; and René Wellek and Austin Warren, *Theory of Literature* (New York: Harcourt, Brace and Company, 1956), pp. 176, 177.

The Wings of the Dove also progresses from images of tastes largely pleasurable to several which are unpleasant. Early in the novel, Densher shows his love of Kate by a long look, "and she took it to its deepest, its headiest dregs" (XIX *WofD* I 69). When Milly accidentally comes upon the two in the National Gallery, she requires "a big dose of inspiration"; then he bravely "tasted of her draught"; and finally "the sweetness of the draught for the time . . . was to feel success assured" (295). Kate tells Densher that Milly just before her death " 'won't smell, as it were, of drugs. She won't taste, as it were, of medicine' " (XX *WofD* II 53). But if the young man will taste no drugs, he will taste something: "His knowledge of American friends was clearly an accident of which he was to taste the fruit to the last bitterness" (31). And overcoming Kate's resistance to his imperious demand upon her yields a rank taste: "It had never yet in life been granted to him to know, almost materially to taste, as he could do in these minutes, the state of what was vulgarly called conquest" (216); later, we read, "He had never . . . tasted, in all his relation with her, of anything so sharp—too sharp for mere sweetness—as the vividness with which he saw himself master in the conflict" (231). But the aftertaste is noxious, and Lord Mark's later presence "only added to what was most acrid in the taste of his present ordeal" (267).[8]

Most of the olfactory images in James are pleasant or at least innocuous, but few are so delightful as the following: "The irrecoverable days had come back to her from far off; they were part of the sense of the cool upper air and of everything else that hung like an indestructible scent to the torn garment of youth" (XIX *WofD* I 119). Many fragrance images have to do with flowers, obviously enough; for example, we read once that a good man's "natural honesty was

8. For some other striking taste figures, see XV "LofM" 73, *OH* 85, XVI "FC" 401, XII "TofS" 309.

like the scent of a flower" (X *SpofP* 102), and elsewhere that "economy hung about like the scent of a garden" (XVII "JC" 439).

Some images of smell are startling, a few even violent. We read of "a whiff too much of the brogue" (II *Ame* 266), "the perfume of Schubert and Mendelssohn" (viii *Bo* I 184), and "old morocco [which] exhaled the fragrance of curious learning" (XVI "AofB" 61). Further, we read of Bight in "The Papers" that "he wouldn't be able not to smell of the wretched man's [Beadel-Muffet's] blood, morally speaking, too strongly for condonations and complacencies" (xxviii "Pap" 177), and in *The Sense of the Past* that "Perry scented his [Pendrel's] cleverness, . . . scented his very act of understanding, as some creature of the woods might scent the bait of the trapper" (XXVI *SeofP* 153).

A great number of James's images are incidentally rather than primarily tactual. For example, Densher's having been the first to know Milly is a fact palpably but only casually present to the young man: "Its influence had been there . . . from the moment she took him to drive, covering them in together as if it had been a rug of softest silk" (XX *WofD* II 186). Further, Adam Verver's love of music may be vague, but when Charlotte plays for him, "the vagueness spread itself about him like some boundless carpet, a surface delightfully soft to the pressure of his interest" (XXIII *GB* I 202).

In the tragic second volume of *The Princess Casamassima*, when Hyacinth feels his fate closing in upon him almost tangibly, we find several instances of the sensation of feeling comprising the principal imagistic factor. Near the readily tactile Milly Henning in church, Hyacinth "felt the brush of a rich unction" (VI *PC* II 329). As he walks into the Poupin home just before receiving the letter, the young man senses a crisis—"It struck him this crisis was in the air, very near—

that he should touch it if he made another movement" (363). When Muniment remarks that Hyacinth now hates having given his promise to the revolutionary Hoffendahl, "the complete reasonableness of his tone itself cast a chill on Hyacinth's spirit; it was like the touch of a hand at once very firm and very soft, yet strangely cold" (212). At the end, Hyacinth turns away forever when "he felt the great hard hand on his shoulder" (419) demanding that he kill.

And how very Jamesian is this final example of a tactual figure: "It wasn't, in a word, simply that their eyes had met; other conscious organs, faculties, feelers had met as well . . ." (XIX *WofD* I 53).

Several of the rather infrequent images making use of sound are interesting. Some are used in simple physical description. Thus, the figure in this passage—"The speech . . . was like a tinkle of bluebells" (XI "InC" 397)—equates literal sound and figurative sound. The following comparison neatly likens visual attractiveness to sound: "The charm of his face was above all in its being . . . alive. You might have seen it in the form of a bell with the long 'pull' dangling in the young man's conscious soul; at the touch of the silken cord the silver sound would fill the air" (II *Ame* 129). Also, in some images sound helps to describe emotional or intellectual states: thus, a joyful pair "let their happy confidence lull them with its most golden tone" (XXIV *GB* II 85); and James's last sensitive hero, Mark Monteith of "A Round of Visits," experiences "a great rush of mere memories, a great humming sound as of thick, thick echoes" (xxviii "RofV" 395).

Synesthetic imagery is rare in James. Most of the few instances involve sound, as when "you seemed to hear the coolness as well as feel it" (iii *Eurs* 112). Also, "The light she had demanded for his altar would have broken his silence with a blare; whereas all the lights in the church were for her too great a hush" (XVII "AofD" 44). Finally, consider this marvelous image which describes the color of crude Sarah Pocock's dress: "a splendour of crimson which affected Strether as the sound of a fall through a skylight" (XXII *Amb* II 165-66).

iv. Children

Most of the children in James's similes and metaphors are in pain; some of course are happy enough, with their lumps of candy, their toys, and their merry-making; and sufficient imagery derives from children's fairy-tales to make us aware that their originator's youthful reading was fortunately not confined to Victorian and French fiction.

Many of the figurative infants and adolescents are unhappy—a proof among much other evidence that James responded imaginatively to the latent hideousness of life.[9] For example, when Mrs. Gereth says something which Flora comprehends only after a lag, we read that the girl "had a pause, that of the child who takes time to know that he responds to an accident with pain" (X *SpofP* 243). When May Bartram becomes thoroughly aware of the true nature of Marcher's horrible fate, she "spoke as with the softness almost of a sick child" (XVII "BinJ" 110). And when Ferdinand Mason, hero of "A Most Extraordinary Case," is racked by his fatal illness, he "put his hands over his face and cried like a homesick school-boy" (xxvi "MEC" 118). Finally, toward the end of *The Wings of the Dove*, James uses a most arresting figure to describe Densher's secret thought that as time passes it is taking away from him forever something ineffably lovely:

He kept it back like a favourite pang; left it behind him, so to say, when he went out, but came home again the sooner for the certainty of finding it there. Then he took it out of its sacred corner and its soft wrappings; he undid them one by

9. See Ward, *The Imagination of Disaster, passim.*

one, handling them, handling *it*, as a father, baffled and tender, might handle a maimed child. But so it was before him—in his dread of who else might see it (XX *WofD* II 395-96).

Of this image, which is characteristic of James's major phase, one can visualize the vehicle more easily than he can understand the tenor, which here remains a little unclear. Densher is obviously torturing himself by reveling in sadness following Milly's death. But who is the mother of the child of his thinking? Did Milly die to bear this thought to him? Does he sense that the product of their spiritual union is at best weak, and inevitably time's early victim?

Of course many of the children in James's imagery are happy. Thus, when a wise tourist in "The Birthplace" explains that certain of his fellow-Americans constantly seek new reasons for raving, James has him put it as follows: " 'You've seen small children laugh to shrieks when tickled in a new place. So there are amiable millions with us who are small shrieking children. They perpetually present new places for the tickler' " (XVII "Bi" 205). Also, when Colonel Assingham humorously indulges his wife in her monotonous search for motives, James sees the man's amusement thus: "It would have made him, for the spectator of these passages between the pair, resemble not a little the artless child who hears his favourite story told him the twentieth time and enjoys it exactly because he knows what is next to happen" (XXIV *GB* II 128). And the aging White-Mason observes with delight the coming of spring in a New York park, where "the quarter about him held its breath after the fashion of the child who waits with the rigour of an open mouth and shut eyes for the promised sensible effect of his having been good" (xxviii "CCor" 323).[10] But there is remarkably little candy in the imagery—perhaps because James feared dentists

10. See also xxvi "Gl" 195.

so![11]—and the following figure may fairly epitomize his frustrated dream-children even as it describes Maisie's sense of being thwarted as she is kept, because of finances, from her French lessons: "She was to feel henceforth as if she were flattening her nose upon the hard window-pane of the sweet-shop of knowledge" (XI *WMK* 137).

The figurative toys are often rather expensive, and when so are usually of the sort that little girls prefer. Thus, a modest house impresses Dr. Sloper as "look[ing] like a magnified baby-house, and [it] might have been taken down from a shelf in a toy-shop" (v *WS* 84), while Lady Barbarina meets an American society woman who "had the appearance of a small but very expensive doll" (XIV "LaB" 128).[12] Less expensive toys, of kinds normally associated with little boys, are also present. For example, at one point Roderick Hudson's mother, "determining for once in her life to hold up her head, was actually flying it like a kite" (I *RH* 435). And the narrator pictures his happy recollections of a past shared with Eugene Pickering as "an ancient cupboard in some dusky corner, and [we] rummaged out a heap of childish playthings —tin soldiers and torn story-books, jack-knives and Chinese puzzles" (xxiv "EP" 248).[13]

Appropriately enough, *What Maisie Knew* has a pattern of child images which is pervasive and intricate. The nearly thirty figures deriving from children's playthings and impressions might possibly be expected in a Jamesian novel about an innocent child betrayed, but the treatment given them constitutes a tour de force. The images are uniformly tender and help greatly to endear little Maisie in every reader's heart. Thus, the doll Lisette, her friendly companion, is pictured as occasionally asking Maisie questions "which re-

11. See pp. 210-11 below.
12. See also iii *Eurs* 34, ix *Bo* II 141, IX *AA* 410, VII *TM* I 295.
13. See also X *SpofP* 234, I *RH* 314-15, XI *WMK* 9, XVII "JC" 475.

produced the effect of her own [questions] upon those for whom she sat in the very darkness of Lisette" (XI *WMK* 34). Maisie stores up impressions—heaps of sights, sounds, and comments—which in her innocence she cannot comprehend all at once, and we read that she therefore

. . . found in her mind a collection of images and echoes to which meanings were attachable—images and echoes kept for her in the childish dusk, the dim closet, the high drawers, like games she wasn't yet big enough to play. The great strain meanwhile was that of carrying by the right end the things her father said about her mother—things mostly indeed that Moddle [her nurse], on a glimpse of them, took out of her hands and put away in the closet. A wonderful assortment of objects of this kind she was to discover there, all tumbled up too with the things, shuffled into the same receptacle, that her mother had said about her father (12).

When her father dramatically tells Maisie that there is money in America, her imagination is stimulated: "This affected her at first in the manner of some great flashing dazzle in one of the pantomimes to which Sir Claude had taken her" (192). Maisie delights in Sir Claude, who talks to her "with a smile of which the promise was as bright as that of a Christmas-tree" (57). But it is Mrs. Wix that the child relies on; that homely, good woman is more comforting even than the handsome Miss Overmore, "on whose loveliness, as she supposed it, the little girl was faintly conscious that one couldn't rest with quite the same tucked-in and kissed-for-good-night feeling" (26). Like the bewildered reader himself, poor little Maisie is baffled by the shuffling about of all the grown-ups, and her thoughts on the subject remarkably conclude as follows: "It sounded, as this young lady thought it over, much like puss-in-the-corner, and she could only wonder if the distribution of parties would lead to a rushing to and fro and a changing of places" (95)!

I cannot turn to another subject without a final apt quotation, in which there is much wisdom in a few words: "Doing one's sum to-morrow instead of to-day doesn't make the sum easier, but at least makes to-day so" (VI *TM* I 262). Children seem to know this instinctively.[14]

v. Games

Of the many images concerned with games, frolics, and sports, Christmas figures are the most frequent. Our friend Maisie, and Mrs. Wix and Sir Claude with her, once revel alone, with all others "simply 'left out' like children not invited to a Christmas party" (XI *WMK* 70); followed by his alter ego, Spencer Brydon feels like "Pantaloon, at the Christmas farce, buffeted and tricked from behind by ubiquitous Harlequin" (XVII "JC" 460); and so on.[15]

Most figures deriving from adult games refer vaguely to cards or gamblers; thus, "she gathered herself as if the words she had just spoken were quite her last hand" ("CE" 380), or "the little lighted carriages . . . always suggested the gamblers he had seen of old at Monte Carlo pushing up to the tables" (XXII *Amb* II 230). When James specifies the type of card game, the image is apt to imply disparagement of idle amusements, as when Nick Dormer describes his mother's distrust of art: " 'She has inherited the fine old superstition that art's pardonable only so long as it's bad—so long as it's done at odd hours, for a little distraction, like a game of tennis or of whist' " (VII *TM* I 18). Occasionally cardplayers are ineffectual or their cards dirty. Ralph Touchett fatally "played the wrong card, and now he had lost the game"

14. For imagery deriving from what has been beautifully dubbed "kiddylit" by innumerable School of Education students, see pp. 117-19 above. For a somewhat fuller treatment of the subject of child imagery in James's fiction, see Robert L. Gale, "Henry James's Dream Children," *Arizona Quarterly*, XV (Spring, 1959), 56-63.

15. See XXIII *GB* I 281, xxviii "CCor" 350.

(IV *PofL* II 141); and brilliantly evoked Lionel Croy "dealt out lies as he might the cards from the greasy old pack for the game of diplomacy to which you were to sit down with him" (XIX *WofD* I 7). Occasionally a gambling image charges the fiction with considerable intensity, as in the following: "The stake on the table was of a special substance and our roulette the revolving mind, but we sat round the green board as intently as the grim gamblers at Monte Carlo. Gwendolen Erme, for that matter, with her white face and her fixed eyes, was of the very type of the lean ladies one had met in the temples of chance" (XV "FinC" 250). In that dramatic manner, James describes the trio seeking Vereker's "figure in the carpet." A vivid gambling image from *The Sense of the Past* almost exactly repeats an earlier one from *The Golden Bowl*. First, Maggie feels that her horrible situation is like a game in which one must be polite:

. . . there was a card she could play, but there was only one, and to play it would be to end the game. She felt herself— as at the small square green table between the tall old silver candlesticks and the neatly arranged counter—her father's playmate and partner; and what it constantly came back to in her mind was that for her to ask a question, to raise a doubt, to reflect in any degree on the play of the others, would be to break the charm (XXIV *GB* II 34).

Maggie's play of course would be to brand Charlotte for what she is, which "card" would destroy Adam Verver. Much later Maggie toys again with the same decisive card: "That hideous card she might in mere logic play—being at this time . . . familiar with all the fingered pasteboard in her pack. But she could play it only on the forbidden issue of sacrificing him . . ." (107). As for *The Sense of the Past,* in it Ralph Pendrel is described as using a suave manner even though he suspects that Perry Midmore judges the action to be unfair.

Let us frankly plead . . . that he found himself affected before this passage lapsed as by the suddenest vision of the possibility of his having to appeal from the imputation . . . of cheating, cheating in that sense which his . . . love of the game, exactly, might expose him to suspicion of; this for all the world as if he were seated with the house of Midmore, not to speak of other company too, at a green table and between tall brave candle-sticks which would at a given moment somehow perversely light the exchange of queer glances from partner to partner at his expense (XXVI *SeofP* 159).[16]

Three-fourths of the images concerning specific sports appear in the fiction after 1890. They are usually not *simpatico*. Thus, the narrator of "The Married Son" says of his brother-in-law, "I can't meet Tom—on that ground, the furious football field to which he reduces conversation, making it echo as with the roar of the arena—one little bit" ("MS" 533). Or consider this long lecture by Lady Grace of *The Outcry:* "'Ah, we can't work sports in our gallery and saloon—the banging or whacking and shoving amusements that are all most people care for; unless perhaps . . . your own peculiar one, as I understand you, of playing football with the old benighted traditions and attributions you everywhere meet: in fact I think you said the old idiotic superstitions'" (*Ou* 42). Or this—and here James ineptly describes the delight that the daughters of Beadel-Muffet of "The Papers" might feel if used by their father for publicity purposes—"'How pleasant for them to find themselves hurtling through the air, clubbed by the

16. This image, from Book IV, Chapter 2, appears well beyond the point at which James set aside the work in 1900. So the image was written in the winter of 1914-15 or a little later. It reflects, therefore, an image from *The Golden Bowl* of ten or eleven years before. See Percy Lubbock, "The War (1914-1916)," in *The Letters of Henry James*, 2 vols. (New York: Charles Scribner's Sons, 1920), II, 380. See also *ibid.*, p. 426; and *The Notebooks of Henry James*, ed. F. O. Matthiessen and Kenneth B. Murdock (New York: Oxford University Press, 1947), p. 361.

paternal hand, like golf-balls in a suburb' " (xxviii "Pap" 85).[17]
It may be that the youthful James felt that he could not
criticize sports without being thought jealous of those more
athletic than he, whereas in his older age he could safely
exploit sports for humor. Further—and I think that this contention is borne out by the fact that three-fourths of the children images come after 1890 also—it seems to me that as James
became surer of his powers as a writer he became more will-
ing to use simpler subjects for his tropes. In this respect, the
early James is more sophisticated than the James of the
major phase.

vi. Cups

James has provided and filled figurative cups of considerable variety. Often these vessels are brimming with sweetness, sometimes with bitterness, even with a measure of poison.
They overflow, are made to spill, may be strenuously drained,
sometimes are dashed frustratingly from the mouth.

What does James intend to symbolize in general when he
repeatedly describes characters as holding cups too full for
easy carrying? Does he suggest thus the brimming sensitivity
of his "supersubtle fry," and their concomitant almost neurotic
surface tension and desire not to jar shifting relationships?
Whatever the answer, here are a few examples: " 'You had filled
my cup too full—I couldn't carry it straight' " (*OH* 200); "both
her elders remained as stiff as tall tumblers filled to the brim
and held straight for fear of a spill" (XI *WMK* 208); and
"she was carrying in her weak stiffened hand a glass filled
to the brim, as to which she had recorded a vow that no drop
should overflow. She feared the very breath of a better wis-

17. "And James had never touched a niblick in his life"; Ford Madox
Ford, "The Old Man," in *The Question of Henry James: A Collection
of Critical Essays*, ed. F. W. Dupee (New York: Henry Holt and
Company, 1945), p. 52.

dom, the jostle of a higher light, of heavenly help itself . . ."
(XXIV *GB* II 298).

But jolts inevitably come: "he was so prepared with a
greeting that he instantly smiled, as a shaken jug overflows"
(XII "Li" 321); for example, "it was for Fleda the shake that
made the cup overflow" (X *SpofP* 243), and "the push was
like a jar that made the vessel overflow" ("CE" 387). Sometimes the cup spills over without any violent inducement:
happy in the Luxembourg Gardens, Strether "passed an hour
in which the cup of his impressions seemed truly to overflow"
(XXI *Amb* I 80).[18]

The other cup images are less provocative, and when taken
together do little but reveal a minor Jamesian mannerism.
Thus, Lady Agnes seizes "those possibilities from which she
still might squeeze . . . the drop that would sweeten her cup"
(VIII *TM* II 226); but Sherringham is more realistic and
hence "flattered himself his hand wouldn't falter on the day
he should find it necessary to drop bitterness into his cup"
(VII *TM* I 314). When Charlotte's arrival at Fawns drives
away other predatory women, Fanny feels obliged to explain
things: "'. . . I don't in the least mean that Charlotte was consciously dropping poison into their cup. She was just herself
their poison, in the sense of mortally disagreeing with
them . . .'" (XXIII *GB* I 194). The narrator of an early
story avoids discussing something unpleasant, because "it
was agreeable to drain the cup of horror without assistance"
("GhR" 666). Finally, the wonder of a girl as to whether her
engagement will be broken is phrased in this way: "could it
be his intention to dash from her lips the sweet, the spiced
and odorous cup of being the wife of a good-natured millionaire?" ("SofM" 140).

18. See also XII "TofS" 237, IX *AA* 327, XX *WofD* II 149, XXVI
SeofP 278.

vii. Jewels

Almost never does James combine his interest in cups and love of jewels to give us a jeweled cup image. It would seem that he regarded cups as functional, and their contents the important thing about them, and further that he looked upon jewels as lushly decorative and not in any utilitarian sense useful. But we do have one highly romantic exception, describing the traveler's progress in the early story "At Isella": "It seemed to me when I reached the Hospice [near the Furca Pass] that I had been winding for hours along the inner hollow of some mighty cup of verdure toward a rim of chiselled silver crowned with topaz" ("AtI" 244).

More than half the numerous jewel figures name specific precious stones, or pearls. Pearls often inspire James to imagery and are mentioned twice as often as diamonds; these two precede a glittering display of sapphires and onyxes, among smaller numbers of other gems. Pearls seem clearly to be lovelier in James's eyes than diamonds, for he uses pearls —as he does not diamonds—in descriptions of artistic work. For example, he twice compares to pearls the elements comprising the precious figure hidden in the carpet of Vereker's writing. The puzzling author approves of the narrator's rug image but then suggests that the hidden figure is " 'the very string . . . that my pearls are strung on!' " (XV "FinC" 241). And later the narrator speaks of " 'the general intention of his [Vereker's] books: the string the pearls were strung on, the buried treasure, the figure in the carpet' " (274). The narrator of "Travelling Companions" describes the chapel of Giotto in Padua as "a mere empty shell, but coated as with the priceless substance of fine pearls and vocal with a murmured eloquence as from the infinite of art" ("TC" 690). Ralph Pendrel, seeking the right attitude, "plunged deeper rather than shook himself free—dived to pick up . . . just the right pearl of cheer . . . [which,] held up between his fingers, threw out its light . . . after the manner of pearls" (XXVI *SeofP* 211-12).[19] Also, being deprived of the dead Milly's letter is to Densher "like the sight of a priceless pearl cast before his eyes . . . into the fathomless sea" (XX *WofD* II 396).[20]

The rhetorical rays of diamond images never probe to any great depth. Thus, Hyacinth's idealism is suggested: ". . . he wanted neither more nor less than to get hold of the truth and wear it in his heart. He believed with the candour of youth that it is brilliant and clear-cut, like a royal diamond . . ." (VI *PC* II 264). James does not much admire hardness in his characters, but when Maggie is obliged to become firm and fine, he praises her resolution in these terms: "hard at this time . . . as a little pointed diamond, the Princess showed something of the glitter of consciously possessing the constructive, the creative hand" (XXIV *GB* II 145).

An endlessly varied type of image makes human eyes resemble gems. They are like "imitation jewels" (XVI "GF" 128), "choice samples of the more or less precious stones called aquamarine" (XXV *IT* 157), "polished agate" (I *RH* 386), and onyx.[21] More extravagantly, a rich old man is said to have eyes "circled with red, but in the battered little setting of their orbits they have the lustre of old sapphires" (xxv "LiM" 217); and when the narrator of "Glasses" learns that young Miss Saunt's lustrous eyes are going blind, "I felt [we read] as if a great rare sapphire had split in my hand" (xxvii "Gl" 196).

Aggressive and flashily dressed women regularly draw James's fire. Maisie's begemmed mother gives the poor little girl a maudlin clasp to her glittering breast, "where, amid a

19. Eugene Pickering and Fleda Vetch are other pearl-divers; see xxiv "EP" 255, X *SpofP* 66.

20. Is there here a suggestion that Densher feels that he has behaved like a swine?

21. XVIII "Ma" 261; XIX *WofD* I 266, 271.

wilderness of trinkets, she felt as if she had suddenly been thrust, with a smash of glass, into a jeweller's shop-front" (XI *WMK* 145). One man's too rapidly acquired second wife strikes a critical narrator as having a "face that shone as publicly as the jeweller's window" (XVII "AofD" 8).

But James surpasses himself in fictive gemmary when he describes the imaginary last liaison between the Prince and Charlotte, the memory of which "might be carried away into exile like the last saved object of price of the *émigré*, the jewel wrapped in a piece of old silk and negotiable some day in the market of misery" (XXIV *GB* II 330).[22]

viii. Court Life

From jewels often fit for crowns to court life is but a single step. James projected himself and his characters with obvious relish into figurative participation in colorful regal scenes—feudal, medieval, Renaissance, exotic. The resulting abundance of court-life imagery may provide us a clue as to the personality of James—he is said to have looked princely, ducal, orientally regal[23]—but it is hard to generalize concerning the functions of such figures in terms of James and his themes. This is so because the four works containing the highest percentage of such images—"Glasses," *Watch and Ward, The Wings of the Dove,* and *The Golden Bowl*—are as replete as they are for totally different reasons. Flora Saunt is a reigning beauty, holding court for her brief hour to slavish admirers. *Watch and Ward* is full of the youthful spirit of faraway romanticism. Milly Theale is persistently

22. This image again shows James's sympathy with the aristocrats of the French Revolution; see pp. 91-93 above.

23. See *The Legend of the Master,* compiled by Simon Nowell-Smith (New York: Charles Scribner's Sons, 1948), pp. 1-2, 7; and "Note on the Cover to This Edition," *The Notebooks of Henry James,* ed. F. O. Matthiessen and Kenneth B. Murdock, A Galaxy Book (New York: Oxford University Press, 1961), opp. p. [i].

envisaged as a princess, aloof and yet responsible—as the best and most mature princesses have been. And *The Golden Bowl* is divided into two volumes, entitled "The Prince" and "The Princess" after the two leading characters.

Flora is twice imaged as holding "her little court" (xxvii "GI" 193) and "her regular court" (198). Geoffrey Dawling, initially far from her real presence, is first smitten romantically because of the narrator's painting of the girl. "He was the young prince in the legend or the comedy who loses his heart to the miniature of the outland princess" (203). The pattern gives way to images of other sorts; then, during the last scene, which occurs at the opera, the narrator sees the beautifully appointed but now blind girl and wonders, "if she had become a person of such fashion, where was the little court one would naturally see at her elbow?" (246).

The adolescent mind of Nora is responsible for most of the prince and princess imagery in *Watch and Ward*. To her, even the ordinary parson Hubert " 'looks like the Prince Avenant' " (xxiv *WandW* 30) from her *Child's Own Book*, while she is " 'a princess in a fairy-tale' " (44). When she is more mature and can travel, she buys a painting from a poor artist, feeling as she does so " 'like some patronising duchess of the Renaissance' " (110). At one point, Lawrence while delirious sees Nora as "a Scheherazade, a Badoura" whose tresses "take on the likeness of a queenly crown" (143). Even the rascally Fenton tells her, " 'I want to treat you, by Jove, as I would treat a queen' " (167), and at one time he ineffectually compares her to " 'a princess on trial for treason' " (174).

The Wings of the Dove has more than a score of images concerning court life. Milly Theale, whose hair is a "crown of old gold" (XIX *WofD* I 109) and whose traveling is once said to resemble "the Empress Catherine's famous progress across the steppes of Russia" (XX *WofD* II 136), is envisaged as a princess in more than a dozen images. Susan sees Milly as "the princess in a conventional tragedy" and herself as "the confidant" (XIX *WofD* I 120), whose "Service was . . . so easy to render that the whole thing was like court life without the hardships" (121). She watches Milly perch on an Alpine ledge "looking down on the kingdoms of the earth" (124) but soon senses that there will be no suicide, because "the future wasn't to exist for her princess in the form of any sharp or simple release from the human predicament" (125).[24] Kate Croy is contrasted to the regal Milly: "what could be more in harmony now than to see the princess waited upon at the city gate by the worthiest maiden, the chosen daughter of the burgesses?" (171). Kate soon regards Milly as "quite the nearest approach to a practical princess Bayswater could hope ever to know" (174). Later, after Milly is imaged as a dove, she remains a royal figure as well: "though a dove who could perch on a finger, one [was] also a princess with whom forms were to be observed" (283). As the colors deepen for the approaching tragedy, Milly becomes in a celebrated figure "the angular pale princess, ostrich-plumed, black-robed, hung about with amulets, reminders, relics," while Kate becomes "the upright restless slow-circling lady of her court who exchanges with her, across the black water streaked with evening gleams, fitful questions and answers" (XX *WofD* II 139). Mrs. Stringham tries to bring Densher into the sprawling metaphor, first by attempting to place him in the glowing Veronese picture of Milly's Venetian palace,[25] then by telling him that Milly's is " 'such a court as never was: one of the

24. This image is the starting point for Jean Kimball's illuminating reading of Milly's problem and her solution to it, in "The Abyss and The Wings of the Dove: The Image as a Revelation," *Nineteenth-Century Fiction*, X (March, 1956), 281-300.

25. Quoted in part p. 123 above; " 'Besides, you're in the picture' " (XX *WofD* II 207), Mrs. Stringham tells Densher.

courts of heaven, the court of a reigning seraph, a sort of a vice-queen of an angel'" (211).

As Francis Fergusson writes, "The beginning of *The Golden Bowl* prepares the very wide stage: Empire, with connotations of rule and loot, is the key word. We feel *la cour, Rome, l'empire*, as in *Bérénice*, and also a more vast and jumbled empire as in *Antony and Cleopatra*."[26] Contributing to this sense are more than twenty images concerning court persons, most of which owe their origin to the actual rank as Prince of Maggie's husband Amerigo. In an early, page-long figure, he is said to resemble "a prince in very truth, a ruler, warrior, patron, lighting up brave architecture and diffusing the sense of a function" (XXIII *GB* I 42). The child of Amerigo and Maggie is "like an infant positively royal" (XXIV *GB* II 24), whose nurse, "in the absence of the queen-mother, was regent of the realm and governess of the heir" (XXIII *GB* I 202). In their ostensible devotion to these "young sovereigns," the Assinghams are "a pair of faithfully-serving subjects" (XXIV *GB* II 149). Adam Verver is regal too: the vantage point of his gigantic financial success "was a platform looking down . . . on the kingdoms of the earth" (XXIII *GB* I 131); yet he is so quiet that he represents force only "as an infant king is the representative of a dynasty" (324). The aroused, suspicious Maggie disconcerts Charlotte, who wisely bears in mind that "though the lady-in-waiting was an established favourite, a little queen, however good-natured, was always a little queen and might with small warning remember it" (XXIV *GB* II 38). Maggie is only too pleased at the end, however, to let Charlotte pretend to be the regal one, and when she and Adam are expected for their farewell call at Portland Place, the Prince and his wife are imaged "as awaiting the visit of Royalty" (354).

26. Francis Fergusson, "The Drama in *The Golden Bowl*," *Hound and Horn*, VII (April-May, 1934), 409.

ix. Astronomical Bodies

A final minor category of figures concerns the sun, moon, planets, stars, and other common astronomical objects, which cluster—if at all—only as rhetorical ornaments, never into imagistic constellations. They hint at no scientific knowledge in their author; no stars or even planets are named, and no lore pertaining to binaries or nebulae, for example, emerges. The comparisons are usually simple, not elaborated.

Stransom sees the candles on his altar as a configuration of stars. "Of course there were gaps in the constellation" (XVII "AofD" 19), he admits. Later, recalling the death of one remembered woman, he thinks that "It was only yesterday that Kate Creston had flashed out her white fire; yet already there were younger stars ablaze on the tips of the tapers" (18), because with each new death he adds "a new star" (29).

Blanche Adney tells how Lord Mellifont, once totally absent from the scene, "'rose before me like the rising sun'" (XVII "PL" 235) at her sudden return. On the other hand, Dencombe of "The Middle Years" when near death has "a smile as cold as a winter sunset . . . on his drawn lips" (XVI "MY" 103-4). Also, another dying man is described as anxious to give away his financial influence: "It's not a bestowal, with him, but a transfer, and half his pleasure in causing his sun to shine is that—being woefully near its setting—it will produce certain long fantastic shadows" (xxv "LiM" 235). The image is a little awkward because it is difficult to translate "sun" to the literal: the shining sun has to do with the man's wealth, but the setting sun clearly refers to the approaching close of his life.

A few moon images interestingly concern the dark portion of the disk when it is only indirectly lighted. For example, a splendid conception describes the hopes of Lawrence, the watcher, with respect to his immature ward Nora, not yet grown into full and radiant maturity: he thinks that other women "shone with a radiance less magical than that dim but rounded shape which glimmered for ever in the dark future, like the luminous complement of the early moon" (xxiv *WandW* 36-37). Lawrence briefly falls in love with a Peruvian beauty, and we read that "It was at Lima that poor little potential Nora suffered temporary eclipse" (37).[27] Benvolio is a kind of split personality, and there is "something grave and discreet in his smile—something vague and ghostly, like the dim adumbration of the darker half of the lunar disk" (xxiv "Be" 305). Something—inexperience, egotism, love, the deceit of others—at first obscures from Isabel Archer's sight the true character of her husband Gilbert: "she had seen only half his nature then, as one saw the disk of the moon when it was partly masked by the shadow of the earth. She saw the full moon now—she saw the whole man" (IV *PofL* II 191).[28] James's whole technique of indirect and sometimes deliberately imperfect revelation is analogous to the astronomical phenomenon known as "earth-shine."

Without exception planet images in James are dull. Strange places are like other planets, and queer people are like creatures from those other planets.[29] Comets are simply phenomena deserving of one's best stare. For example, "The idea . . . now loomed large. She threw back her head a little; she stared at it as if it had been a comet in the sky" (IV *PofL* II 433); "he dangled, more than once, . . . at the tail of the human comet" (XVII "Bi" 143); and "her existence was made manifest through her long train of good deeds,—just as the presence of a comet is shown by its tail" ("SofY" 273).

27. The word "eclipse," a rather popular one in James, is not figurative unless elaborated.

28. This is an eclipse not an earth-shine figure; see also iii *Eurs* 158.

29. See "GdeB" 56, XIII "PP" 388, XIII "MofF" 455-56, XXIII *GB* I 25.

Conclusion

So much for the most important minor categories of Jamesian metaphors and similes. Fire figures suggest the crescendo and the diminuendo of passion, the leaping up of intellectual illumination, the flickering of memory, and the oxidation of things warm and alive to cold ashes. Metal imagery is used to praise strength but also to deplore inflexibility and repellency; to suggest the objects of searchers for the rare but also the curse of those possessing it. Varied sensation images conduct a grand dialogue, pleasant ones opposing unpleasant. And so with children tropes: many figurative infants shriek with laughter, but others are in unspeakable pain. Similes concerning games and sports reveal a sedentary, observant author often critical of the idly amused and the noisily strenuous. Cup figures cater to James's love of the ambivalent: beneath the speciously calm surface of the mysterious fluid in the ornate vessel, is there sweetness or swift poison? Pearls too help express his awareness of ambivalences and deceptive appearances in life; they seem to be softer hued, more palpable and perhaps more subtly iridescent, and more illuminating of the evolution of beauty and art out of irritating life, than pure, simple, hard, mathematically neat diamonds—which perennial bachelor James may often have unconsciously shied away from mentioning in his fiction! Court-life imagery is pervasive throughout James's fiction, used notably to suggest the lushness of youthful romantic imaginations, the beauty and sovereignty of some women, and the accursed splendors of great wealth and power. Astronomical tropes are disappointing in James, who may reveal in them a commendable enough literary bent but almost no scientific or mathematical acumen.

Taken together, the nine most significant minor categories of imagery in James contribute abundant evidence attesting to the daring of his imagination and his unwillingness to leave plain and unenriched any strand of the glowing carpet of his fiction. A more exhaustive examination of its warp and woof might turn up figures concerned with colors, death, deserts, diseases, food, handwriting, heights, letter-writing, mechanical devices, mirrors, pickpockets, photographs, schools, sewing, weather, and weddings. And of course other analyses would treat other allusions still.

IX · THE MYSTIC SCROLL

I did laugh, I'm sure, as I remembered this to be the mystic scroll I had scarcely allowed poor Mr. Morrow to point his umbrella at (XV "DofL" 149-50).

Introduction

Since all writing reveals something of the writer, if only of his world, every group of images examined thus far has contributed to a fuller understanding not only of the individual works and of James's fiction as a body, but of James's personality as well. We have incidentally learned already that James was a seasoned traveler, a lover of gardens, and a devoted student of literature, painting, and the drama. Further, we have seen that he was surely no soldier or athlete, and that he did not respond to music with much passion. And we have noted his delight in children, his sensitivity to various sensations, and his wonderfully warm and sympathetic response to women. Much of all this we can obviously verify by reference to James's autobiography and his letters, and by recourse to contemporary accounts of his striking personality. Still, the imagery is a source of new light—not oddly angled, to be sure—on an old and familiar portrait. To illuminate that picture a little further, we ought to consider those groups of figures significant less because they are parts of categories or patterns than because they highlight James the man, and occasionally do very little else.

i. America

James appears to have had two purposes in writing his many figures of speech which make comparisons to things American: to criticize some of the gaudier elements of the American tradition and the American personality, and to poke often witty fun at frequently misunderstanding Europeans. Fully as important, these images reveal their author to be warmly American, but also sometimes too anxious to make humor at the expense of his native land.[1] *The American* and *The Portrait of a Lady* contain figures which clearly show the dual purpose of James's American imagery and also his fundamental loyalty to the land of his birth. When Mrs. Tristram calls Newman " 'the great Western barbarian,' " he objects; whereupon she adds, " 'I don't mean you're a Comanche chief or that you wear a blanket and feathers. There are different shades' " (II *Ame* 45). Isabel is similarly satirical when she tells Warburton, " 'It's a pity you can't see me in my war-paint and feathers' " and " 'if I had known how kind you are to the poor savages I would have brought over

1. James responded jingoistically, however, when foreigners ridiculed the United States; see Oscar Cargill, *The Novels of Henry James* (New York: The Macmillan Company, 1961), p. 45 and p. 56, n.15 and n.16.

my native costume!'" (III *PofL* I 96). Newman as a youth in San Francisco is ludicrously described: "If he did not, like Dr. Franklin in Philadelphia, march along the street munching a penny loaf it was only because he had not the penny loaf necessary to the performance" (II *Ame* 27). To Newman, who urges him to drop Noémie, Valentin says, "'Don't brandish your tomahawk at that rate'" (237). And the rugged American once criticizes something as "'worse than a free fight in Arkansaw'" (476); more sensitively, he thinks that "Madame de Cintré's face had . . . a range of expression as delightfully vast as the wind-streaked, cloud-flecked distance on a Western prairie" (183). This prairie image, coming in the original 1877 edition of *The American*,[2] like some of Cooper's effects was not based upon first-hand observation, since James did not tour the American West until 1905. Other wild-west images are also only imagined, and often not accurately so either. For example, "She herself could but . . . remind herself really of people she had read about in stories of the wild west who threw up their hands on certain occasions for a sign they weren't carrying revolvers" (XXIV *GB* II 310-11).[3] Somewhat more accurately, James twice compares predatory women to Indians whose belts display "the scalps of . . . enemies" (xxiv *WandW* 8).[4]

In and out of imagery, James was concerned with the implications of the American skyscraper. John Wheelwright has

2. Henry James, *The American* (New York and Toronto: Rinehart & Co., Inc., 1949), p. 127. A similar image from "Fordham Castle" also appeared before James's Western tours; see XVI "FC" 408 and the identical original text in *Harper's Monthly Magazine,* CX (December, 1904), 152. See Charles R. Anderson, "Henry James's Fable of Charleston," *South Atlantic Quarterly,* LIV (April, 1955), 249-57, for criticism of similar fictional treatment of aspects of America James had not personally observed.

3. In this age of television, we all know that hands are put into the air to place them out of the reach of slung or pocketed weapons.

4. See also xxvii "GI" 207; for a foolish image concerning cannibalistic American Indians, see XXVI *SeofP* 169.

said that James "was not buffaloed by the skyscraper before which Pennell the etcher and the members of the architectural profession were preparing to fall down in worship. He anticipated [in *The American Scene*] the criticisms of the skyscrapers which architects have come to, though they dismiss with professional philistinism the opinion of literary critics."[5] Thus, Prince Amerigo in James's 1904 *The Golden Bowl* compares his inefficient old moral sense with one that might exist in Fanny Assingham's modern world: "'. . . it's no more like yours than the tortuous stone staircase—half-ruined into the bargain!—in some castle of our *quattrocento* is like the "lightning elevator" in one of Mr. Verver's fifteen-storey buildings'" (XXIII *GB* I 31). Only a few years later, significantly after his 1905 American tour, James's imagistic buildings are much taller, for in the 1909 "Crapy Cornelia" White-Mason suggests that the past is "'so different from any of *these* arrangements of pretended hourly Time that dash themselves forever to pieces as from the fiftieth floors of skyscrapers'" (xxviii "CCor" 349).

James indulged in a good deal of humorous imagery deriving from things American. Thus, when he describes a pair of former social pariahs now tolerated as oddities in England, he writes that "They were engaged for a fixed hour, like the American imitator and the Patagonian contralto" (X "Ch" 497). Further, the unique patois which the Moreen family speaks in "The Pupil" contains "tough cold slices of American" (XI "Pu" 520). When Maggie feels socially without tradition compared to the ensconced Prince, we read that she finds herself "in the fashion of a settler or a trader in a new country; in the likeness even of some Indian squaw with a

5. John Wheelwright, "Henry James and Stanford White," *Hound and Horn*, VII (April-May, 1934), 481. See also Joseph Pennell, *The Adventures of an Illustrator: Mostly in Following His Authors in America & Europe* (Boston: Little, Brown, and Company, 1925), p. 264, for the report of a comment by James on skyscrapers.

papoose on her back and barbarous bead-work to sell" (XXIV *GB* II 323-24). More simply, James once wrote that something uninspired "was like singing . . . to a Boston audience" (XVII "Bi" 199).[6] It seems unfortunate that the few images deriving from American fiction[7] could not have been augmented by other favorable tropes which might, for example, have drawn upon American history and scenery, American pioneering, and even the best in the American industrial spirit.[8]

ii. Money

The abundance of imagery concerning money, investments, and general wealth corroborates what we already know—that James enjoyed his income and only wished that it were greater.[9] Stephen Spender has forcefully argued that "the fascination of gold in his [James's] books is that it is at once the symbol of release from the more servile processes of the world in which we live, and also supremely the symbol of the damned";[10] however, the ambivalence of James's obsession is not, I think, evident in the money imagery.

6. See also II *Ame* 41, VIII *TM* II 193, X "LL" 342, XIII "MdeM" 277, XIII "Bi" 193, XVIII "Pan" 132, XXI *Amb* I 267, XXV *IT* 209, xxv "NEW" 53, xxvi "So" 313, "CE" 332.

7. See pp. 107-8, 110 above.

8. I feel that many of James's highly conscious images deriving from America tend to counter much of Marianne Moore's impressionistic portrait of James as characteristically American; see "Henry James as a Characteristic American," *Hound and Horn,* VII (April-May, 1934), 363-72.

9. See Edwin T. Bowden, "Henry James and the Struggle for International Copyright: An Unnoticed Item in the James Bibliography," *American Literature,* XXIV (January, 1953), 537-39; Bowden, "Henry James and the International Copyright Again," *American Literature,* XXV (January, 1954), 409-500; and Alfred R. Ferguson, "The Triple Quest of Henry James: Fame, Art, and Fortune," *American Literature,* XXVII (January, 1956), 475-98.

10. Stephen Spender, *The Destructive Element: A Study of Modern Writers and Beliefs* (London: Jonathan Cape, 1935), p. 60; see also p. 62. See my discussion of gold and gem imagery above, pp. 171-73, 188-90. See also Bradford A. Booth, "Henry James and the Economic Motif," *Nineteenth-Century Fiction,* VIII (September, 1953), 141-50.

Money held safely at several removes from the workaday world of commerce was not unpleasant to James. Thus, Newman likes to hear civilities "so syllabled and articulated that they suggested handfuls of crisp counted notes pushed over by a banker's clerk" (II *Ame* 323); and of young Brookenham in *The Awkward Age* an observer says, " 'Here's Harold, precisely . . . as clear and crisp and undefiled as a fresh five-pound note' " (IX *AA* 391). Figurative coins ring hygienically through the fiction to the very end: in 1909 one woman's "house . . . had . . . that glare of a piece fresh from the mint and ringing for the first time on any counter" (xxviii "CCor" 326-27), while a woman in a 1910 story "brought out and caused to ring . . . the heaviest gold-piece of current history she was to pay him with for having just so felicitously come back" (xxviii "RofV" 379).[11]

Counterfeit coins inspire an intriguing little hoard of images. Colonel Capadose's lies are inevitably "his false coinage," which his wife appears to be dangerously taking "at his own valuation" (XII "Li" 346). When someone tries a reproof on him, "Harold [Brookenham] turned this over as if it were a questionable sovereign" (IX *AA* 161). Charlotte assumes the task of entertaining for Verver and for Maggie both, knowing that there will be "arid social sands, the bad quarters of an hour, that turned up like false pieces in a debased currency, of which she made . . . very nearly as light as if she hadn't been clever enough to distinguish" (XXIII *GB* I 317). And Perry stares at Pendrel's manner "as if it were a counterfeit coin or a card from up his sleeve" (XXVI *SeofP* 159). One might expect *The Ivory Tower*, which is—as Newton Arvin has pointed out—"a directer grappling than James elsewhere attempted with the theme of money-making, of ac-

11. See also XV "DofL" 107, XV "CF" 305, XIX *WofD* I 295-96, XXI *Amb* I 112, XXIII *GB* I 333.

quisition on a vast piratical scale,"[12] to contain many money images, but there are only a few and they are simple.[13]

The large proportion of shaky and failing stock in the imagery perhaps reveals a concern in James as to the purchasing power of his fixed and unearned patrimonial income; in addition, it probably represents an unconsciously critical comment on the capitalistic system itself which had nurtured the young son and brother so comfortingly. Only a few figures are based on blithe faith in the market; more than a proper quota hint at a fear of crashes. The images having to do with successful investments are humdrum: "she had on hand a small capital of sentimental patronage for which she desired a secure investment" (xxiv *WandW* 86); of Kate Croy's presence, her tough aunt says, " 'I've been saving it up and letting it, as you say of investments, appreciate' " (XIX *WofD* I 82); and the Misses Frush of "The Third Person" regard the ghost that comes with their inherited house as "an indescribable unearned increment" (xxvii "TP" 424). But to counterbalance these few images of fortunate securities, there are several like the following pair: "he might have been speaking of 'shaky' shares" (VI *PC* II 338); and secrets are "things as depressing and detestable as inferior securities" (II *Ame* 244), thinks stock-expert Christopher Newman.

Like many of his characters, James in his imagery looks down his nose at the busy, noisy, often unpleasant world of commerce. Often it is the characters themselves, for example, the Bellegardes, who eschew contact with the commercial— such as rich Newman, who is imaged as soiled and tainted by hard work in the oppressive atmosphere of business. However, enough other similar imagery exists to suggest an authorial prejudice. Thus, we read of a well-furnished house

12. Newton Arvin, "Henry James and the Almighty Dollar," *Hound and Horn*, VII (April-May, 1934), 442.

13. See XXV *IT* 23, 47, 239 for the best of the mediocre lot.

that "Everything on every side had dropped straight from heaven, with nowhere a bargaining thumb-mark, a single sign of the shop" (IX *AA* 349); that " 'She's as common as a dressmaker's bill' " (XIII *Re* 78); and of Morgan Moreen's father and brother that "They were good-natured, yes—as good-natured as Jews at the doors of clothing-shops. But was that the model one wanted one's family to follow?" (XI "Pu" 554).[14]

Dealings which are actually or supposedly sordid often suggest money metaphors. Thus, Adam Verver feels guilty of showing off when he takes Charlotte along to see Mr. Gutermann-Seuss's Damascene tiles, because, after all, "a man of decent feeling didn't thrust his money, a huge lump of it, in such a way, under a poor girl's nose" (XXIII *GB* I 217). And when Densher muses on Kate's visit to his rooms—in fulfillment of a decidedly commercial bargain—he feels engaged anew to fidelity: "The force of the engagement, the quantity of the article to be supplied, the special solidity of the contract, the way, above all, as a service for which the price named by him had been magnificently paid, his equivalent office was to take effect—such items might well fill his consciousness where there was nothing from outside to interfere" (XX *WofD* II 237).[15]

iii. Travel

It is not surprising that the author of six books of travel should have scattered through his fiction many figurative ref-

14. James's mild anti-Semitism is pervasive and is worth some study. See, for a good deal of evidence, "Ad" 181; XIII *Re* 27, 28; X *SpofP* 13; IX *AA* 70; XI *WMK* 91; XI "InC" 487; XXI *Amb* I 199, 230; XXIII *GB* I 18, 34, 359; XXIV *GB* II 223, 256.

15. I feel that James's rather consistent anti-commerce imagery invalidates much of Bradford A. Booth's "Henry James and the Economic Motif." Of course in James's fiction there is often a scramble for money, but it is usually for capital accrued through the offending labor of others. Hyacinth Robinson of *The Princess Casamassima*, the clerk of "In the Cage," and Herbert Dodd of "The Bench of Desolation" are exceptionally hard workers in James.

erences to foreign scenes and also to the responsibilities and pleasures of the confirmed tourist.

Through his imagery James shows his awareness of problems attendant upon rail travel. One character "relapsed . . . into silence very much as he would have laid down, on consulting it by mistake, . . . some superseded time-table" (II *Ame* 250). Another "rose in the doorway with the manner of a person used to arriving on thresholds very much as people arrive at stations—with the expectation of being 'met'" (IX *AA* 47). Still another "was as content to say nothing as if . . . she had been keeping her mouth shut in a railway-tunnel" (X *SpofP* 26). And during his famous lament, Strether says, " 'And it's as if the train had fairly waited at the station for me without my having had the gumption to know it was there. Now I hear its faint receding whistle miles and miles down the line'" (XXI *Amb* I 217).[16]

Images so often reflect details of travel and sight-seeing that they reveal James as an habitual traveler. Thus, "he felt as if to settle down to an unread author were very like starting on a journey,—a case for farewells, packing trunks, and buying tickets" (xxiv *WandW* 46-47);[17] "Father . . . has after all a sharp nerve or two in him, like a razor gone astray in a valise of thick Jäger underclothing" ("MS" 533); and "he felt himself a cicerone showing a church to a party of provincials" (VII *TM* I 354).[18]

In the aggregate, places named in the imagery tell more of James than of his characters. He can make convincing little figures of Clapham Junction, the Rhine, an Alpine sun-

16. See also xxviii "MM" 292, xxvii "WofT" 101, VIII *TM* II 246, XVII "PL" 243.

17. Note that in this image, in which the traveler says farewell to casual friends before packing, James implies that his friends—as the decades advanced there were fewer and fewer relatives—did not see him off at the station or the pier.

18. See also II *Ame* 17, 136; I *RH* 434; "CE" 390.

rise, Scotch moors, the Villa Borghese.[19] On the other hand, his faraway images are simple and general: "'Her charming manner is . . . the wall of China'" (VII *TM* I 370); "'Florence seems to me a very easy Siberia'" (XIII "MofF" 442);[20] and the like.

iv. Wine

The figures of speech suggest that James preferred wine to other drinks.[21] Admittedly, some of the wine usages are poetic and general, as in the following: "the wine of life flowed less free" (XI "InC" 486), and "'Ours was everything a relation could be, filled to the brim with the wine of consciousness'" (XXIV *GB* II 329). But other images show closer experience: "'. . . at the bottom—down at the bottom in a little place as small as the end of a wine-funnel—I agree with you!'" (II *Ame* 394); "'I am filled with this feverish

19. III *PofL* I 421, VIII *TM* II 187, IX *AA* 168, XI "InC" 428, xxv "DofD" 196.

20. Although James saw intimately and learned to love London, Geneva, and especially Venice and Florence and Rome (see Robert L. Gale, "Henry James and Italy," *Nineteenth-Century Fiction*, XIV [September, 1959], 160), it was inspiring Paris which was the tenor of the most resplendent imagery relevant here. Strether learns to listen to "the tick of the great Paris clock" (XXI *Amb* I 79) and to appreciate the glowing city as it hangs "before . . . , the vast bright Babylon, like some huge iridescent object, a jewel brilliant and hard" (89). See also xxviii "VG" 231. Elsewhere, Paris is personified: Nick Dormer learns to appreciate "every fine feature of that prodigious face [of Paris]" (VII *TM* I 88). But others do not like its grimace (see VII *TM* I 165, XIII "MdeM" 320, XIV "PofV" 596). Perhaps, commercial bazaar as it is (see II *Ame* 356, VII *TM* I 100), inevitably "'Paris eats your head off'" (XI *WMK* 233).

21. In his notebooks, James records his delight in the companionship of Herbert Pratt, who was with him in Venice during the spring of 1880: "I remember one evening when he took me to a queer little wine-shop, haunted only by gondoliers and *facchini*, in an out of the way corner of Venice. We had some excellent muscat wine . . ."; *The Notebooks of Henry James*, ed. F. O. Matthiessen and Kenneth B. Murdock (New York: Oxford University Press, 1947), p. 31. See also *Henry James and Robert Louis Stevenson: A Record of Friendship and Criticism*, ed. Janet Adam Smith (London: Rupert Hart-Davis, 1948), p. 226.

sense of liberation; it keeps rising to my head like the fumes of strong wine'" (xxiv "EP" 254); and—best of all—aged Abel Gaw of *The Ivory Tower* has a pallor which "suggested at this end of time an empty glass that had yet held for years so much strong wine that a faint golden tinge still lingered on from it" (XXV *IT* 12).

Non-vinous drink imagery is unattractive or vague. Thus, effete Osmond comes to feel that having something to show for his abilities is "like the swallowing of mugs of beer to advertise what one could 'stand'" (IV *PofL* II 12). Further, a buyer tells a young man that his art theory "'began to work in you, sir, like a very strong drink!'" (*Ou* 81). Finally, in the absence of the Princess Casamassima, Hyacinth finds that "his thoughts rattled like the broken ice of a drink he had once wistfully seen mixed at an 'American Bar' . . ." (VI *PC* II 395).

v. Circuses

James like Huck Finn happily never became too sophisticated to confess—albeit often only in imagery—his undying love of circuses. Still, in his fiction it is only the lowbrows who literally go, at least in Paris.[22] But many noisy and glittering images derive from circuses, carnivals, side-shows, and other sub-literary theatricals.

The circus image may be short, as when little Maisie compares her father's new brown lady to "a dreadful human monkey in a spangled petticoat" (XI *WMK* 193). On the other hand, it may be immense, as is this one which pictures Maggie becoming an adept society entertainer under Fanny's tutelage:

Fanny Assingham might really have been there at all events, like one of the assistants in the ring at the circus, to keep up

22. See XIII *Re* 45-50, 171; XXII *Amb* II 133, for two charming examples.

the pace of the sleek revolving animal on whose back the lady in short spangled skirts should brilliantly caper and posture. That was all, doubtless: Maggie had forgotten, had neglected, had declined, to be the little Princess on anything like the scale open to her; but now that the collective hand had been held out to her with such alacrity, so that she might skip up into the light even, as seemed to her modest little mind, with such a show of pink stocking and such an abbreviation of white petticoat, she could strike herself as perceiving, under arched eyebrows, where her mistake had been (XXIV *GB* II 71).

Often, as in the case of *The Golden Bowl*, small patterns of circus imagery emerge.[23] Thus, Maggie regards the manner in which she and her friends live as a kind of public show; from their privacy, "a great overarched and overglazed rotunda where gaiety might reign," are "doors . . . which opened into sinister circular passages" (288); only one of these doors "connected . . . with the outer world, and, encouraging thus the irruption of society, imitated the aperture through which the bedizened performers of the circus are poured into the ring" (289). Later Maggie is again likened to a circus artist, this time "the overworked little trapezist girl—the acrobatic support presumably of embarrassed and exacting parents" (302). Subordinate performers in this circus include the linguistically adept Charlotte, who "juggled [with tongues] as a conjuror at a show juggled with balls or hoops or lighted brands" (XXIII *GB* I 54), and also helpful Fanny, whose uninvolved husband watches her attempt to seek motives in others "very much as he had sometimes watched at the Aquarium the celebrated lady who, in a slight, though tight, bathing-suit, turned somersaults and did tricks in the tank

23. Austin Warren rightly isolates the circus pattern as a significant one in this novel; "Myth and Dialectic in the Later Novels," *Kenyon Review,* V (Autumn, 1943), 561.

of water which looked so cold and uncomfortable to the non-amphibious" (65).[24]

As a rule, however, the circus images do not group into patterns but are instead simple and isolated. The uncomplicated little comparison is usually stated and then dropped: "'She looks as if she belonged to a circus troupe'" (xxiv *WandW* 15); and "'Don't you remember how she turned up that day like the clown in the ring?'" (XII "Li" 384). Only slightly more developed are several images which makes mature women grotesquely resemble dazzling ladies in tights. Mrs. Brookenham of *The Awkward Age* so pictures herself: "'I often feel as if I were a circus-woman, in pink tights and no particular skirts, riding half a dozen horses at once'" (IX *AA* 188). And Mrs. Beever senses that her son so images her, after she has been lecturing him on his chances in love: "She paused a moment; she felt, before her son's mild gape, like a trapezist in pink tights" (*OH* 96).

vi. Toothaches and Dentists

The sizable group of figures concerning toothaches and visits to dental parlors undoubtedly has its root in James's own unpleasant personal experience.[25] When Owen Gereth suddenly experiences unhappiness, he "might have been a fine young man with a bad toothache, with the first even of his life" (X *SpofP* 86). Forced to his knees, poor Guest groans "like a man with a violent toothache" ("GuC" 397). When sick Milly emerges from the illustrious physician's office, we read that Kate, who has been waiting, "rose for her with such a face of sympathy as might have graced the vestibule of a dentist. 'Is it out?' she seemed to ask as if it had been a ques-

24. Several of these images reinforce James's related metaphor of high society as life in a goldfish bowl; see p. 33 above.

25. In "A Small Boy and Others" James speaks of various joyful "holidays on which we weren't dragged to the dentist's"; *Autobiography*, ed. Frederick W. Dupee (New York: Criterion Books, 1956), p. 89.

tion of a tooth" (XIX *WofD* I 232). Adam Verver's Parisian hotel court is likened to "some critical apartment of large capacity, some 'dental,' medical, surgical waiting-room, a scene of mixed anxiety and desire, preparatory, for gathered barbarians, to the due amputation or extraction of excrescences and redundancies of barbarism" (XXIII *GB* I 233). An aggressive journalist who is interviewing a novelist keeps his notebook "slightly behind him, even as the dentist approaching his victim keeps the horrible forceps" (XV "DofL" 115). Maisie's early violent separation from Mrs. Wix is like the recent literal pulling of one of the little girl's teeth; the unduly protracted image, which also has the phrase "the horrible forceps," concludes with a rare dangling Jamesian participle: "Embedded in Mrs. Wix's nature as her tooth had been socketed in her gum, the operation of extracting her [Maisie] would really have been a case for chloroform" (XI *WMK* 29). Amid all these images of pain,[26] one of relief stands out: "Peter was in the state of a man whose toothache has suddenly stopped—he was exhilirated by the cessation of pain" (VIII *TM* II 130).[27]

vii. Arithmetic

The three score or more of images deriving from simple arithmetic and geometry, which occasionally dot the fiction, show James unconsciously harking back, I should say, to unpleasant hours of drill in sums and angles, his animosity perhaps reinforced by memories of his brother William's success in mathematics. The complete absence of geometric progressions,

26. See also VII *TM* I 115, xxviii "CCor" 351.

27. Does this image stem from personal experience or possibly from a recent reading of Chapter XXVIII of *Huckleberry Finn* (published five years before *The Tragic Muse*)?—"I see I had spoke too sudden, and said too much, and was in a close place. I asked her to let me think a minute; and she set there, very impatient and excited, and handsome, but looking kind of happy and eased-up, like a person that's had a tooth pulled out."

asymptotes, and vectors, all of which might be expected to appeal to a mind seeking new and valid comparisons, reveals an unawareness of the more imaginative elements of higher mathematics. Here are the most complex figures from James's entire book of numbers: "These excellent people might indeed have been content to give the circle of hospitality a diameter of six months" (XV "CF" 281); "'You're the most charming of polygons!'" (III *PofL* I 213); "He early measured the angle of convergence, as he called it, of their two projections [the collaborators' music and poetry]" (xxvii "Col" 178); "If her various graces were . . . the factors in an algebraic problem, the answer to this question was the indispensable unknown quantity" (iii *Eurs* 137); and finally "'It's a kind of fourth dimension. It's a presence, a perfume, a touch. It's a soul, a story, a life'" (X *SpofP* 249).

It will be recalled that James once opined that "Doing one's sum to-morrow instead of to-day doesn't make the sum easier, but at least makes to-day so" (VII *TM* I 262).[28] When combined with other images similar to it, that one suggests, I believe, James's feeling toward arithmetic. Other terms in the equation include the following: "Mrs. Luna glanced at him from head to foot, and gave a little smiling sigh, as if he had been a long sum in addition . . . he even looked a little hard and discouraging, like a column of figures" (viii *Bo* I 4); "Her choice . . . was there before her like an impossible sum on a slate" (XI *WMK* 341); "poor Roderick's muddled sum was a mystifying page" (I *RH* 450);[29] "He [Paul Overt] felt

28. See p. 183 above.

29. Stephen Spender quotes an earlier, non-imagistic passage from *Roderick Hudson* which also concerns sums and then inaccurately generalizes as follows: "The last sentence [quoted from I *RH* 313] has an air of self-importance and of irrelevance to Roderick Hudson: where it is relevant is to James's later heroes, who are doomed for ever to be reckoning up such 'sums'"; "The School of Experience in the Early Novels," *Hound and Horn*, VII (April-May, 1934), 34. As a matter of fact, sum images appear very regularly throughout James's fiction, as

as if some of the elements of a hard sum had been given him and the others were wanting: he couldn't do this sum till he had got all his figures" (XV "LofM" 88-89); and " 'You seem to me to see her as a column of figures each in itself highly satisfactory, but which, when you add them up, make only a total of doubt'" (xxvii "GrC" 271).

Puzzling figures symbolize confusing places. Thus, "The city of New York is like a tall sum in addition, and the streets are like columns of figures. What a place for me to live, who hate arithmetic!" (xxiv "IofC" 370), opines the narrator of "The Impressions of a Cousin." And another character "wondered how London could be so endlessly big and if one might ever know a tenth of the items in the sum" (X "LL" 356).

All types of characters, then, are made to express confusion in arithmetical terms, from little Maisie to the celibate novelist Paul Overt. And only one of James's innumerable personae likes mathematics: ". . . they were as interesting as the factors in an algebraic problem. This is saying a good deal; for [Robert] Acton was extremely fond of mathematics" (iii *Eurs* 136). Q.E.D., James had no passion for addition.

viii. Medicine

It is somewhat surprising that James has so few images deriving from medicine. His brother William studied medicine at Harvard beginning in 1863 and after several interruptions obtained his degree in 1869; James was in the Boston area most of that time. But the following pair of medicinal tropes from *Watch and Ward* are typically general and dull: Hubert "administered his spiritual medicines in homeopathic doses" (xxiv *WandW* 78), and "prosperity [for Mrs. Keith] . . . acted on her moral nature very much as a medicinal tonic—quinine or iron—acts upon the physical. She was in a com-

the best examples, which I have quoted chronologically, clearly show. See also "SofM" 6 (1868), xxiv *WandW* 160 (1871).

fortable glow of charity" (86). Newman's unweakened financial wizardry is well suggested in the following image, which is nonetheless only general: "He asked half a dozen particular questions which, like those of an eminent physician enquiring for particular symptoms, proved he was master of his subject" (II *Ame* 529). In an awkwardly technical image, James tells how a retired sea captain tries to learn whether a listener will swallow a given sea yarn: "he will auscultate, as it were, his auditor's inmost mood, to ascertain whether it is in condition to be practised upon" (xxv "LaP" 359). The final notable figure, however, is glaringly unprofessional: at one point Maggie senses that the Prince's anxiety "was shut in there between them, the successive moments throbbing under it the while as the pulse of fever throbs under the doctor's thumb" (XXIV *GB* II 183-84). Here again, as with the arithmetic images, James is perhaps reacting adversely to his brother William and therefore to that unconscious rival's profession of medicine.

ix. Law

The case is not vitally different when it comes to law images, for which James might conceivably have drawn upon his admittedly dilatory Harvard Law School attendance. True, he describes going from Newport down to Cambridge in 1862 to enter this phase as "one of the oddest errands, I think, that, given the several circumstances, I could possibly have undertaken."[30] His probable discomfort in the role of law scholar and his definite lack of success with law perhaps combined to make him want never to express directly or indirectly any aspect of the "errand." Still, one might have hoped to find—if only because the law experiment bore no other

30. Henry James, "Notes of a Son and Brother," in *Autobiography,* p. 411.

fruit—more than the infrequent and usually conventional legal figures which we do have in his fiction.

The American has more than its expected legacy of legal images, probably because it was written rather shortly after James attended law school and also because he wished to present Newman in a somewhat commercial light, as the following images certainly help to do: " 'It sounds quite foolish [Newman says]—as if I were to get my pleasure somehow under a writ of extradition' " (II *Ame* 131). Next, "she had a slight reversionary property in herself" (253). Also, "in her philosophy a servant was but a machine constructed for the benefit of some supreme patentee" (531). Finally, as he listens to the testimony of Mrs. Bread, "Newman felt as if he had been reading by starlight the report of highly important evidence in a great murder case" (456-57).

Without exception, the other law images are routine, and some appear to have been seen through the eyes of a novelist, a dramatist perhaps, or even a painter, rather than those of a former law student. Thus, when Morris Gedge of "The Birthplace" returns to those awaiting his report on the outcome of his interview with Mr. Grant-Jackson, they remind him of "a sentimental print, seen and admired in his youth, a 'Waiting for the Verdict' " (XVII "Bi" 211).[31]

x. Chess

I wish that James had been a competent amateur chessplayer. He would have been a ponderous adversary, immovable in defense, imaginative in attack, almost telepathic as he stroked his beard or—later—felt his bald head. His advance would have resembled his famous conversation, uncheckable, irresistible, and surprising. His few chess images, however, prove clearly that he knew little or nothing about the game.

31. See also xxvi "MW" 210, XXVI *SeofP* 217.

Only a novice without a rating would write of chess the way James does in the two passages which follow. "The gentleman on his left at last risked an observation as if it had been a move at chess, exciting in Lyon however an apparent wantonness. This personage played his part with difficulty: he uttered a remark as a lady fires a pistol, looking the other way. To catch the ball Lyon had to bend his ear . . ." (XII "Li" 320). And "The figures on the chessboard were still the passions and jealousies and superstitions and stupidities of man, and their position with regard to each other at any given moment could be of interest only to the grim invisible fates who played the game—who sat, through the ages, bow-backed over the table" (VI *PC* II 104). Now, the first image is inappropriate because the conversationalist in the story is adept in his field, whereas a chess-player is not if he "risks" a move simply to note its effect—to say nothing of "looking the other way" while doing so. And the second figure, though more dramatic than the first, is still general, and in addition betrays James's unawareness that the slow game of hunched chess-players can be of interest to vast audiences —if not to James.

If James had been an experienced chess-player, he might have brilliantly pictured the central situation in "The Figure in the Carpet"—the literary critic's search for the pattern hidden in the novelist's work—in chess-play terms. Instead, we have only this:

The hours spent there by Corvick [the critic] were present to my fancy as those of a chessplayer bent with a silent scowl, all the lamplit winter, over his board and his moves. As my imagination filled it out the picture held me fast. On the other side of the table was a ghostlier form, the faint figure of an antagonist good-humouredly but a little wearily secure—an antagonist who leaned back in his chair with his hands in his pockets and a smile on his fine clear face. . . . He [the critic] would take up a chessman and hold it poised a while over one of the little squares, and then would put it back in its place with a long sigh of disappointment (XV "FinC" 245).

But we all know that in professional and even competent amateur chess tilts no player ever touches a piece without moving it. James must not have been aware of this universal rule, as may be further shown if we look at another image, this from *The Golden Bowl*, the plot of which would have challenged the trope-making fancy of a chess-playing novelist, having an aging American—rich as King Croesus—his powerful young "queen," and a *principe* (not an Italian king, to be sure). The Bloomsbury shopman dots his counter with precious old wares, and as he displays their virtues to Charlotte and the Prince, his hands "touched them at moments, briefly, nervously, tenderly, as those of a chess-player rest, a few seconds, over the board, on a figure he thinks he may move and then may not" (XXIII *GB* I 107).

Finally, James did not understand the intricate maneuvers of chess knights, as will be clear after a glance at the complex simile by which he tries—but fails—to suggest that Lizzie Crowe envisages her life as the battleground of a psychic struggle between two gentlemen who love her:

These two figures stood like opposing knights (the black and the white,) foremost on the great chess-board of fate. Lizzie was the wearied, puzzled player [but she has no opponent]. She would idly finger the other pieces [illegally], and shift them carelessly hither and thither; but it was of no avail: the game lay between the two knights. She would shut her eyes and long for some kind hand to come and tamper with the board; she would open them and see the two knights standing immovable, face to face ("SofY" 272).

The image is faulty. No game of chess is likely to involve a duel of knights. Further, Lizzie has one knight—either the white one or the black—on her side and can fight with it against the opposition, which includes the other knight. Yet James wrongly suggests that the girl is playing only against herself and also that for some reason she must touch neither knight.

Clearly James was not a chess-player. His was the loss, and so is ours.

xi. Unconscious Sexual

Most of the major categories of Jamesian imagery contain elements capable of being interpreted as sexually symbolic. Thus, followers of Freud would argue that water references often relate unconsciously to the amniotic fluid and that swimmers are symbols of the male, ships the female. Flowers may represent the male or the female, depending upon the part stressed, but the gardens producing them or inviting one to linger are unquestionably female symbols. Some animals and their actions may be emblematic of one sex or the other. And war involves gaping wounds caused by flourished knives and pistols, all of which are genital symbols.[32] In addition, the categories of art and religion contain figures which readers of Freud regard themselves as especially qualified to elucidate. However, little can be accomplished by showing again, what many individuals began to accept at least as early as the time of Freud's *Traumdeutung* (1900),[33] that most of the heterogeneous mass of things in this world may be regarded as sexual symbols. On the other hand, something valuable about James can be deduced, I feel, by analyzing the nearly two

32. See Sigmund Freud, *A General Introduction to Psychoanalysis,* trans. Joan Riviere (Garden City, New York: Garden City Publishing Company, Inc., 1943), pp. 136-47.

33. The first English translation, by A. A. Brill, of *The Interpretation of Dreams,* was published in 1913. There are no references in James's published letters or notebooks, I believe, to Freud. His brother William James, however, met Freud in Worchester, Massachusetts, in 1909; see Ralph Barton Perry, *The Thought and Character of William James,* 2 vols. (Boston: Little, Brown, and Company, 1935), II, 122-23.

hundred fictional images used to describe men and women, and their relationships, when the contexts as well as the terms appear sexual or at least suggestive.

Images containing male symbols are rather rare in James. They often concern keys and bolts, as for example when the narrator of "Adina," wondering how Scrope can tolerate Adina Waddington's boisterous mother, suddenly understands: "The key to the mystery was the one which fits so many locks; he was in love with Miss Waddington" ("Ad" 39). More closely linked to its plot is an extended metaphor by which Peter, returning to Miriam after an absence, is pictured as finding her ability as an actress improved, perhaps because of her contact with Basil Dashwood. "And the assurance flowed over him [Peter] again that she had found the key to her box of treasures. In the summer, during their weeks of frequent meeting, she had only fumbled with the lock. One October day, while he was away, the key had slipped in, had fitted, or her finger at last had touched the right spring and the capacious casket had flown open" (VII *TM* I 338). It would be foolish to suggest that a sexual interpretation could explain all of the elements in this curious passage. As usual, the figure aids the general plot. Still, the metaphor provides a hint that Miriam and Dashwood may be lovers in the first volume; at the end of the second, we learn that they have married one another. *The Portrait of a Lady* has three apt images concerning keys and bolts. Shortly after they first meet, Gilbert smoothly remarks to Isabel, "'. . . I'm perfectly aware that I myself am as rusty as a key that has no lock to fit it. It polishes me up a little to talk to you—not that I venture to pretend I can turn that very complicated lock I suspect your intellect of being!'" (III *PofL* I 371). Later, the description of Isabel's emotional response to Osmond's profession of love certainly has sexual overtones: "The tears came into her eyes: this time they obeyed the sharpness of the pang that suggested to her somehow the slipping of a fine bolt—backward, forward, she couldn't have said which" (IV *PofL* II 18). Throughout the novel, devoted but sick Ralph is aware that his keys are not for Isabel, whom he nonetheless has always regarded as "a beautiful edifice," which "He surveyed . . . from the outside and admired . . . greatly; he looked in at the windows and received an impression of proportions equally fair. But he felt that he saw it only by glimpses and that he had not yet stood under the roof. The door was fastened, and though he had keys in his pocket he had a conviction that none of them would fit" (III *PofL* I 86-87).[34]

Other images having obviously male parts are less numerous than those concerning keys and bolts. The following few examples incidentally reveal an occasional naïveté in their author. Felix in discussing his desired marriage to Gertrude Wentworth says rather awkwardly to her father: "'Of course with me she will hide her light under a bushel, . . . I being the bushel!'" (iii *Eurs* 193). Angela of *Confidence* tells Bernard of her annoyance that his friend Gordon should have asked him to comment on her suitability for marriage: "'Did it ever strike you that my position . . . was a charming one? —knowing that I had been handed over to you to be put under the microscope—like an insect with a pin stuck through it!'" (iv *Con* 195). Even worse is the comment of the narrator of "The Beldonald Holbein" to the beautiful, heartless Lady Beldonald: "'That's the way, with a long pin straight through your body, I've got you'" (XVIII "BH" 388).[35] Finally, with a clear, brief sexual image James pictures Nora's fascinated

34. R. W. Stallman calls the last part of this image "pre-Freudian" and "unwittingly witty"; *The Houses That James Built and Some Other Literary Studies* ([East Lansing]: Michigan State University Press, 1961), p. 7.

35. This image was considered in the insect category also; see p. 79 above.

gaze at Fenton: "She regarded her cousin with something of the thrilled attention which one bestows on the naked arrow, poised across the bow" (xxiv *WandW* 60). The figure, appearing early in the novel, hints at the excitement and the pain which are to be Nora's lot at Fenton's hands.

Occasionally a figure emphasizes male and female elements equally. Thus, we read that Osmond, once possessed of Isabel, can afford to take pleasure in torturing Caspar, whom he therefore once patronizingly flatters, then adds, " 'I'm talking for my wife as well as for myself, you see. She speaks for me, my wife; why shouldn't I speak for her? We're as united, you know, as the candlestick and the snuffers' " (IV *PofL* II 309). Osmond consciously regards himself as a luminous wit and his wife a damper; less consciously, he may be confessing that Isabel has quenched his ardor. And it may not be too extravagant to add that James may also be suggesting that Isabel, who does not shine in her husband's presence, is really of firmer stuff. Herbert Dodd of "The Bench of Desolation" recognizes that Kate Cookham (note the last name) has trapped him: he must marry her or pay her off. "And it had all been but the cheapest of traps—when he came to take the pieces apart a bit—laid over a brazen avidity. What he now collapsed for . . . was the fact that, whatever the trap, it held him as with the grip of sharp, murderous steel. . . . He shouldn't get out without losing a limb. The only question was which of his limbs it should be"[36] (xxviii "BofD" 415-16). "The Turn of the Screw" yields only one figurative passage containing elements in the least Freudian; oddly,

36. This is the only partially sexual image in which there is any suggestion of a castration motif. The absent fingers of the alter ego in "The Jolly Corner" represent the same theme symbolically but not imagistically used. This paucity is surprising in the light of the fact that James's father lost a leg by fire and James himself injured his back fighting a fire. See Saul Rosenzweig, "The Ghost of Henry James: A Study in Thematic Apperception," *Character and Personality,* XX (December, 1943), 81-84, 92-93.

though it appears in a context of some emotional intensity, the sequence has juxtaposed male and female elements which contribute nothing to any sexual interpretation. When Flora asks, "'And where's Mike?'" the governess is highly suspicious and feels her taunt nerves snapping: ". . . these three words from her were in a flash like the glitter of a drawn blade the jostle of the cup that my hand for weeks had held high and full to the brim and that now, even before speaking, I felt overflow in a deluge" (XII "TofS" 277).[37]

Images predominantly concerned with female symbols are very numerous and mainly have to do with doors, windows, gates, buildings, and flowers. Musing on his power over his ward, Lawrence says, "'I can open the door and let in the lover'" (xxiv WandW 47). Hyacinth feels an overmastering need for fickle Millicent Henning, wishing that "he might at least feel the firm roundness of her arms about him. He didn't exactly know what good this would do him or what door it would open, but he should like it" (VI PC II 421). Overt is shocked to learn that the young lady he was counseled by St. George to give up has become Mrs. St. George: "He had renounced her, yes; but that was another affair—that was a closed but not a locked door. Now he seemed to see the door quite slammed in his face" (XV "LofM" 88). Knowing that Isabel has refused Warburton as well as Goodwood, her cousin is at first only amused by the prospect of Osmond as "a fresh suitor at her gate. . . . Ralph looked forward to a fourth, a fifth, a tenth besieger; he had no conviction she would stop at a third. She would keep the gate ajar and open a parley; she would certainly not allow number three to come in" (III PofL I 395).[38] But Osmond does go in and tries to

37. This imagistic use of blade and cup has an interesting coincidental relationship to the symbolic use in the same story of tower and lake; see Edmund Wilson, "The Ambiguity of Henry James," *Hound and Horn,* VII (April-May, 1934), 387.

38. See also xxvii "GI" 217-18, XXVI SeofP 8.

annex the garden beyond, with the idea of "rak[ing] the soil and gently water[ing] the flowers" (IV *PofL* II 200).

Not merely doors, windows, and gates, but whole buildings of various sorts are involved in imagistic treatment of women. In "The Pension Beaurepas," M. Pigeonneau says of Aurora Church, "'Mees Cheurch? I see; it's a singular name. Ça veut dire "église," n'est-ce pas? Voilà a church where I'd willingly worship!'" (XIV "PB" 420). Osmond even more wildly employs unconscious double-entendre when he describes Warburton's really not reproachable conduct toward Pansy:

"He comes and looks at one's daughter as if she were a suite of apartments; he tries the door-handles and looks out of the windows, raps on the wall and almost thinks he'll take the place. Will you be so good as to draw up a lease? Then, on the whole, he decides that the rooms are too small; he doesn't think he could live on a third floor; he must look out for a *piano nobile*. And he goes away after having got a month's lodging in the poor little apartment for nothing" (IV *PofL* II 287).[39]

Love as an assault over the defenses of a stronghold is a harmless enough little conceit, but James occasionally uses it rather ludicrously. Thus, overactive little Léon Verdier in "A Bundle of Letters," misunderstanding the ingenuous forwardness of Miranda Hope, writes to an old friend in a way less accurate than suggestive: "I almost owed her a grudge for having deprived me of that pleasure of gradation, of carrying the defences one by one, which is almost as great as that of entering the place" (XIV "BofL" 522-23). And Maud of "The Papers" might become responsive to Mortimer Marshal, we learn, if it were not for his lack of romantic dash: "He wouldn't

39. Stallman discusses in great detail house symbolism (but not imagery to any great extent) in *The Portrait of a Lady; The Houses That James Built*, pp. 3-33.

rage—he *couldn't,* for the citadel might, in that case, have been carried by his assault; he would only spend his life in walking round and round it, asking everyone he met how in the name of goodness one did get in" (xxviii "Pap" 151).[40] Perhaps the most grotesque sexual image in all of James appears in *Watch and Ward:* ". . . Roger caught himself wondering whether, at the worst, a little precursory love-making would do any harm. The ground might be gently tickled to receive his own sowing; the petals of the young girl's nature, playfully forced apart, would leave the golden heart of the flower but the more accessible to his own vertical rays" (xxiv *WandW* 58).[41]

Finally, it may be of incidental interest that among the numerous unconsciously sexual figures are several highly peculiar ones which in my opinion permit no other conclusion than that James was in some ways naïve. Here are four examples. "It was as if she had lifted him first in her beautiful arms, had raised him up high, high, high, . . . pressing him

40. These and other citadel and castle images are considered as part of the category of war images, pp. 90-91 above.

41. This peculiar specimen, together with a few others like it from the same novel, contributes to the validity of the following remark by F. W. Dupee: "Like all the early stories, *Watch and Ward* is strewn with images so palpably and irresistibly erotic as to imply a whole resonant domain of meaning beyond anything he [James] could have intended"; *Henry James,* American Men of Letters Series ([New York]: William Sloane Associates, 1951), p. 61. See also xxv "PR" 428, in which Miss Whittaker is compared to a blockaded port in whose waters Richard wants to cast his anchor; VII *TM* I 62, in which Gabriel Nash opines that Mrs. Rooth must be hoping that her daughter will not be overturned and smashed like "a precious vase"; and XXI *Amb* I 277, in which Little Bilham, calling himself a " 'farthing candle,' " says that young Jeanne de Vionnet is like a flower with " 'pale pink petals . . . folded up,' " which will open only " 'to some great golden sun' " (three books later, Mamie Pocock, "a flower of expansion" [XXII *Amb* II 147], awaits Little Bilham). I think that Stephen Spender is correct in castigating the author of *The Ambassadors* and *The Golden Bowl* for writing "novels about sexual subjects [in which] the vulgarity consists in the sexual act being referred to only as the merest formality"; "The School of Experience in the Early Novels," p. 425.

to her immortal young breast while he let himself go . . ."
(xxviii "VG" 233). Next, "the reassurance she had extorted
there . . . hadn't only poured oil on the troubled waters of
their question, but had fairly drenched their whole intercourse with that lubricant" (XXIV *GB* II 279).[42] Also, "He
had hesitated like an ass erect on absurd hind legs between
two bundles of hay" (xxviii "CCor" 337). Finally, "What
was confounding was her disparities—the juxtaposition in her
of beautiful sun-flushed heights and deep dark holes" (XVI
"MG" 275).

Most of the images quoted in this section appear in works
dated before 1890. As James grew older, he may have become
so much more aware of the problem of sex in human relationships that these unconsciously motivated figures were more
and more carefully avoided during the actual writing and
rewriting. But the fact that James was measurably naïve
even in the 1900's is evident, I think, when we realize that the
last four images, quoted just above, are from works published
between 1900 and 1910.

xii. Eyes

Eyes do not often appear in the figurative half of images
in James, but literal eyes—like real Paris—inspire graphic and
occasionally unusual similes and metaphors.

James often compares the vivid quality of the eye to some
kind of light: a spark, a smouldering fire, a smoky torch, a
fitful lamp, a glowing coal, and so on. Miriam Rooth's attractive eyes are said at one time to be "full of their usual
sombre fire" (VII *TM* I 339), while villainous Urbain de
Bellegarde's eyes once "flickered like blown candles" (II *Ame*
433). When Juliana Bordereau catches the narrator of "The

---

42. Note also the following non-figurative phrase: "lubrication of
their intercourse by levity" (XXI *Amb* I 162). What does such wording
prove but naïveté in its author?

Aspern Papers" snooping through her desk, she virtually hypnotizes him with "her extraordinary eyes. They glared at me [he goes on]; they were like the sudden drench, for a caught burglar, of a flood of gaslight; they made me horribly ashamed" (XII "AP" 118).[43]

Human eyes—usually in women—often inspire animal, bird, insect, and fish imagery by James. Thus, Spencer Brydon shamefully stalks his alter ego "like some monstrous stealthy cat; he wondered if he would have glared at these moments with large shining yellow eyes" (XVII "JC" 458). Madame de Mauves is charmingly pictured: "Her throat and bust were slender, but all the more in harmony with certain rapid charming movements of the head, which she had a way of throwing back every now and then with an air of attention and a sidelong glance from her dove-like eyes" (XIII "MdeM" 217). Mrs. Gracedew, another charming American woman, is somewhat similarly described: "Her beautiful wandering eyes played high and low, like the flight of an imprisoned swallow, then, as she sank upon a seat, dropped at last as if the creature were bruised with its limits" ("CE" 271). Buggy eyes in James usually belong to people whom others regard as unpleasant but who are really as harmless and even attractive as most insects. Thus, old Mrs. Wix's glasses seem hideous to Maisie, who at the outset looks at the kind woman carefully: "She wore glasses which, in humble reference to a divergent obliquity of vision, she called her straighteners, and a little ugly snuff-coloured dress trimmed with satin bands in the form of scallops and glazed with antiquity. . . . With the added suggestion of her goggles it reminded her pupil of the polished shell or corslet of a horrid beetle" (XI *WMK* 25). When Flora Saunt must wear disfiguring glasses, the narrator reports: "All I saw at first was the big gold bar crossing each

43. See also "SofB" 772, xxv "LiM" 244, XVII "OW" 311, XV "FinC" 265-66.

of her lenses, over which something convex and grotesque, like the eyes of a large insect, something that now represented her whole personality, seemed, as out of the orifice of a prison, to strain forward and press" (xxvii "Gl" 234).[44] And we read that the supercilious socialite Lady Castledean in *The Golden Bowl* "didn't distinguish the little protuberant eyes of small social insects, often endowed with such a range, from the other decorative spots on their bodies and wings" (XXIV *GB* II 50).

As we have seen, James images high-society as life in a gold-fish bowl, and many are the poor fish there. Strether and Waymarsh, thrown together and then pushed about by social currents, seem to be in a "fathomless medium [which] held them . . . and our friend felt as if they passed each other, in their deep immersion, with the round impersonal eye of silent fish" (XXI *Amb* I 172). The journalist Bight regards publicity-seekers as dumb fish which "'leap straight out of the water themselves, leap in their thousands and come flopping, open-mouthed and goggle-eyed, to one's very door. What is the sense of the French expression about a person's making *des yeux de carpe*? It suggests the eyes that a young newspaper-man seems to see all round him . . .'" (xxviii "Pap" 85).

James frequently likens somewhat unpleasant people's eyes to man-made objects in a grotesque or comical way. Thus, repulsive Mrs. Crawford in the poor story "Crawford's Consistency" has "a small dark eye, of a peculiarly piercing quality, set in her head as flatly as a buttonhole in a piece of cotton cloth" ("CCon" 578); Henrietta Stackpole has eyes "like polished buttons—buttons that might have fixed the elastic hoops of some tense receptacle" (III *PofL* I 117); and Nick Dormer helps to dissuade himself from a political career

44. See also 189, 195, 196.

by comparing the massed faces of his fat constituents to
"'an enormous sofa, with the cheeks for the gathers and the
eyes for the buttons'" (VII *TM* I 243). Finally, Eugene Pickering distortedly views Anastasia Blumenthal's eyes as "'shining
through it ["'a sort of mist of talk'"] opposite to me, like
fog-lamps at sea'" (xxiv "EP" 267-68).[45]

Water is involved in a few other images dealing with eyes.
The artificially bright Lady Beldonald, for example, "looks
. . . new, as if she took out every night her large lovely varnished eyes and put them in water" (XVIII "BH" 378); Warburton's demure sisters have "eyes like the balanced basins,
the circles of 'ornamental water,' set, in parterres, among the
geraniums" (III *PofL* I 104); and we read that when Flora
Saunt is asked an embarrassing question, "her eyes darkened
to the purple of one of the shadow-patches on the sea" (xxvii
"Gl" 199). By contrast, of the frigid spinster Olive Chancellor's eyes we read that their "curious tint . . . was a living
colour; when she turned it on you, you thought vaguely of
the glitter of green ice" (viii *Bo* I 435).[46] More tenderly, in
"Benvolio" Scholastica's blind and aged father's blue eyes
are described as "sitting fixed beneath white brows like patches
of pale winter sky under a high-piled cloud" (xxiv "Be" 332).

Expressionless if not sightless eyes occasionally suggest to
James the incomplete orbs of statues: concerning one attractive but unsympathetic woman, he points out "the quietness
of her deep eyes, which were as beautiful as if they had been
blank, like those of antique busts" (XIV "LaB" 128); he en-
dows a more admirable heroine with "the blurred absent eyes,
the smoothed elegant nameless head, the impersonal flit of a
creature lost in an alien age and passing as an image in worn

45. See also XV "DofL" 112.
46. The eyes, however, of Olive's near-victim Verena Tarrant are
vibrant with warm life: "She had curious, radiant, liquid eyes (their
smile was a sort of reflection, like the glisten of a gem)" (69-70).

relief round and round a precious vase" (XXIII *GB* I 187); and, he sketches an odd mother in this way—"she had no eyebrows, and her eyes seemed to stare, like those of a figure of wax" (viii *Bo* I 134).

James compares the inpenetrable or merely vacant expression of a number of his characters to windows that show only a masking light or reflect light from outside and thus do not reveal much that is going on inside. For example, Henrietta's "remarkably open eyes, lighted like great glazed railway-stations, had put up no shutters" (IV *PofL* II 282). Prince Amerigo's "dark blue eyes were of the finest and, on occasion, precisely, resembled nothing so much as the high windows of a Roman palace, of an historic front by one of the great old designers, thrown open on a feast-day to the golden air" (XXIII *GB* I 42).[47] We read at one point of dull Owen Gereth that "his impatience [was] shining in his idle eyes as the dining-hour shines in club-windows" (X *SpofP* 47). And the expression of massive Mrs. Churchley of "The Marriages" is somewhat similarly imaged, when James writes that her "pupils reflected the question as distinct dark windows reflect the sunset" (XVIII "Ma" 261).

Massive women and their seemingly little eyes evoke in James some of his most fantastic rhetoric. Of the dozen or so descriptions of such persons, the one portraying Mrs. David E. Drack—a monumental presence in the short story

47. Thus, if Adam Verver has masses of New World gold, Amerigo still comes from the Italy of "the golden air." A less subtle contrast is provided by the description of Adam Verver's simpler American eyes, when his face is said to resemble "a small decent room, clean-swept and unencumbered with furniture, but drawing a particular advantage . . . from the outlook of a pair of ample and uncurtained windows" (170). It seems to me that this type of image in James owes much to Hawthorne's *The House of the Seven Gables*. For a brilliant discussion of the differences between Adam's and Amerigo's "gold," see J. A. Ward, *The Imagination of Disaster: Evil in the Fiction of Henry James* (Lincoln: University of Nebraska Press, 1961), pp. 149-50.

"Julia Bride"—is especially rich: "she presented a huge hideous pleasant face, a featureless desert in a remote quarter of which the disproportionately small eyes might have figured a pair of rash adventurers all but buried in the sand. They reduced themselves when she smiled to barely discernible points— a couple of mere tiny emergent heads—though the foreground of the scene, as if to make up for it, gaped with a vast benevolence" (XVII "JB" 515).

Finally, once in a while James daringly compares eyes to flowers. Thus, one of the lovers of Maisie's busy mother makes the observant little girl think "it nice when a gentleman was thin and brown—brown with a kind of clear depth that made his straw-coloured moustache white and his eyes resemble little pale flowers" (XI *WMK* 147). More charming is this description of aging but still spry Colonel Assingham: "The hollows of his eyes were deep and darksome, but the eyes within them were like little blue flowers plucked that morning" (XXIII *GB* I 66-67). Still better, foolish Louis Leverett writes home in "A Bundle of Letters" about "a lovely English girl with eyes as shy as violets and a voice as sweet" (XIV "BofL" 502).[48]

Conclusion

If we have read the mystic scroll correctly, the image of Henry James the man is now a little clearer. He emerges more sharply as thoroughly American if at times slightly self-conscious and rarely reluctant to spoof his native land. It is also clearer that he was attracted by clean money but was

48. For descriptions of James's penetrating eyes, see Alice Boughton, "A Note by His Photographer," *Hound and Horn*, VII (April-May, 1934), 478; and *The Legend of the Master*, compiled by Simon Nowell-Smith (New York: Charles Scribner's Sons, 1948), pp. 2, 5, 6, 8. For comments on James's powers of observation, see Leon Edel, "The Art of Seeing," *Henry James: The Conquest of London: 1870-1881* (Philadelphia and New York: J. B. Lippincott Company, 1962), pp. 53-58.

a bit jittery about the imminence of stock-market crashes; further, that he was an experienced and free-spending traveler who especially loved Paris. James liked a little wine, and the glitter and blare of a good circus with attractive trapezists in pink tights. He appears to have cared little for ciphers or for sitting in a dentist's parlor. He was the reverse of stimulated by the professions of medicine and law, undoubtedly because of repressions having to do with Dr. William James and also the Harvard Law School.[49] James was no chess player, and it must be said that he was somewhat naïve sexually. Finally, he was almost transcendental in his respect for the insatiable human eye and its powers of penetration and revelation.

49. See Edel, *Conquest of London,* pp. 135-51, 418-20, for illuminating information and conjectures relating to Henry James's unconscious rivalry with his brother William.

X · SUCH WAS THE IMAGE

Such was the image under which he had ended
by figuring his life (XVII "BinJ" 79).

In conclusion, there are six major categories and several minor categories of images in James, whose personality in addition is incidentally revealed in still other similes and metaphors. Three of the major categories—water, flower, and animal—are subsumed under the large class of nature images; the other three major categories—war, art, and religion—fall into the great class of man images. The minor groups concern fire, metals, sensations, children, games, cups, jewels, court-life, and astronomical bodies. Figures revealing aspects of James's personality relate to his attitudes toward America, money, travel, wine, circuses, dentists, arithmetic, medicine, law, chess, sex, and eyes. Still other images fall into other classes, since no meaningful grouping can capture all of his 16,902 tropes.

The water imagery in James is pervasive and distinctive. The figurative water is often in movement, bearing passive drifters willingly or unwillingly while others, equally passive but perhaps more curious intellectually, stand on the shore and watch. Knowledge occasionally comes to James's characters in breaking waves of awareness. His tides rise, turn, and ebb, as events of men and women wax, alter, or subside sadly. Water often moves out to sea, bearing elements to a loss or to release. Time is manneristically imaged often as a flux, while the process of partially conquering time through reminiscence is seen as remounting the stream.

There are numerous images of travel by water. Some are conventional and romantic, concerning wind in the sails, gurgling wakes, and the like. Perhaps because ocean-going in modern steamers was always a routine activity to James, he often makes his metaphorical vessels somewhat archaic; he does, however, honestly image sea sights usually from the vantage point of comfortable passenger rather than deck-hand or stoker.

Danger is latent in most of James's plot situations, which fact is reflected in much of his water imagery, concerned as it often is with wind-rent canvas, ships dashed on rocks, panic in lifeboats, drowning passengers, flotsam, jetsam, and so on. Occasionally James suggests mental illumination amid social confusion by lights-at-sea figures; also he sometimes describes the shock of his naïve characters in suddenly becoming aware of the depths of darkness, cold, and evil about them by metaphors concerning bathers suddenly caught by chilling currents and quickly lost.

James also makes figurative use of the pleasures of bathing, in sweet-smelling and even tinted waters, in tepid tanks, and in bracingly cool streams. Many a Jamesian character tries to escape, to float and shine in silvery seas; almost without exception, however, they are dragged back, engulfed, and drowned.

James's plashing fountains are infrequent, and his metaphorical fishermen are never professional. Ice imagery curiously enough is reserved exclusively for his naïvely serene and rigid, chilly American characters. His seashell usages almost always concern the faint message from the past which can be heard by patient and sensitive ears. The need for water in those whose lives are arid sandy tracts inspires occasional figures having to do with frustration, while victims of emotional exploitation are sometimes the sacred founts of those who drain them of vitality.

By water imagery, then, James suggests carefree pleasure, drift, and change within the social sea, the cost and consequence to others and one's self of joy, the ever-present danger of being pulled from heights and sucked under, and the brooding mystery and flux of all things.

The flower imagery is usually more pleasant than the water figures. Gentle winds comb fragrances from lovely gardens; and if flower-like people—usually thin-waisted, flexible, radiant-faced young ladies—bend to the gale, harsh winds do not wreak havoc among the banks of blossoms. However, some passions are fierce and sirocco-like; when they sweep by, fragility is often blighted and blasted.

Steady fruitful productivity, whether artistic or merely conversational, James images in flower terms, and he can also wax comic and with conscious grandiloquence limn the romantically faraway with garden imagery which is inappropriate in actual context. But it is another matter when he tenderly describes *jeunes filles en fleurs:* they are folded buds awaiting golden suns, lithe flowers of plasticity, and only once in a while autumnally tawny. James reserves thorny barbs for over-cultivated and florid women of middle-age; however, aged and frail ladies are always tenderly handled. Flowery men in James are never so vigorous and admirable as Chaucer's fine "yong squier," who was "Embrouded . . . as it were a meede / Al ful of fresshe floures, whyte and reede." Such men in James are usually closer to plain pansies.

James's fruit imagery is less frequent than his flower figures but functions similarly. Tiny patterns of blight and withering run through the fiction. Artificiality in appearance and behavior evokes artificial-flower metaphors in James, who loathed hypocrisy, over-dressing, and other concealments of natural beauty and grace. He disliked meddling also, and he suggests the propriety of privacy by a curious little set of garden-wall figures.

And so through his flower tropes James pictures the sweetness, the petal-like delicacy, and—if you will—the fragrance of persons, places, and situations that are allowed to develop naturally. But since such evanescence is ever at the mercy of exploitation, acridity, and the sickle of Father Time, he cannot always avoid breeching the garden wall and introducing blight.

James compares men and women to scores of beasts, birds, fish, and insects lower in the scale than "the paragon of animals." Again, his purpose is two-fold: to suggest that human beings are noble, graceful, supple, strong, and attractive when they behave naturally, and yet with all of this to degrade men by pointing out their measure of bestiality and low cunning.

James employs the nobility and sleekness of horses in imagery occasionally, but more often he drafts their stolid Clydesdale strength and utility. In fact, he even uses admirable prancing and curveting of horses in rhetorical flourishes which have the effect of ridiculing human and equine behavior both. The routine of much of this world's necessary activity James makes more galling by means of harness and halter figures. Runaway-horse metaphors portray the drama of human events which, despite man's rationality, cannot always be controlled by the participants.

James's figurative sheep are naïve, passive, and stupid. Usually it is innocent young girls who are compared to sheep, with evil in a wolfish ring about them. Often such sacrificial victims are ignorant of what lies ahead, sometimes they smell blood and bleat in uncomprehending terror; but sooner or later, and regardless of the efforts of any shepherds who may be near, they are fleeced or slaughtered.

Dogs in our imagistic kennels are of several breeds. Independent, foreign-acting persons are like sleek greyhounds; unsophisticated, good-natured people resemble spaniels; those dominated by their masters are likened to poodles. And the sluggish fidelity of dogs to undeserving owners occasions a few more similes. James must have regarded most cats in real life as unfortunate; in his imagery they are regularly terrified, starved, sick, or blind. When circumstances for his characters are uncontrollable and fate is unkind to them, he sometimes has recourse to a starved cat or a blind kitten figure.

James's figurative lions and tigers are more admirable—because of their hypnotic suppleness and silent ferocity—even if his tigerish human characters richly merit our reproof. His free-ranging predators are amoral and swift to seize and destroy their victims. His sheep-like innocents are typically remembered as resembling Christian martyrs soon overwhelmed by beasts in the arena, and all under the amused gaze of society which likes a good show.

Several women in James are likened to birds, vividly feathered, raucous, quick-eyed, beating hurt wings in vain attempts to get away from something which has surrounded them too rapidly for comprehension, and caught and caged. James's favorite bird was the dove, with its pearly hues and soft sounds, wonderfully winged, capable of fine flights. The fish and bug images are uniformly disappointing, especially the former; a few times, harmlessly bustling little people are likened to grasshoppers, worms, and fleas, while a few attractive but inconsequential women, shimmering and long-limbed perhaps but certainly insubstantial, are caught in insect metaphors.

In all of this imagery stemming from aspects of the animal kingdom, as well as in water and flower figures, James implies that brute nature, outer and inner, stands ready at all times to dash to pieces, wither, and devour the higher, more aesthetic, more spiritual aspects of man. At the same time, this nature imagery can suggest the evanescent quality of natural human pleasure and beauty. The most basic message from such imagery, it seems to me, is two-fold: that joy, attractiveness, and simple innocence must pass; but further, that conscious heroism, intellectual and creative endeavor, and spiritual values have a chance of abiding, in spite of the whelming wave, the careless gardener, and the fanged beast.

Man-centered images—as opposed to nature-centered ones like those having to do with water, flowers, and animals—usually concern war, art, and religion. As for the first group, James does not often extend himself to make much rhetorical use of classical war imagery. To be sure, we have a Hannibal and an Attila or two, a few Rubicons and phalanxes; but James is clearly not at his best here. Medieval and Renaissance knight figures are far more attractive and worthy of attention. Some of James's figurative knights are ineffective, but a few of his strong silent men are well imaged as self-sacrificing fighters in armor. The glitter of similes and metaphors having to do with weaponry adds to the richness of James's texture, while the pitiless conflicts both personal and social which make poniards and pistols necessary suggest that James viewed human relationships as battles very often indeed. Sometimes a lonely, eminent, immobile object of the desires or ambitions of others is aptly imaged as a castle—tempting, rich if occasionally decadent, massive. The fact that modern guns rarely appear in James's imagery is perhaps owing to his streak of romantic rather than realistic adventuresomeness. A curious cluster of French Revolution tropes challenges the reader: in each case the subject is a doomed aristocrat—a sensitive young woman, a talented artist, a person seeking social approbation, or one quietly awaiting inevitable doom at the hands of stronger but less cultured foes.

Much irony accompanies the many figures specifying military rank: sometimes James sardonically suggests that would-be female fighters ought to lay down their arms and be more lady-like; almost as often their assumed mannishness seems simply comic.

In sum, James uses war imagery to make graphic the fact that reality is shot through with perils and sudden ruination, further to evaluate degrees of authoritativeness and subservience within and between social strata, and also to dramatize poignantly the need, but with it the incapability, of the sensitive and meek to protect themselves in the war called life.

James's figures of speech stemming from the various arts —literature, painting, the drama, music, sculpture, the dance, and architecture—are among his most representative and rewarding. James is often challenging when he likens one of his characters to a specific or general personage from a British novel, an Italian painting, a French play, or when he points up the particular quality of a given voice by means of a music image, catches what is eternal in a passing gesture by means of a sculpture trope, or lights up a formal relationship by an allusion to architecture.

Most of the specific literary references in the imagery are to British novelists, with Thackeray and Dickens in the undisputed lead. But James does pay some homage to Hawthorne, the one American novelist whom he genuinely admired, if with some reservations. Keats he also uses in imagery, but only very casually. It should be added that James hardly ever made serious use in figures of speech of any poets, beyond echoing certain tags of lines probably memorized in his youth. He did recall that Shakespeare had immortalized a vacillating Hamlet, a heath-roaming Lear, a Cleopatra of infinite variety; but he made use of rather little else in this area. As for French writers other than Balzac, whom he revered, James alludes in imagery mainly to the nineteenth-century dramatists. However, his numerous little references to aspects of popular classical literature—Homeric goddesses, Hercules, Medusa, and their friends—are employed with occasional brilliance but such frequency as almost to constitute a little mannerism; further, since few of James's characters can aptly be called Jovial, there is irony in many figures of this sort. It is a different story when we consider the tropes stemming from children's literature. They refreshingly paint the atmosphere of mystery and awe hovering over his naïve characters. They suggest both the precocious maturity of many of his fictive children and the childishness of some of his adults. And in addition they serve, as Mark Twain's works do, to remind us of what we should not forget, that we were all once boys and girls in a pain-swept but golden childhood not long ago. A final type of book imagery concerns pages, margins, bindings, revisions, and translations—all of which goes to prove that James was a highly bookish writer.

The painting images glow and beckon throughout the entire range of the fiction. Titian emerges statistically as the favorite of James, who must have responded instinctively, artist to artist, to that painter's daring innovations in point of view, composition, and color. Veronese's sweeping gorgeousness and Holbein's gnarled intensity may seem strange when found side by side in a catalogue of James's art imagery, but together they attest to his ambition to produce crowded, radiant canvases intricately finished. James aimed at Gainsborough effects too, as the English wing of his gallery of fair ladies reveals. Indeed, there is such variety in his characterizing brush-work that he often has recourse to similes and metaphors evoking lesser-known painters as diverse as Longhi and Boucher. In addition, James often seeks a pictorial effect without naming an artist as analogue but instead by suggesting that his grouped figures are of the sort that might have been caught by, say, an anonymous Spanish painter in Naples or a nameless pastelist of the time of Louis XV.

Figures of speech by James which draw upon the theater are usually disappointing. Shakespeare surprisingly accounts only for routine comparisons totally lacking in ingenuity and depth. More understandably, classical drama provides the trope-making James with little to his purposes. Unfortunately, it was the French stage to which he went for many similes of this kind, and most of his readers today inevitably ignore the implications of his occasional allusions to Augier and his contemporaries. The several images deriving from technical stage-terms are natural enough in the light of James's biography, and they surely help to demonstrate that for much of his professional life James did indeed adjure himself to dramatize, dramatize! The numerous drama images focused from the darkened side of the footlights reflect his lifelong practice of attending plays, while his almost mannered mask figures reinforce many ingenious critical theories having to do with Jamesian ambivalences and points of view.

The music images, like the drama ones, are somewhat disappointing, but for different reasons. They show no technical competence, rarely name composers, and reveal that James evidently wished not to point up—by figurative language, at least—the subtle relationships between his fictive rhythms and those of musical composers. It is curious that Willa Cather should have written in this respect so very differently from the manner of one of her acknowledged masters. James best employs his infrequent music tropes to suggest delicately balanced sensibilities, odd-timbred voices, regrettable deafnesses in the insensitive, and—rarely—the operatic staginess of some melodramatic plot elements.

Occasionally James hits upon a brilliant sculpture figure to make graphic the physical appearance of a character, often a hard, cold woman, but sometimes a merely fragile one not yet warmed into life. Men so imaged are usually grotesque. Enigmatic, fine-featured women are sometimes limned in bright coin and carved gem imagery. Finally, the quality of the architecture figures is as poor as that of much drama imagery. James fails completely to group his caryatids, cornices, keystones, and lozenges in any functional manner, all of which is surprising in the light of the fact that in his prefaces he images himself repeatedly as a master-builder of fine houses of fiction.

To conclude, the amazing variety and abundance of his art imagery helps to place James in the main stream of western artists like Dante, Michelangelo, and Goethe who sought to show that the Palace of Art might have many rooms but is built upon one foundation.

The religion imagery is so eclectic that it helps to rule out the idea that James was attracted to any one dogma; at the same time it is so pervasive and moving that it supports the contention that he was highly aware of spiritual essences.

The religion of the Greco-Roman world James uses very often in imagery. Its gods and goddesses, sacrifices to them, oracles whispering their divine messages, their direct intervention in the lives of mere Endymions—all of this finds frequent expression. Still, the relatively fewer Hindu, Buddhist, Egyptian, and Mohammedan similes are often far more dramatic and vivid.

In the many usages involving idols and altars James shows tolerance enough for sincerity but with it scorn for any un-Grecian excessive zeal. Many dramatic images spring like sparks from the clash of pagan and Christian beliefs, most memorably in the pattern of similes comparing naïve victims destroyed by amused society like Christian martyrs fed to beasts in the Roman arena. James clearly suggests that society is crass and spiritually blind, and that only a few people in any group possess the abiding virtues.

James appropriately enough makes only limited use of Biblical allusions. Although he saw Catholicism only from the outside, he approached it, at least in his imagery, most respectfully, using saint, priest, monk, rosary, and kindred figures with no contempt whatever; on the other hand, perhaps because he was a formal Protestant himself, he occasionally allowed himself to use Protestant images with jibing frivolity.

By varied imagery exploiting elements of diverse religions James achieves pictorial and dramatic effects, casts light into the spiritual recesses of many of his characters, and in the reflection of that light reveals himself as possessed of no formal creed but assuredly of profound spiritual depths.

The rest of James's imagery is useful to us here for two

main reasons. First, the amazing variety and vitality of innumerable figures which do not readily fall into any of the six major classes encourage us to conclude that James so writes as to discomfit those who would limit him by catalogue techniques. And second, in spite of himself James incidentally tells us much about himself through still other types of figures.

Through fire and sensation images James suggests the light and heat of life and the thrill which people feel who respond fully to it. Metal and gem figures help to support his opinions concerning the ambivalences of reality. Tropes making use of court-life and childhood reinforce his notions that at all social levels responsibilities and pains are weighty. Other images, falling into minor groups or none, attest to the force of James's imagination and the persistence of his determination to enrich his stylistic carpet.

If we turn over the grand carpet of James's four million words of fiction, we find many loose bits of varicolored thread used in the figures on the surface normally exposed to public view. These hidden snippets have their message about the weaver. Many images show James as critic of and yet apologist for elements in the American tradition and the American personality. His many expensive tastes are faintly reflected in several wine and travel tropes, and his fear at inability to earn enough by writing to cater to those tastes—as well as his probable guilt at inheriting more money from his wealthy father than most of his fellow-writers ever possessed —had much to do with his similes and metaphors concerning shaky investments and impending stock-market declines. It is revealing to collect James's allusions to circuses and chess: he enjoyed the one because it was a noisy, colorful show, but he must have dismissed the other as a potential threat to creative thought and stimulating conversation. Through his imagery James stands revealed as measurably naïve in matters sexual, in addition as no scholar of the law, mathematics, or astronomy, and further as no intimate friend of physicians or dentists. Finally, his infinitely varied eye imagery provides indirect additional proof of what all readers of his fiction and travel essays know, that he was creatively observant.

Images by James appear with amazing regularity in his fiction, published through half a century. He varied rather little from a norm of four images per one thousand words, or about one image per page (Table I). During the quarter-century from 1890 to 1915 he achieved the greatest density of imagery, which is particularly high during his major phase in the middle of that time. The decade of the 1880's was notable for intense realism, less so for figurative patterns (Table II). James was most imagistic when writing quite short stories and rather long novels, somewhat less so when amid various difficulties he composed long short stories and nouvelles (Table III). The works he revised for the New York Edition, when compared to those which he left unrevised, have a slightly greater density of imagery in a considerably greater word bulk (Table IV). He was somewhat more stimulated toward trope-making when his plots were cast in England (with which scene almost half of his fiction is exclusively concerned) rather than in France; surprisingly, his beloved Italy evoked rhetorical images less than America did (Table V). If the imagery is a reliable guide in this respect, James's interest in human phenomena—war, art, and religion, mainly—declined slightly through the years, while his interest in natural objects—mainly water, flowers, and animals—dropped less from their norms; however, all of this may mean only that James when he arrived at artistic maturity grew discontented with more stereotyped figures of speech and then succeeded in becoming much more varied in imagery in the early 1900's. For example, he must have sensed the limitations of art imagery, which was surely over-used to a degree in the 1870's but which became a rich if not so frequent resource in the 1900's. Water figures remain at a steady level. Animal images are somewhat more numerous in James's frustrated 1890's. Flowers perhaps rightly belong to an author's youth. But James's interest in religion—if we may draw conclusions of this sort from his imagery—declined inexorably as he went his way from the circle of his family. War imagery is densest immediately following the Civil War, but—unlike any of the other major groupings—does not drop in the 1910's (Table VI).

Unintentionally, I have quoted or referred to proportionately more of the figures from the stories under 25,000 words in length and from the novels of more than 75,000 words. Also, I have quoted relatively more often from the revised than from the unrevised works. Finally, the images from the 1900's and from the 1870's are more abundantly represented here than those from other decades are. These facts tend to prove what we instinctively accept: that James's long novels —especially those of the major phase—and his so laboriously compressed short stories deserve the closest study. Yet the bulk of the quotations suggests something else too, which may be a little surprising: that the style of certain of James's works in the 1870's—notably *Watch and Ward* and *The Europeans,* both often ignored in favor of *Roderick Hudson* and *The American*—deserve to be examined more carefully. Among the novels of the 1880's, I have quoted rather little from *The Bostonians* and *The Tragic Muse,* while *The Princess Casamassima* (though sparser in imagistic count) is abundantly represented by quotations showing variety and charm. "Owen Wingrave," "The Beldonald Holbein," "The Impressions of a Cousin," "The Private Life," and especially "The Altar of the Dead," "Glasses," "The Birthplace," and "The Velvet Glove" have seemed to warrant surprisingly frequent quotation. On the other hand, the following novels and short stories have been disappointing for my purposes: *The Spoils of Poynton, The Outcry,* and *The Ivory Tower,* and "An International Episode," "The Visits," and "Miss Gunton of Poughkeepsie." Scarcely more interesting are "De Grey, A Romance," "The Sweetheart of M. Briseux," "The Path of Duty," "The Modern Warning," "The Given Case," "Maud-Evelyn," "The Tree of Knowledge," and "The Story in It."

We find that James's vast world of figures is a mythically dualistic one. We have the world of nature: out of the land which surrounds and is surrounded by a constantly changing watery element flowers and beasts have sprung up. And we have the world of men: ever fighting, creating, and worshipping. This cosmic dualism is repeated within the individual major categories of tropes. In fact, James's images are dramatic polarizations of the inherent conflicts of life. Thus, water helps James show that life is alternately—and sometimes simultaneously—pleasant and terrifying, warmly delightful and mortally chilling, twinklingly sunny and profoundly bleak. We begin in water, go down gelidly to death, and sometimes are accorded a watery rebirth. Life is also a fragile flower, fragrant but evanescent in an environment criss-crossed by all sort of rigid sickles. Tender beauty, fine sense, embattled decency, and even the verities are threatened with nullity by the black powers of the jungle. The beasts themselves are similarly divided: the kitten, the spaniel, and the lamb balance precariously in the great scale; over against them are serpent, cormorant, and tiger. Animals may be graceful or gauche, cunning or fumbling, soft and furry or plated to endure. Eternal warfare is waged by the strong against the weak. The

strong may fight nobly or ignobly, singlehandedly or in re-
sistless phalanxes, with attractive arms or crude clubs; the
meek may run and hide, or stand stoically and pitifully, may
ignorantly move down to doom or clutch at straws and shriek.
In the world of art it is the same: doers and seizers oppose
the makers, who themselves may see in life the quiescent picture or the moving drama, an isolated marble figure or a
harmony of colors. But art seems the best means to arrest
and focus the otherwise unresting, cacophonous processes of
meaningless change. Art hence is at the service of the gods,
who themselves, however, seem uncertain and divided, as are
their devotees. Venus clashes with Mars, pagan with Christian, thoughtful communicant with frenzied priestess.

James's images in toto are mythopoeic. Men and women
crossing vast oceans battle ceaseless waves, move on through
forest and jungle, here taking a rose and admiring a graceful
bird, there suffering a sting or a torn throat. Through it all
they hear the clamor of arms, pause to shape a legend or a
tale, draw a picture, carve an icon. They beat back the big
woods, make a clearing and a fane, lift their eyes beyond
the eclipsing branches to the pure heavens.

The minor images reinforce these fundamental contrasts.
Fire holds the cold at bay and lights the darkness; metals
cut through softness and retain the shape which passing men
give them. Sweet and sour sensations fall on the sensitive
and miss the dull; children gurgle with delight and sob in
pain or terror. Games are fun or deadly serious, and someone
always loses to the noble or vicious victor. Cups may hold
plain water, mead, or poison, may fall and shatter or survive
the hand of the potter. Jewels may be meretricious or precious, deservingly held or clutched by the dirty robber or the
spotted monarch in his high clean court or a soiled inner

chamber. The stars themselves may be steady or twinkling, solitary or in clusters, red or blue, propitious or obscure.

The images which light up James's personal character are likewise often curiously ambivalent. Why did James avoid an America to which he still remained loyal? Was money to him liberating or damning? Did the sedentary novelist only force himself to travel? How could the sophisticated writer stoop to gaudy circus figures? Did the highly cerebral and ascetic man irrationally fear pain, forget medical and legal lore completely, unconsciously reveal deep longings? And does he, when he speaks of the eye, as he so often does, mean the physical or the inner?

These fundamental contrasts form a pervasive basis in support of the dramatically contrasting symbols on the levels of action and topic. The juxtaposing of the New World and the Old is reinforced by much of the water imagery and the animal imagery, among other sorts; the role of the poet, who opposes the doer, is clarified by innumerable tropes, including those of art and religion; the good and the evil of society are suggested by war, water, garden, and other figures. The actions of contrasting types of characters, balanced in picture and motion, are made to have more symbolic import by virtue of myriads of metaphors and similes. Innocence—experience, youth—age, riches—poverty, love—isolation, appearance—reality, garden—house, fire—darkness, noise—silence, pearl—brummagem, circus—arithmetic, candy—dentist, travel—medicine, princess—burgher—the list is endless.

A return now from it to the fiction of James will show that its imagery is an important element but only one element of his varied, elaborate, and masterfully articulated style. The admirably challenging personality of the master emerges from these figures, never objectionably, to heighten the colors of sketch and gesture, never to blur our view of either. But it is the fiction in all its varied complexity of style and content to which we must return, for it is this which lastingly mirrors the image of the curious world which passed before the profoundly penetrating vision of Henry James.

TABLES

TABLE I

Abbreviations for Fiction of Henry James

The following is a list in alphabetical order of every fictional work by Henry James, preceded by my abbreviation for it and followed by the year in which it originally appeared or began to appear, the number of images in it, the estimated number of words, and the number of images per one thousand words. The Roman numerals indicate, if in capitals, the volume or volumes in which the work appears in the New York Edition (New York: Charles Scribner's Sons, 1907-17) or, if in lower case, the volume or volumes in the New and Complete Edition (London: Macmillan and Company, 1921-23). If neither form of numerals appears after a title, full reference to it may be found in the bibliographical note in this Table below.

"AofN"	"The Abasement of the Northmores"	1900	56	7,100	7.9	XVI
"Ad"	"Adina"	1874	53	16,100	3.3	
"AofD"	"The Altar of the Dead"	1895	94	13,100	7.2	XVII
Amb	The Ambassadors	1903	706	147,600	4.8	XXI, XXII
Ame	The American	1876	618	136,700	4.5	II

"AP"	"The Aspern Papers"	1888	68	35,300	1.9	XII
"AtI"	"At Isella"	1871	48	12,100	4.0	
"AofB"	"The Author of Beltraffio"	1884	79	17,400	4.5	XVI
AA	*The Awkward Age*	1898	408	130,400	3.1	IX
"BinJ"	"The Beast in the Jungle"	1903	125	16,700	7.5	XVII
"BH"	"The Beldonald Holbein"	1901	65	7,700	8.3	XVIII
"BofD"	"The Bench of Desolation"	1909	92	18,200	5.1	xxviii
"Be"	"Benvolio"	1875	59	16,600	3.6	xxiv
"Bi"	"The Birthplace"	1903	91	20,200	4.5	XVII
Bo	*The Bostonians*	1885	669	150,500	4.4	viii, ix
"BW"	"Broken Wings"	1900	33	6,500	5.1	XVI
"Br"	"Brooksmith"	1891	33	6,300	5.2	XVIII
"BofL"	"A Bundle of Letters"	1879	54	12,800	4.2	XIV
"Ch"	"The Chaperon"	1891	50	15,800	3.2	X
"Col"	"Collaboration"	1892	40	7,800	5.1	xxvii
Con	*Confidence*	1879	171	74,200	2.3	iv
"CE"	"Covering End"	1898	161	34,200	4.7	
"CF"	"The Coxon Fund"	1894	113	21,300	5.3	XV
"CCor"	"Crapy Cornelia"	1909	74	10,700	6.9	xxviii
"CCon"	"Crawford's Consistency"	1876	61	11,700	5.2	
"DM"	"Daisy Miller"	1878	43	23,100	1.9	XVIII
"DofD"	"A Day of Days"	1866	23	8,600	2.7	xxv
"DofL"	"The Death of the Lion"	1894	104	13,400	7.8	XV
"DeG"	"De Grey, A Romance"	1868	45	13,000	3.5	
"DofM"	"The Diary of a Man of Fifty"	1879	13	11,900	1.1	xxv
"EP"	"Eugene Pickering"	1874	93	17,300	5.4	xxiv
"Eur"	"Europe"	1899	22	7,200	3.1	XVI
Eurs	*The Europeans*	1878	123	59,700	2.1	iii
"FinC"	"The Figure in the Carpet"	1896	96	13,900	6.9	XV
"Fl"	"Flickerbridge"	1902	64	7,400	8.6	XVIII
"FC"	"Fordham Castle"	1904	45	7,800	5.8	XVI
"FM"	"Four Meetings"	1877	34	11,400	3.0	XVI
"FofF"	"The Friends of the Friends"	1896	27	9,700	2.8	XVII
"GdeB"	"Gabrielle de Bergerac"	1869	79	22,300	3.5	
"GeR"	"Georgina's Reasons"	1884	62	23,700	2.6	xxv
"GhR"	"The Ghostly Rental"	1876	39	12,600	3.1	
"GiC"	"The Given Case"	1898	26	9,400	2.8	xxvii
"Gl"	"Glasses"	1896	87	17,300	5.0	xxvii
GB	*The Golden Bowl*	1904	1,092	192,200	5.7	XXIII, XXIV
"GrC"	"The Great Condition"	1899	47	14,500	3.2	xxvii
"GGP"	"The Great Good Place"	1900	83	9,200	9.1	XVI
"GF"	"Greville Fane"	1892	41	6,500	6.3	XVI
"GuC"	"Guest's Confession"	1872	106	21,700	4.9	

"IofC"	"The Impressions of a Cousin"	1883	54	27,300	2.0	xxiv
"IE"	"An International Episode"	1878	56	29,300	1.9	XIV
"InC"	"In the Cage"	1898	177	32,800	5.4	XI
IT	*The Ivory Tower*	1917	351	66,800	5.3	XXV
"JD"	"John Delavoy"	1898	71	12,900	5.5	xxvii
"JC"	"The Jolly Corner"	1908	84	12,700	6.6	XVII
"JB"	"Julia Bride"	1908	136	13,300	10.2	XVII
"LaB"	"Lady Barbarina"	1884	86	35,600	2.4	XIV
"LaP"	"A Landscape Painter"	1866	51	13,200	3.9	xxv
"LofV"	"The Last of the Valerii"	1874	58	11,100	5.2	xxvi
"LofM"	"The Lesson of the Master"	1888	81	23,600	3.4	XV
"Li"	"The Liar"	1888	85	19,600	4.3	XII
"LiM"	"A Light Man"	1869	63	11,500	5.5	xxv
"LL"	"A London Life"	1888	109	40,700	2.7	X
"LoM"	"Longstaff's Marriage"	1878	23	11,100	2.1	xxiv
"LoB"	"Lord Beaupré"	1892	38	20,600	1.8	xxvii
"LoP"	"Louisa Pallant"	1888	29	14,000	2.1	XIII
"MdeM"	"Madame de Mauves"	1874	132	29,600	4.5	XIII
"MofF"	"The Madonna of the Future"	1873	90	14,200	6.3	XIII
"Ma"	"The Marriages"	1891	46	12,000	3.8	XVIII
"MS"	"The Married Son"	1908	66	10,600	6.2	
"MEu"	"Master Eustace"	1871	71	10,700	6.6	xxvi
"MEv"	"Maud-Evelyn"	1900	29	10,200	2.8	xxviii
"MY"	"The Middle Years"	1893	46	7,500	6.1	XVI
"MG"	"Miss Gunton of Poughkeepsie"	1900	20	5,000	4.0	XVI
"MW"	"The Modern Warning"	1888	41	24,100	1.7	xxvi
"MM"	"Mora Montravers"	1909	88	21,800	4.0	xxviii
"MEC"	"A Most Extraordinary Case"	1868	44	15,200	2.9	xxvi
"MrsM"	"Mrs. Medwin"	1901	20	8,100	2.5	XVIII
"MrsT"	"Mrs. Temperley"	1887	14	12,300	1.1	xxvi
"MFB"	"My Friend Bingham"	1867	12	8,100	1.5	
"NEW"	"A New England Winter"	1884	91	21,400	4.3	xxv
"NT"	"The Next Time"	1895	126	15,100	8.3	XV
"NV"	"Nona Vincent"	1892	48	11,600	4.1	xxvi
"OR"	"Osborne's Revenge"	1868	61	15,300	4.0	
OH	*The Other House*	1896	289	70,500	4.1	
Ou	*The Outcry*	1911	243	56,400	4.3	
"OW"	"Owen Wingrave"	1892	36	12,600	2.9	XVII
"Pan"	"Pandora"	1884	54	18,500	2.9	XVIII
"Pap"	"The Papers"	1903	134	35,000	3.8	xxviii
"PP"	"A Passionate Pilgrim"	1871	166	25,800	6.4	XIII
"Pas"	"Paste"	1899	18	5,900	3.1	XVI
"Pat"	"The Patagonia"	1888	32	21,300	1.5	XVIII

"PofD"	"The Path of Duty"	1884	34	13,500	2.5	xxv
"PB"	"The Pension Beaurepas"	1879	53	20,000	2.7	XIV
"PofV"	"The Point of View"	1882	47	16,800	2.8	XIV
"PR"	"Poor Richard"	1867	62	22,300	2.8	xxv
PofL	The Portrait of a Lady	1880	668	217,300	3.1	III, IV
PC	The Princess Casamassima	1885	480	197,800	2.4	V, VI
"PL"	"The Private Life"	1892	58	12,800	4.5	XVII
"Pr"	"A Problem"	1868	20	5,800	3.4	
"PF"	"Professor Fargo"	1874	62	15,200	4.1	
"Pu"	"The Pupil"	1891	71	16,500	4.3	XI
"RRT"	"The Real Right Thing"	1899	20	4,900	4.1	XVII
"RT"	"The Real Thing"	1892	45	9,600	4.7	XVIII
Re	The Reverberator	1888	157	53,000	3.0	XIII
RH	Roderick Hudson	1875	642	133,100	4.8	I
"RofC"	"The Romance of Certain Old Clothes"	1868	18	7,400	2.4	xxvi
"RA"	"Rose-Agathe"	1878	11	7,100	1.5	xxv
"RofV"	"A Round of Visits"	1910	60	10,600	5.7	xxviii
SF	The Sacred Fount	1901	408	71,300	5.7	xxix
SeofP	The Sense of the Past	1917	327	71,800	4.6	XXVI
"SofL"	"The Siege of London"	1883	98	32,000	3.1	XIV
"SirD"	"Sir Dominick Ferrand"	1892	57	20,200	2.8	xxvi
"SirE"	"Sir Edmund Orme"	1891	18	10,700	1.7	XVII
"So"	"The Solution"	1889	38	18,000	2.1	xxvi
"ST"	"The Special Type"	1900	18	6,800	2.6	xxviii
SpofP	The Spoils of Poynton	1896	334	65,000	5.1	X
"SinI"	"The Story in It"	1903	23	6,400	3.6	XVIII
"SofM"	"The Story of a Masterpiece"	1868	36	13,500	2.7	
"SofY"	"The Story of a Year"	1865	84	15,000	5.6	
"SofB"	"The Sweetheart of M. Briseux"	1873	41	12,000	3.4	
"TP"	"The Third Person"	1900	50	11,900	4.2	xxvii
"TofT"	"The Tone of Time"	1900	26	7,700	3.4	xxvii
"TofE"	"A Tragedy of Error"	1864	28	8,000	3.5	
TM	The Tragic Muse	1889	804	199,600	4.0	VII, VIII
"TC"	"Travelling Companions"	1870	55	16,800	3.3	
"TofK"	"The Tree of Knowledge"	1900	31	5,400	5.7	XVI
"TofS"	"The Turn of the Screw"	1898	144	39,600	3.6	XII
"TF"	"The Two Faces"	1900	24	5,300	4.5	XII
"VG"	"The Velvet Glove"	1909	72	10,600	6.8	xxviii
"Vi"	"The Visits"	1892	9	6,000	1.5	xxvii
WS	Washington Square	1880	143	62,200	2.3	v
WandW	Watch and Ward	1871	257	56,200	4.6	xxiv
WMK	What Maisie Knew	1897	364	89,200	4.1	XI

"WofT" "The Wheel of Time"   1892   28   17,100   1.6   xxvii
WofD   The Wings of the Dove   1902   893   172,100   5.2   XIX, XX

Totals: 135 works of fiction, 16,902 images, 4,189,800 words, 4.0 images/1000 words.

Bibliography of uncollected fiction by Henry James:

"Adina," *Scribner's Monthly*, VIII (May, June, 1874), 33-43, 181-91.
"At Isella," *Galaxy*, XII (August, 1871), 241-55.
"Covering End," *The Two Magics: The Turn of The Screw and Covering End* (New York: The Macmillan Company, 1898), pp. 215-393.
"Crawford's Consistency," *Scribner's Monthly*, XII (August, 1876), 569-84.
"De Grey, A Romance," *Atlantic Monthly*, XXII (July, 1868), 57-78.
"Gabrielle de Bergerac," *Atlantic Monthly*, XXIV (July, August, September, 1869), 55-71, 231-41, 352-61.
"The Ghostly Rental," *Scribner's Monthly*, XII (September, 1876), 664-79.
"Guest's Confession," *Atlantic Monthly*, XXX (October, November, 1872), 385-403, 566-83.
"The Married Son," *The Whole Family*, Part VII, *Harper's Bazaar*, XLII (June, 1908), 530-44.
"My Friend Bingham," *Atlantic Monthly*, XIX (March, 1867), 346-58.
"Osborne's Revenge," *Galaxy*, VI (July, 1868), 5-31.
The Other House (Norfolk, Conn.: New Directions, 1948).
The Outcry (New York: Charles Scribner's Sons, 1911).
"A Problem," *Galaxy*, V (June, 1868), 697-707.
"Professor Fargo," *Galaxy*, XVIII (August, 1874), 233-53.
"The Story of a Masterpiece," *Galaxy*, V (January, February, 1868), 5-21, 133-43.
"The Story of a Year," *Atlantic Monthly*, XV (March, 1865), 257-81.
"The Sweetheart of M. Briseux," *Galaxy*, XV (June, 1873), 760-79.
"A Tragedy of Error," *Continental Monthly*, V (February, 1864), 204-16.
"Travelling Companions," *Atlantic Monthly*, XXVI (November, December, 1870), 600-14, 684-97.

TABLE II

Density of Images by Decades

Decade	No. of Images	No. of Words	Images/1000 Words
1860's	626	179,200	3.5
1870's	3,232	830,100	3.9
1880's	4,023	1,295,500	3.1
1890's	3,392	813,900	4.2
1900's	4,648	865,500	5.4
1910's	981	205,600	4.8
	16,902	4,189,800	4.0

TABLE III

Density of Images by Length of Works

short stories	5,370	1,319,000	4.1
long short stories	1,385	397,200	3.5
short novels	2,803	707,100	4.0
long novels	7,344	1,766,500	4.2
	16,902	4,189,800	4.0

TABLE IV

Density of Images in Unrevised and Revised Works

unrevised	5,757	1,588,800	3.6
revised	11,145	2,601,000	4.3
	16,902	4,189,800	4.0

TABLE V

Density of Images by Scene of Works

England	8,422	1,969,200	4.3
France	1,880	449,200	4.2
United States	3,018	754,600	4.0
Italy	1,792	502,500	3.6
Switzerland and Germany	249	57,900	4.3
Evenly mixed	1,541	456,400	3.4
	16,902	4,189,800	4.0

TABLE VI

Percentages of Images by Categories

	1860's	1870's	1880's	1890's	1900's	1910's
water	8	8	7	8	9	7
flower	4	5	5	3	4	3
animal	4	6	5	7	6	5
war	7	4	5	5	4	4
art	11	14	13	11	11	8
religion	9	7	5	4	4	3

INDEX